Crystals and Crystal Grids

Tapping into the Power of Healing Stones, and Sacred Geometry for Protection, Spirit Communication, Love, and More

© Copyright 2023 - All rights reserved.

The content contained within this book may not be reproduced, duplicated, or transmitted without direct written permission from the author or the publisher.

Under no circumstances will any blame or legal responsibility be held against the publisher, or author, for any damages, reparation, or monetary loss due to the information contained within this book, either directly or indirectly.

Legal Notice:

This book is copyright protected. It is only for personal use. You cannot amend, distribute, sell, use, quote, or paraphrase any part, or the content within this book, without the consent of the author or publisher.

Disclaimer Notice:

Please note the information contained within this document is for educational and entertainment purposes only. All effort has been executed to present accurate, up-to-date, reliable, and complete information. No warranties of any kind are declared or implied. Readers acknowledge that the author is not engaging in the rendering of legal, financial, medical, or professional advice. The content within this book has been derived from various sources. Please consult a licensed professional before attempting any techniques outlined in this book.

By reading this document, the reader agrees that under no circumstances is the author responsible for any losses, direct or indirect, that are incurred as a result of the use of the information contained within this document, including, but not limited to, errors, omissions, or inaccuracies.

Free Bonus from Silvia Hill available for limited time

Hi Spirituality Lovers!

My name is Silvia Hill, and first off, I want to THANK YOU for reading my book.

Now you have a chance to join my exclusive spirituality email list so you can get the ebooks below for free as well as the potential to get more spirituality ebooks for free! Simply click the link below to join.

P.S. Remember that it's 100% free to join the list.

~~$27~~ FREE BONUSES

-  9 Types of Spirit Guides and How to Connect to Them
- 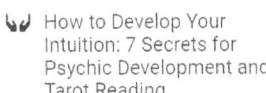 How to Develop Your Intuition: 7 Secrets for Psychic Development and Tarot Reading
- 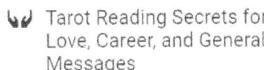 Tarot Reading Secrets for Love, Career, and General Messages

Access your free bonuses here
https://livetolearn.lpages.co/crystals-and-crystal-grids-paperback/

Table of Contents

PART 1: CRYSTALS AND HEALING STONES 1
   INTRODUCTION 2
   SECTION ONE: CRYSTAL BASICS 4
   CHAPTER 1: HOW ARE CRYSTALS AND MINERALS CREATED? . 5
   CHAPTER 2: THE HEALING PROPERTIES OF CRYSTALS 14
   CHAPTER 3: TYPES OF CRYSTAL SHAPES 26
   CHAPTER 4: 13 MUST-HAVE CRYSTALS FOR BEGINNERS 37
   CHAPTER 5: 16 MORE-ADVANCED CRYSTALS TO OWN 50
   CHAPTER 6: USING CRYSTALS FOR PROTECTION 65
   CHAPTER 7: CRYSTAL CLEANSING AND MAINTENANCE 76
   SECTION TWO: CRYSTALS AND THE ZODIAC SIGNS 85
   CHAPTER 8: CRYSTALS FOR EARTH SIGNS 86
   CHAPTER 9: CRYSTALS FOR AIR SIGNS 96
   CHAPTER 10: CRYSTALS FOR FIRE SIGNS 105
   CHAPTER 11: CRYSTALS FOR WATER SIGNS 113
   SECTION THREE: USING CRYSTAL GRIDS 122
   CHAPTER 12: UNDERSTANDING CRYSTAL GRIDS 123
   CHAPTER 13: CRYSTAL GRIDS AND THE STARS 133
   CHAPTER 14: ACTIVATING YOUR CRYSTAL GRID 143
   CHAPTER 15: CARING FOR YOUR CRYSTAL GRID 150
   CONCLUSION 157
PART 2: CRYSTAL GRIDS 159
   INTRODUCTION 160

CHAPTER 1: CRYSTAL HEALING EXPLAINED 162
CHAPTER 2: WHAT IS A CRYSTAL GRID? 171
CHAPTER 3: CRYSTALS AND OTHER TOOLS FOR GRIDWORK 180
CHAPTER 4: CREATING YOUR FIRST CRYSTAL GRID 192
CHAPTER 5: CRYSTAL GRIDS FOR LOVE AND RELATIONSHIPS 200
CHAPTER 6: CRYSTAL GRIDS FOR MONEY AND CAREER 211
CHAPTER 7: CRYSTAL GRIDS FOR HEALTH AND HEALING 222
CHAPTER 8: CRYSTAL GRIDS FOR PSYCHIC DEVELOPMENT AND PROTECTION 233
CHAPTER 9: CRYSTAL GRIDS FOR SPIRIT COMMUNICATION 241
CHAPTER 10: CRYSTAL GRIDS FOR THE HOME 249
CHAPTER 11: CRYSTAL GRID USES AND MAINTENANCE 259
CONCLUSION 265
APPENDIX 1: A-Z CRYSTALS AND THEIR PROPERTIES 267
APPENDIX 2: A-Z CRYSTALS AND MINERALS 273
HERE'S ANOTHER BOOK BY SILVIA HILL THAT YOU MIGHT LIKE 280
FREE BONUS FROM SILVIA HILL AVAILABLE FOR LIMITED TIME 281
REFERENCES 282

Part 1: Crystals and Healing Stones

Everything from Must-Have Crystals, Minerals, and Gemstones for Different Zodiac Signs, to How to Use a Crystal Grid for Healing

Introduction

Crystals have been recognized as an aid used for healing since ancient times. They are found all over the world in many shapes and sizes. They vary from place to place, with some crystals more common than others. Each crystal has its own energy, which reacts to different types of people and heals them in specific ways. They have been used to improve the flow of spiritual energy, help in meditation, and cleanse the body. Having crystals in your home is an excellent idea for many reasons.

Crystals are said to be used by shamans, healers, and psychics worldwide. They have been used for thousands of years to cleanse, protect, and energize the body, mind, and spirit. As we continue to become more aware of our need for a greater connection with the Earth, it is normal to seek out these powerful healing crystals. This book has been designed to help you get started in the wonderful world of crystals.

This book is not intended as a scientific treatise on crystals and their effects, as many aspects of crystals are still unknown. Rather, it is designed to give you an understanding of the power of crystals and their potential healing properties, as well as some elementary ritualistic methods for helping heal yourself with crystals.

As you become more aware of your own energy field, it will be easy to know what kind of crystal will resonate with you or help your healing process in a particular situation. This book represents a seamless introduction for the beginner and a comprehensive reference for the advanced user. Everyone is different, and so are the crystals used in their healing journey. The more you learn about crystals, the more you can tailor your own personal crystal journey to suit your needs.

Section One: Crystal Basics

Chapter 1: How Are Crystals and Minerals Created?

It is common to see the words "crystal," "mineral," and "gemstone" being used interchangeably. However, it is vital to understand that they are not necessarily the same things. While they are related and often placed together, crystals, minerals, and gemstones have very different properties that can be observed under the microscope.

Crystals and minerals have different properties.
https://unsplash.com/photos/cVt0u781VGo

Crystals

Only a small percentage of the materials that make up our world are crystals, and, as such, there are few ways to pick them out. They are produced by a natural process called crystallization. Still, it isn't always easy to find a crystal with so many other materials being formed through this process. They are usually found in igneous rocks, which were formed through volcanoes and different mineral processing, or they can also be found in sedimentary rock. Some examples of crystals include salt, sugar, and snow.

Minerals

A mineral is a generic term for a naturally-occurring substance formed of one or more elements; it does not include natural objects such as rocks. Minerals can be any number of different materials but are usually defined by their chemical composition and crystal structure. They are usually found in igneous rock beds and can be distinguished by various physical properties such as hardness, color, and density. Minerals come in many shapes and sizes. However, most have a unique look which makes them easy to spot. Some examples are gold, silver, iron, and calcium.

Gemstones

These are the most colorful and interesting of the three but are also the hardest to find. Gemstones differ from other minerals in that they are primarily used both in jewelry making and decorative design. They must also only be found in certain places and must not contain impurities or defects. It is rare to find a genuinely natural gemstone, as it must either be mined or grown artificially under laboratory conditions. Diamonds, emeralds, rubies, and sapphires are all commonly known gemstones. They are mostly found in igneous rock formations but can also be mined from metamorphic and sedimentary rocks.

Crystallization

Crystallization is a natural process in which crystalline substances form through changes caused by heat, pressure, and time. When liquid water is subjected to very high temperatures, it can turn into a gas and then begin to cool. This cooling process occurs on the element's surface, leading to tiny crystals or grains forming. These grains can then be melted together and affect other molecules, causing them to grow. This growth process is known as nucleation. It is a process where the molecules of a substance can grow and form grains by removing themselves from liquids or by adding molecules from another substance. These grains then can grow in size, eventually becoming large enough to be detectable to the naked eye. Nucleation occurs when an atom or molecule becomes tightly bound to something else, such as when one molecule attaches itself to another molecule within a liquid or gas. Crystals and gemstones are the results of nucleation.

Types of Crystallization

There are three different types of crystallization:

- *The first type is known as the "mushroom" or lamellar crystal.* This process takes place on the surface of an element. A liquid or vapor can nucleate and grow into a crystal when it touches the surface. This type is used in many processes, such as producing salt and sugar. These crystals tend to be very small, expressed visually through their atomic structure as having needle-like points to their particles. They are also very fragile and prone to shattering, making them difficult to use in many applications where high strength is required.

- *The second type is the "spherulite."* In this process, atoms or molecules become linked in a chain-like structure. Those closest to each other continue to grow and can eventually arrange themselves in a visually recognizable pattern to scientists. This process is known as "growth" and occurs at temperatures of 300-500C. An example of this type of growth would be snow, which crystallizes when water is cooled enough to freeze. This growth process can occur at any temperature, although the rate is much greater at temperatures close to the freezing point. Snow crystals are very common, and their visual expression reveals clusters of grains that seem like lightbulbs above a sea of white.

- *The third type of crystallization is also known as precipitation.* This process occurs with the help of a nucleus. A nucleus is an area surrounded by lines of atoms or molecules, such as a crystal. This forms when two elements meet in an environment that is rich in water. The two elements are separated into their salt and metal components, which can then combine with other free atoms in the water to form new ions. These ions can then interact with ions from the other element to form a new substance, settling and growing into a new crystal.

Each type of crystallization may produce crystals or grains of different sizes and shapes, depending on the conditions present at the nucleation point and the amount of time it takes for growth to occur. Crystals can be used in various applications, from producing useful materials to decorating our homes. They are an outstanding way rocks can be changed into other materials and are a truly fascinating process to understand.

Crystal Lattice

The crystal lattice is what allows the crystalline structure in minerals to grow. It is made of tightly packed atoms and can sometimes be considered a combination of a molecular lattice and an atomic lattice. A molecular lattice is when weak bonds between atoms occur, holding the molecules in place over long periods. An atomic lattice exists for much shorter periods but provides a strong bond between atoms in its structure. Combining these two allows the crystal lattice to form, giving crystalline substances their unique properties.

A crystal lattice exists in a three-dimensional arrangement of atoms known as *the space group*. This can be thought of as a grid, with the atoms forming layers, and each layer has similar atoms. However, there are differences in the types of bonds and their positions within the crystal lattice. All space groups have an A point defined by the number and orientation of atoms in the top layer. The A point represents awareness or order within a crystal. For example, only one atom can be at this point, as it can only bond to one element at once. This atom either forms a weak bond or is surrounded by others with different bonds. The A point is special in the crystal lattice.

A crystal can be thought of as a three-dimensional object, with the atoms that make it up arranged in a way that allows them to bond together. The atoms in a crystal lattice have different types of bonds and positions, allowing them to take on multiple forms. These are determined by the order of the atoms found within each layer. This order is determined by the spacing between each layer in space group notation. The space group notation is essential because it tells scientists about which types of bonds exist between groups of atoms and also where they are located within the three-dimensional lattice structure.

Types of Crystal Lattices

There are three types of crystal lattices: Quasi-crystals, body-centered cubic, and space groups. The first two types were discovered in the early 20th century. However, there was a long period when scientists thought all crystals were identical. This led to many experiments being done incorrectly to try and prove that all crystals had the same structure. However, it was only after research into properties that are unique to crystals that scientists began to realize just how vital and unique these structures were. Their position within the lattice was also important, as each could be found in multiple positions within a lattice structure with its own unique property.

- **Quasi-Crystal:** The first type of crystal lattice is a quasi-crystal. This is also known as a non-repeating structure, meaning that the pattern it follows does not repeat itself. Although they look very complex, they are very simple to understand. Every structure within the crystal lattice can be found in every other layer that makes up the crystal. An excellent way to understand this structural pattern is by looking at reflections from a moving object. When you see your reflection through a moving object such as water or glass, it would appear to be stationary and perfectly symmetrical, even though it is not in reality. This is an example of how quasi-crystals can be thought of. Every atom in the crystal lattice is placed in the same position, which makes it appear to have symmetry in its structure.

However, this is not the case, as true symmetry does not exist within a quasi-crystal structure.

- **Body-Centered Cubic:** The second type of crystal lattice is the body-centered cubic lattice. This is also known as a symmetric space group, and it has sublattices within it that are known as body-centered cubic sublattices. A body-centered cubic structure has many layers within it, unlike quasi-crystals, which have just one layer for every atom in its lattice. This is because body-centered cubic structures have different properties.

- **Space Group:** The third type is the space group. This is the most common type of crystal lattice and can be found in most crystals. There are many types of space groups, each with its unique set of properties. They all have a high level of symmetry and have symmetries that are similar to each other; however, they are not identical as there are slight differences between them.

Crystal System

Crystal systems are highly important when discussing crystalline substances and their structure. The word crystal is from the Latin word *crystallum*, which refers to *ice*. Ice is a form of matter, but it also has a crystalline structure, and this is a direct reference to minerals. Crystals have been around for millions of years, so how do scientists know they resemble snowflakes? A crystal system allows scientists and researchers to determine the properties of minerals that appear the same but are very different. Just like the appearance of snowflakes can vary, so can their structures and arrangement. Although they have the same basic structure, snowflakes vary in shape, size, and number of arms. This is similar to crystals, which are made of the same elements but have different properties and arrangements. There are seven crystal system types: triclinic, monoclinic, orthorhombic, hexagonal, tetragonal, trigonal, and cubic systems. However, only the three first mentioned are commonly known. The following are the seven different crystal systems in use today, and an explanation of each so that it can be a bit clearer:

Triclinic System: The triclinic system is only one of the crystal systems divisible by a single angle; all the rest are divisible by more than one angle. The triclinic crystal system consists of three-axis of unequal length, which form angles to each other, which are at 120 degrees. The angles between them are usually the same, and they form equal angles to each other in relation to the lattice points. Examples of minerals in this category are turquoise, feldspar, and kyanite.

Monoclinic System: The monoclinic crystal system is divisible by two angles and has three unequal lengths. The angles between them are different, and each of the three axes is at equal angles to the lattice points. Examples of minerals that fall into this category are borax, jadeite, and gypsum.

Orthorhombic System: The orthorhombic system is a crystal system with one axis of unequal length and two perpendicular axes. The two perpendicular axes are equal in size, and there is a center of symmetry in this system somewhere in the middle. This is the most commonly found crystal system in minerals, as it is more stable than the other systems. Examples of minerals in this category are topaz, cerussite, and olivine.

Hexagonal System: To describe this type of structure, scientists refer to it as a rhombohedral substructure. This means that there are six axes at right angles to each other, arranged in a cube with six faces. Each face can be described as an equilateral triangle where they meet at the four corners of the cube. They are also described as octahedrons that form a hexagonal lattice. Examples of minerals that fall into this category are zincite and aquamarine.

Tetragonal System: The tetragonal system consists of four axes at right angles to each other and has equal lengths. The axes are arranged in a tetrahedron and have two equal planes that run perpendicularly. Each plane meets the four axes at the corners of the cube. As well as having a center of symmetry, a plane runs along the middle of each axis, and both sides meet it. Examples of minerals in this category are wulfenite, apophyllite, and rutile.

Trigonal System: The trigonal system is also known as trigonal antiprism. This structure consists of three equal-length axes arranged in a cube with three equal-length facets. These facets can be described as hexagonal prisms, which are triangles that meet at the cube's corners. As if these three identical facets are not enough to make up this system, there is also a center of symmetry that runs through the middle of each face. Examples of minerals that fall into this category are agate, tiger's eye, and calcite.

Cubic System: The cubic system is one of the most stable, strongest, and hardiest of all crystal systems. It consists of four axes of unequal length. They are arranged in squares that are at right angles to each other and have four corners on them. Finally, a center runs through the middle of each axis. Lastly, these squares can be placed in a cube as they all meet at the corners exactly at right angles. Examples of minerals in this category are fluorite, spinel, and diamond.

Many other types of crystal structures have been discovered throughout time, and more than one type of crystal structure could exist at once within a mineral. The difference between a mineral's crystal structure and that mineral's structure when it is melted is highly significant. This is because when a substance is molten, it can have a completely different crystal structure compared to its solid form. This makes it very important for scientists to know the different crystal structures of certain minerals to be able to identify them correctly. This allows them to predict the properties and characteristics belonging to that specific piece of rock and classify them for further research. This is essential for scientists to be able to develop new ways of processing and using minerals and create better super-strong materials with improved qualities. It also opens up new possibilities for extracting useful metals from these minerals.

In addition, the fact that minerals exist in six different crystal systems can cause confusion. This is because, in most cases, the form of a mineral does not match its actual crystal structure. For scientists to figure out what structure it belongs to, they have to break it down into small fragments and study them individually. This is known as the process of chemical analysis, and it can be extremely time-consuming. Scientists make use of x-ray crystallography to understand a mineral's crystal structure, as this is an extremely important method to determine a mineral's properties.

In conclusion, the crystalline structures of minerals play an important role in the study of matter. They are very useful when it comes to developing new technologies, as well as being able to compare and contrast these minerals with each other. It is also essential for scientists to know what sort of crystal system a mineral belongs to be able to classify them accurately, which is necessary for them to create effective new technologies. This is why crystal structures are so important and deserve more recognition.

Crystal structure analysis is not limited only to minerals but can also be used with gemstones such as sapphire, amethyst, rubies, and emeralds. This is because gemstones are crystalline, meaning that they also have a unique crystal structure. Although gemstones are not minerals - as minerals are made of metals and non-metallic elements - certain gems can be considered either metallic or non-metallic. This is because some gemstones may contain metal atoms or non-metal atoms, in addition to some organic molecules. This can affect their crystal structures, but gemstones generally fall into one of the six major crystal systems. With this thorough understanding of precious stones and their peculiar structure, you are now ready to move on to something far more intriguing — the healing properties contained within these stones.

Chapter 2: The Healing Properties of Crystals

Crystal healing is not just spiritual or magical thinking. It is a deeply scientific process with a long history, and it's been used to treat illnesses and injuries by many cultures around the world. Crystals can be programmed, charged, and lend their properties to the person who works with them. There are different schools of thought about how exactly these stones do this, but it's clear that something about the physical composition of crystal energies allows for transformation at a different level than other forms of medicine or healing. This has been shown through many studies on people who've tried using crystals in conjunction with the usual treatments for illnesses that range from the common cold to illnesses as serious as cancer.

Crystals have been used for healing extensively throughout history.
https://unsplash.com/photos/YRrj9QMbv9o

Crystals aren't the only tools that can be used to heal, but they do have properties that make them particularly well suited for this task. It's reasonable to assume that the other conventional medicines used in these studies also affected the disease, but they didn't work nearly as well as when combined with these special stones. The best theory on how that happens is by some kind of energy transfer or resonance between the person and the crystal during their treatment, and this can work in different ways, even without any psychic ability on the part of the person.

How Crystals Work with Our Energy

Crystals are made up of a lattice of atoms and molecules that are arranged in a very specific pattern that repeats throughout the entire stone. The way these molecules vibrate at different frequencies allows them to carry out various actions in various ways. Most stones have a physical effect on us when we come into contact with them, but the most significant effects we experience from crystals stem from their vibrations. These vibrations interact with our bodies" electromagnetic energy field and can help regulate the flow of qi (or chi, prana, ki, or other terms you may have heard) that flows throughout our bodies.

If those vibrations are out of balance or weak, they can be rebalanced through treatment with an appropriately-vibrating crystal. This effect can extend to a person's entire energy field or only affect specific areas needing healing. When crystals are used as part of holistic treatment, they provide a full spectrum of benefits that go far beyond that produced by isolated beta-carotene pills and ibuprofen.

Qi, Frequency, and Crystals

Many people are familiar with the idea that qi energy flows within our bodies but aren't sure what it means. Qi is a type of energy that originates in the core of our being and spreads out through our physical body, surrounding aura, and meridians that carry this life force throughout our system. If you're not familiar with qi, you can think of it as the vital force in all living things responsible for animating plants and animals. It's also important to understand that this qi is vibrating at a particular frequency. It takes time, and practice, to learn how to detect this energy and utilize it in our lives. You can think of the vibration of qi as a cosmic internet connecting everything. When the energetic waves of qi are at their strongest, it acts as this superhighway for the information that all living things share. The more qi you can keep flowing throughout your system, your physical body will be more coordinated. The stronger the overall qi flow is within you, the more talents, traits, and abilities you're likely to have. In practice, the best way to take advantage of your qi is by using crystals that resonate at the frequency of the qi you want to enhance.

The electromagnetic field surrounding us is not as hard or rigid as we think. It expands and contracts at different times and in different seasons. Our bodies carry frequencies from all electronic devices and appliances we use, from television sets to microwave ovens. This same energy comes in through the skin and travels around our bodies through meridians, where it can then flow outwards and interact with other people's fields and systems. You can use crystals to interact with your qi and bring your body back into balance. When you work with crystals, you need to set the intention in your mind and then program the crystal to carry out that purpose. Crystals are very good at carrying out specific functions and tasks when properly programmed, charged, or prepared for use within an energetic structure.

Aura

The aura is an electromagnetic field that exists around your physical body. It can be perceived by the naked eye, although you may have to train yourself to see it. The aura can be influenced by many things, from disease and negative emotions to electromagnetic forces and crystals. The aura's energetic flow depends upon the balance of its different layers, and each layer has a particular meaning and color. These layers also affect the overall shape of the aura itself. The shape or type of aura doesn't say anything about one's personality, health, or spiritual progress, but it does say something about how that person interacts with their physical environment and other people around them. Knowing how to see auras and how your aura interacts with crystals is an important skill to have. It is especially useful if you plan to use a crystal for personal healing because it can reveal the best way to work with it to achieve the most effective results.

Aura colors are a good indicator of an individual's health and the spirit with which they interact with the world around them. Knowing the colors of your aura can help you determine how to work with different types of stones and how to use your crystals for purposes that best serve you. This also involves learning about the aura's layers, their movement, and whether something is wrong. We all have three layers:

The most important layer of the aura is the etheric layer. This is the layer closest to your body, and it is made up of tiny filaments that give your etheric double its shape and form. If this layer becomes damaged or misaligned, then your physical body may also be affected. The etheric layer is responsible for your connection to the physical world, and it is responsible for your inner authority. Due to its proximity to the physical body, energy imbalances in this layer directly impact your physical health. If you are sick or have a weakened immune system, you can be sure that there are issues with your etheric layer. One of the most effective ways of healing the etheric layer is through the use of crystals because they act as energy conduits, have a profound effect on the aura, and can help restore balance to its damaged layers.

The second layer of the aura is known as the emotional or astral body, which allows you to feel emotions. This layer is made up of tiny fibers that vibrate very fast and are responsible for your emotional well-being. There is a great deal of emotional energy in the astral body, which makes it susceptible to outside influences. This is why you need to be careful about how you use crystals around other people. Suppose you want to enhance your emotional energy to provide yourself with more clarity, enthusiasm, and joy. In that case, you can choose crystals with the corresponding energies. Some crystals that can help you in this way are rose quartz, opal, light citrine, and lapis lazuli. The best way to work with these stones is to have a specific purpose in mind and focus on that purpose as you meditate or hold the stone.

The final layer of the aura is the mental body or etheric double. This layer appears as a kind of mist surrounding your body, defining your boundaries and providing you with an innate sense of your individuality. The etheric double doesn't allow any energy to pass through it except for those energies that you have previously agreed to experience. This sense of individuality is an important part of your self-identity and allows you to know that you are separate from everyone else. The mental body is also responsible for your reasoning abilities and your level of understanding. It tells you what to think and helps you develop a particular point of view on every situation. The mental body also protects the higher energy centers of the human body, which are located in the head area. Protecting your higher centers is a key element to overall health and well-being. On the matter of energy centers, the human body has seven such centers, and they are known as chakras.

The Seven Chakras

The human body is made up of sacred energy centers in constant flow, providing a vital link between the physical and spiritual realms. These energy centers are located in areas of special sensitivity to the physical body. They are joined by a subtle substance known as *nadi*, which provides channels that allow kundalini to flow through the body. These channels run along the spine, causing it to become erect like a tree trunk or pole. The spine is therefore considered our staff or cosmic axis, and it connects us to the higher worlds above us. This cosmic axis also connects us with the Earth below us, providing a vital channel for our nutrients and energies to pass through to help sustain our lives here on Earth.

There are seven chakras.
https://pixabay.com/es/illustrations/chakras-cuerpo-yoga-7271423/

Chakras are the basis for our thinking, feeling, sensation and vitality. They also provide us with a source of clairvoyance, clairaudience, and telepathy. They are also responsible for our sense of autonomy and individuality and providing us with a source of power. A key element to overall health is the balance of all these energy centers. Therefore, it is important that we understand their importance and how to open them up to gain more access to healing energies.

The opening of our chakras is called a Kundalini awakening. This is the process of awakening your internal psychic powers, which is necessary to achieve long life, perfect health, and well-being. Suppose you are interested in Kundalini awakening and how it can help you achieve a greater sense of self-control and inner strength. In that case, there are many ways you can go about it, but in this book, we will be taking the crystal route. There are seven main chakras in the human body, which are connected to vital organs, and they are located in this order:

1. The first chakra is known as **Muladhara**, located at the spine's base. Its primary function is to control our physical, financial, and reproductive functions.
2. The second chakra is known as **Svadhisthana**. It is located right under the navel, and its primary function is to help us with self-control.
3. The third chakra is known as **Manipura**, and this chakra controls our sense of self-identity and power. It is located in the stomach.
4. The fourth chakra, known as **Anahata**, is responsible for our heart and the organs within the chest. This chakra also regulates our breathing, immune system, and emotional health. It is located in the middle of the chest.
5. The fifth chakra is known as **Vishudda**. It is located at the base of the throat and regulates our sense of sound and communication.
6. The sixth chakra is known as **Ajna**, located between the eyebrows. Its primary function is to regulate our intuition, psychic powers, and clairvoyance.
7. The seventh chakra, known as **Sahasrara**, is located at the head's crown. This chakra is our main connection to spirituality and is responsible for our enlightenment.

Now that we know the location of all seven chakras, we can begin to work with them through the use of crystals. The first step is to determine which crystal corresponds to each chakra and then focus your attention on that crystal as you meditate or go about your day.

The first chakra, Muladhara, corresponds to the color red –a grounding color. Red crystals are known for providing us with physical energy, vitality, and strength. They are grounding stones that help us become more aware of our physical surroundings and provide protection against external forces. A few examples of red crystals are red tiger's eye quartz and red jasper.

The second chakra, Svadhisthana, corresponds to the color orange. Orange crystals are powerful ray crystals that help us with self-control, sensuality, and sexuality. They also help us to become less self-centered and more in touch with our spiritual nature. A few examples of orange crystals are citrine and tiger's eye quartz.

The third chakra, Manipura, corresponds to the color yellow. Yellow stones help us with mental clarity, decision-making, and logic. They help us become more resourceful and increase our overall vitality through the use of practicality and frugality. Yellow stones also promote a sense of justice, equality, and fairness, as well as provide a balance between our physical and spiritual health. A few examples of yellow crystals are amber and lemon quartz.

The fourth chakra, Anahata, corresponds to the color green. Green stones help us with a sense of compassion and love, which is crucial in our spiritual journey. They are also known for their ability to regulate our emotions and give us greater awareness of what's happening around us. A few examples of green crystals are emeralds, green amethyst, and jade.

The fifth chakra, Vishudda, corresponds to the color blue. Blue crystals help us regain harmony within ourselves and with others. They also help us experience heightened feelings within our heart chakra due to the color of their energies. A few examples of blue crystals are lapis lazuli and aquamarine.

The sixth chakra, Ajna, corresponds to the color indigo. Indigo stones help us with self-control, and they also help us attune to greater levels of knowledge and wisdom through clairvoyance and telepathy. A few examples of indigo crystals are turquoise and celestite.

The seventh chakra, Sahasrara, corresponds to the color violet. Violet stones help us become more spiritualized through a sense of enlightenment and serenity. A few examples of violet crystals are amethyst, purple fluorite, and purple sapphire.

How Do Crystals Heal?

The crystalline structure of stones is an important part of their potential as medicine, but it isn't the only thing that matters. Crystals do more than influence our bodies in ways they might seem, even without contact with us. The stones use their powers to create effects in our environment. They can be considered miniature weather systems that influence the world around us, including us. The energy they carry can significantly impact those sensitive to the energies of crystals, especially if they are placed in areas where people gather. Putting a crystal somewhere affects what's around it because you have placed an energetic signature in the area.

So, putting a crystal on top of your phone, computer, or any other electronic device may cause it to start doing something weird. That's because the crystal emits a field of energy that influences how these machines work. It might slow down your computer or interfere with its signal, or it might do nothing at all, but it is doing something, and if you're sensitive to this kind of thing, you can feel it in your body. This is because the crystal is connected to your body, and your body's electromagnetic field affects all crystals near it. So, when you put a crystal near something like a phone or computer, that object is on the receiving end of whatever qi the crystal emits.

The body has been referred to as a map of the universe, but it's also a representation of the world we live in since what is outside us is also invariably inside us. When we explore our inner self through medical procedures and diagnostic tests, we are also exploring our external world. All things are part of this whole experience. So, when we diagnose or treat any aspect of our body, we also treat every part that makes up who we are.

Our bodies contain all the influences that play upon us from all around us. Our bodies -and how we interact with the environment - are affected by what energy we are given. How we feel about our lives and ourselves is affected by the energy we take in from the environment daily. What you bring into your life is mirrored back to you in the form of affecting your health. Your emotional state affects your body's health just as much as your physical state affects your emotional health. That's because they're all interconnected. Everything you perceive as part of yourself influences every other aspect of yourself — including how you feel physically, mentally, and emotionally.

Your health is a direct reflection of your life as a whole and also of the way you think about yourself. If you feel good about yourself, then your body will feel good. If you don't feel good about yourself, then your body will not be able to function in the way you want it to, and even when it does, there will be a lot of blockages and imbalances in your body. It takes a certain strength of character to truly take care of your health, and doing so is the only cure for the illness that is part of who you are. It takes a certain kind of courage to choose sanity over insanity. It takes a deep level of respect for your own body to remember that it is not just the sum of everything about you but also a part of something much larger than itself. Your physical body is composed of many systems, an amalgamation of all kinds of energies. These systems are not only connected but also connect to the electromagnetic field that surrounds us. How we interact with the environment and our bodies is affected by what energy we are given. Hence, the direct influence of crystals in healing.

Factors That Influence a Crystal's Healing Properties

Many factors influence a crystal's healing properties. The following is a list of what I feel are the most important factors. It isn't an exhaustive list, but it does give you a clear idea of how stones work and why they do what they do.

Shape: Crystals come in all shapes and sizes, and how they are cut affects how they work. Any type of chunk of stone will contain its own inherent patterns. If a crystal is cut in a certain way, it can resonate with the chemical processes that are taking place within the body. This is one theory behind how certain stones have a healing effect on particular ailments. There are also general trends in shapes, such as being square or cubical. These are thought to indicate certain properties such as grounding and centering or being open to new ideas and expression.

Color: Crystals come in many colors and have been used alongside conventional healing methods. For example, there is some evidence that red crystals regulate blood pressure, while blue crystals increase mental clarity and promote positive outlooks on life. Green is generally thought to be healing and protective, and red crystals have been used for their empowering qualities.

Composition refers to a crystal's makeup and the material that crystallizes out of the ground when it forms. This can be influenced by many things, such as man-made pollutants or natural forces, including the sun and moon cycles. Crystals that develop in violent ways are sometimes considered to have stronger earth healing powers than those that form in calm conditions. This is because crystals often store and emit earth energies, and how they were formed affects how they do this.

Frequency: Crystals can be tuned to specific frequencies, affecting how their energy is stored and taken in. Many crystals have their healing properties tuned to the human body's wavelength so that energy can be absorbed more easily. Other crystals can be tuned to specific frequencies, such as those of the Earth or cosmic energies, and these can be used for larger applications like being an environmental protective agent or representing an aspect of the Divine.

Crystal Piezoelectricity

Piezoelectricity is the idea that certain crystals can produce an electrical charge in response to physical disturbances. This is often visualized as a crystal "firing" energy in response to acoustic vibrations, mechanical stress, or even the body's electrical system. Piezoelectricity is an important subject of discussion regarding crystals and healing. However, it can be applied more generally in terms of how crystals interact with other forms of energy. Crystals are affected by many kinds of energies. Some of them are good for healing, and others are not.

It is important to be aware of these differences so that you can choose a crystal with the healing properties you need. Some stones can influence the body's metabolic processes through sound waves, while others can be used to enhance mental clarity and promote positive outlooks on life. For example, the Sacred Geometry Center uses special tuning forks to enhance the piezoelectric potential in crystals, which are then placed on acupuncture points or other areas of the body that need healing. According to their theory, this directly affects the human system and produces immediate results.

There is no single universal theory of how crystals can be used to heal. Many different factors come into play and are considered for each specific application. One of the best indications of whether a stone is healthy for you or not is to look at its color and observe how it reacts when it comes in contact with your skin. While many different qualities can be associated with stones, the best indicator of their healing powers is their actual effect on you.

Chapter 3: Types of Crystal Shapes

The shape is an important factor in determining a crystal's properties. Crystals come in various shapes and sizes, each with a meaning and energy signature of its own. Most crystals come from the earth and can be found everywhere, from sandy beaches to deep caverns below mountains. These natural formations may grow for thousands or millions of years before being removed by miners or crystal enthusiasts. Depending on their shape and formation, certain crystals are believed to possess certain characteristics that play a crucial role in transmitting their energy.

How a crystal is shaped is important when it comes to healing.
https://unsplash.com/photos/EUIALcbnQYI

The shapes of crystals are typically determined by how they are formed in the earth or how miners and collectors cut them. Many people are interested in crystal shapes, as understanding their properties can help them to make informed decisions when purchasing crystals of their own or for others. Depending on the shape, it may be more likely to have certain healing qualities or specific benefits for the interested individual. For example, a person looking to buy an amethyst as a gift may want to give an amethyst with a six-sided point if the person they are buying it for is struggling with anxiety or stress. Likewise, if they are hoping that the recipient will feel more grounded and calmer, they may want to get an amethyst whose point is wider at one end than the other.

The shape of a crystal tells you a lot about the type of energy you should expect from it. The energy of a crystal can be described as vibrations, which come from the crystal's internal structure. Even though these vibrations remain within the crystal, they can be shared with other objects and beings. Depending on the shape and how it relates to the energy being transmitted, crystals can be used for healing, balancing, and strengthening the body's chakras or even soothing an individual who is feeling anxious or stressed.

The shape of a crystal can also provide information about how it was formed. For example, a rough exterior may indicate that the crystal has been exposed to high temperatures and tremendous pressure to form as it did. If these conditions were caused naturally, the crystal would likely have very strong vibrations. However, suppose these conditions were created by man (such as in a mine when the rock was heated to make it easier to remove). In that case, there may be less energy present in the crystal because some of its energy was lost during the removal process.

Many charts are used to describe the energies of crystals based on their shape and appearance. Some look at the whole crystal, whereas others look specifically at the cut-off end. Depending on the appearance, some crystals may be stronger than others when it comes to transmitting energy. For example, a crystal cut with a hexagon point is often considered very powerful because there are many different angles and surfaces from which energy can transmit. However, a different chart may consider a crystal with a much less defined point to be more powerful because its crystal properties have not been disrupted by tampering with sharp instruments.

In terms of healing properties, some crystals may be stronger in certain areas than others. A crystal with many facets on the top may be able to focus energy in certain areas while reducing energy in others. In some instances, the energy differences between various crystal shapes will be subtle and not noticeable to some. However, certain people may have a keen sense of what is happening within the crystal and how it interacts with their energy. These people can use their awareness to help determine which crystals will work best for them and why. Not everyone can do this, and that is fine. For those in need of a little help, you will find below a list of common crystal shapes, what they generally mean, and how you can use them:

Tumbled Stones

Tumbled stones are also called polished stones because when they are made, the rough exterior is ground down to create a smooth surface. This process can take quite a long time, but the result is a smooth and seemingly perfected stone with many uses. If you are looking to work with crystals in your home or on your person, tumbled stones could be an appropriate choice as they are often easy to hold and carry around with you. They may not be as impressive as other crystals, but that doesn't mean that they don't have amazing properties.

Meaning: Tumbled stones are all about grounded energy. You may feel stable and safe when you are near one of these crystals. They can be excellent aids if you need to stay focused at work or school or in any situation where you need to keep yourself calm and feel secure. The tumbled stone is also a good choice if one of your chakras needs energizing, as it will ensure that the flow of energy moving into the body remains steady and consistent.

Pros: They are often inexpensive and easy to find. You can easily put them in your home to help you stay grounded or have them on hand if you need to stay calm. The tumbled stone is also an excellent piece for someone who feels hurt or upset, as it can help them to take out their frustrations and sadness. It is a good piece for anyone who wants to generate positive energy around themselves and anyone who needs a long-term healing crystal, especially if they have started developing negative energy.

Cons: The tumbled stone is not the best choice if you are looking for a crystal that will get your energy moving or going in the right direction quickly. It can take some time to catch on to the energy emitted by a tumbled stone, but once you do, you will probably never feel better. The tumbled stone is also not an excellent choice if you want a crystal to help you release stagnant energy. Since they are naturally very calm, they are not ideal for helping you release what may be stuck in your aura or chakras. They may be good for releasing specific emotions, but they will not necessarily help with the transition from one emotion to the next.

Another drawback of the tumbled stone is that it does not contain many facets. A crystal with many facets can create more energy within itself as it is being worked on, which can positively affect your aura. However, the tumbled stone will not have many facets, so the amount of energy it will emit may be rather small. This can make working with a tumbled stone somewhat arduous, as you may have to spend more time just getting used to the energy being transmitted than you would have if you had a crystal with more facets.

Raw Shape

Raw shapes are uncut, unpolished pieces of a crystal. Although they are not as polished as tumbled stones, they could be cut and polished to make them into tumbled stones or used as is to create a unique piece of jewelry or other objects.

Meaning: Raw crystals are all about amplifying your energy. They can energize you if you need a boost and can be excellent tools when working with the universe to ensure that things move along smoothly. Some raw stones may also have a high amount of energy, which means they will release this energy quickly once you start working with them. Thus, you may want to be careful if you are trying to focus on one particular aspect of your life when this particular problem needs more attention than the rest.

Pros: The raw stone is a good place for those interested in working with stones in their home or on the body because it is relatively easy to handle and carry around. They are also inexpensive and will not take up much space in your home or on your person.

Cons: The wavy look of a raw stone can make it challenging for someone to decide what shape they want to make the piece into.

Wand Shape

A wand crystal has been shaped into a wand. They have always been used for divination purposes and can be found in most old-world magic books. It is believed that the energy emitted from this crystal travels back and forth from your aura to the crystal and back again, creating a constant flow of energy.

Meaning: The energy emitted by a wand stone is often very powerful, so if you are looking for something to help eliminate negative emotions or stagnant energy in your life, this could be an excellent choice. They can do this because much of the power emitted by these stones comes from their ability to manipulate your aura and release any negative emotions or feelings that you may have. They are also excellent sources of energy when you are trying to focus on your life and make a change. They can help you strengthen your aura or your chakras and have the ability to help calm you down if you are feeling overwhelmed or stressed.

Pros: The wand stone is good for those who struggle with stagnant energy. It is also good for those who need a little extra help dealing with negative emotions, as it will make sure that these energies do not overwhelm them. When used in conjunction with other crystals, the wand stone can help release trapped positive energy from the aura or chakras so that it may flow outward freely and easily.

Cons: The wand stone can take some time to get used to. If you are trying to focus on something specific about your aura or chakra, it may help to work with the wand stone by itself for a while before adding another crystal or putting it into water or jewelry. This will help ensure that you are comfortable with the energy it releases before going forward.

Generator Stones

A generator crystal is a stone that can help you create more of your energy. These crystals have been known to aid in meditation, enhancing your spiritual growth and ability to manifest. Generator stones are often rough and unpolished, with six facets of equal size and a single central point. They are very powerful when used properly, emitting rare and intense energy. They will allow you to feel things from within yourself in a way that makes it seem natural and easy. This stone has been used for many years by both practitioners of magic and people interested in the healing power of crystals.

Meaning: If you are looking to enhance your energy, the generator crystal is an excellent choice. It can help with healing by releasing positive energy from your aura and helping you to use this energy in all aspects of your life. Generator crystals can also help with meditation and be used to help open your mind up so that you can learn things more easily. Due to generator stones being known to increase your ability to feel things, they can also help open up pathways in the brain so that you may become more sensitive emotionally or spiritually.

Pros: The generator crystal is an excellent stone for healing and increasing your general knowledge. They can be used for increasing spiritual awareness and making you feel more comfortable with the idea of working with your spiritual side than many other types of crystals. Thanks to this stone's ability to help you become more sensitive, it is assured to improve your clarity on what you want in life. If you are working on your inner strength and power, the generator crystal may be a good choice for you as well.

Cons: The generator crystal may take some time to get used to because it can be intense. It may also be uncomfortable when you first start using it because the energy can feel foreign, although it will eventually open your mind and make you more comfortable working with your spiritual side.

Pyramid Shape

Pyramids are believed to be very powerful and affect your energy in a uniquely effective way. This crystal shape has been referred to as a "power stone" because it has been able to increase energy throughout the body and help other crystal shapes function more easily. Natural pyramids and other crystals that are cut like pyramids will often emit a small beam of energy out of the top when placed on a surface for healing purposes.

Meaning: This shape represents power, intelligence, and healing because it is considered to be a symbol of the human soul. It is also known to represent the Earth, as it is made up of all the energy in the universe. It can help you tap into your mind by channeling the power within the crystal and focusing it on your thoughts and emotions.

Pros: The pyramid shape is mostly beneficial for those who are looking to increase their power in their life. It can help you embody power and confidence, which can be very helpful when trying to define your life purpose. It can also help increase your energy so that you begin to feel better overall, which can make working toward that power a much easier task because of how strong and healthy you will feel.

Cons: The pyramid shape can take some time to get used to, as it may feel a little intense at first. It can also be uncomfortable because it will open up your mind and make you more aware of your thoughts, which may be overwhelming.

Cluster Shape

Clusters are often used for their energy, ability to work together, and the beautiful shapes they can make. They can also help to heal, balance, and enhance chakras. Cluster stones are also excellent for grounding and promoting mental purity. They can be described as a "condensed energy" stone and are believed to be able to enhance one's psychic abilities. These stones are often used in meditation because they work to help you connect with your higher self.

Meaning: Cluster-shaped crystals represent the unity of all things. They are also a symbol of Earth and can help open up your chakras so you may feel a renewed sense of connection to the surrounding nature. They are also believed to increase the power of crystals in contact with them.

Pros: Cluster stones are excellent for releasing bad energies from your aura, chakras, and mind. They will help you become more aware of what you want out of life, increasing clarity. They can also help you feel more relaxed because cluster stones are believed to promote healing, mentally and physically. They are wonderful for anyone who wants to work on their health and sense of well-being.

Cons: These stones may be a little intense at first and can feel uncomfortable, especially if you are not used to feeling so open.

Sphere Shape

Spheres are often used for spiritual purposes and are known to emit energy when held. They are often believed to be able to help with astral travel, psychic abilities, and insomnia. They can also be helpful for healing, increasing energy levels, relieving stress, and allowing you to connect with your subconscious mind.

Meaning: The sphere stone is a powerful symbol of divine feminine energy because it is round and open in the center. Its circular shape will allow your aura to expand so that you may achieve higher states of consciousness and become more aware of your spirituality. Because it can allow you to travel outside your body and into the astral plane, it can help with spiritual manifestations and psychism.

Pros: The sphere-shaped crystal is a powerful tool that increases your awareness and helps you achieve spiritual goals because of its ability to bring spirituality into the present moment. It is excellent for helping those who experience anxiety and insomnia because the stone will help them attain a sound sleep through meditation. It will also increase the energy within your aura, making you feel empowered and more self-confident.

Cons: The sphere stone can feel a little too much at first, especially if you are not used to feeling so expanded within your aura. It may take some time for you to get used to, and there may be an adjustment period when you do decide to start using the sphere stone.

Egg Shape

Eggs are often used for their beauty, connection to yin and yang, and ability to balance the body. They are also believed to be able to help you with change and healing.

Meaning: This shape symbolizes the third eye, the pineal gland, and the pituitary gland.

Pros: Egg-shaped crystals can help you protect yourself from harm by increasing your physical and spiritual strength. They can help you to cope with changes in your life because they have a natural ability to retain energy. Egg-shaped crystals will also help smooth out any energetic imbalances in your life so that there will not be as much stress or blockages within it.

Cons: One would not want to use this stone if they were looking to stop the flow of life; rather, they should be trying to flow with it.

Heart Shape

Heart-shaped crystals are often used as a symbol of love and affection. They can help to promote loving feelings and connect with your heart chakra. Hearts can also help you to achieve meaningful dreams, channel psychic abilities, and increase self-awareness. Many people believe that hearts are good for healing because they can align with the solar plexus chakra and help restore balance after an illness or injury.

Meaning: Heart-shaped stones will help you to connect with the divine love and affection within you. By working with this type of crystal, you can learn how to achieve emotional balance and truly feel in tune with your inner self. Heart-shaped crystals are also very powerful when it comes to dispelling negative energies, which can be useful for those who feel as if they are struggling in their lives because of anxiety or other negative emotions. They will also remove any existing blockages within the body so that healing can occur more easily.

Pros: Heart-shaped crystals have a better ability to rid the body of negative energy than other stone shapes, making them highly effective when helping to heal on many levels.

Cons: It can be difficult to work with heart-shaped crystals if you are not used to feeling compassionate and loving toward yourself.

Hexagonal Shape

Hexagonal crystals can be described as perfect six-sided crystals that are as powerful as they look. They have a very strong connection with the Earth, which can be felt through the energy that they emit and the way that they look. Hexagonal crystals often intensify emotions and energy to promote healing, cleansing, and protection. These stones are often placed on third eye chakras to help aid with psychic abilities.

Meaning: This crystal shape represents truth, abundance, and balance. Using hexagonal stones can help you achieve a perfect balance and find your inner truth.

Pros: It is believed that these crystals will help you to open up your mind and allow you to see things from a different perspective. They can also be used for protection, especially when paired with the solar plexus chakra. In addition, hexagonal crystals can increase creativity, making them very useful if you are searching for an alternative way of thinking or feeling.

Cons: These crystals can be a bit intense and off-putting at first, making it difficult to fully comprehend what they are telling you.

Cube Shape

Cube-shaped crystals are mostly used for their beauty and the way that they look. They are often associated with protection and healing because of the way that they appear to hold everything together. These crystals can help promote mental clarity while also helping to create stability within your life.

Meaning: Cube-shaped crystals represent wisdom and knowledge, as well as security.

Pros: Cube-shaped crystals are often used for protection and healing because of their ability to defend against harmful energies. They can also help with physical healing through their ability to promote the creation of new cells in the body.

Cons: These stones are powerful and can be a bit intense if you are not used to feeling like you have all the answers.

Chapter 4: 13 Must-Have Crystals for Beginners

Something is comforting about the idea of carrying a crystal, and it is no surprise that many people find them to be powerful tools for self-expression, healing, and intuition. The vast world of crystals is fascinating — there are approximately twelve thousand known varieties. So, you may be thinking, "Where do I even start?" Well, before you get overwhelmed with all the choices out there, just take a deep breath and prepare yourself for an in-depth journey with these 13 must-have crystals for every beginner.

Selenite

As one of the most important crystal varieties, this magnificent mineral exhibits a creamy white color and is often used in crystal healing because of its powers of purification. Carrying or wearing selenite can help you to get rid of negative energy that may be holding you back.

Selenite.
https://upload.wikimedia.org/wikipedia/commons/3/3a/Gypse-s%C3%A9l%C3%A9nite_3.jpeg

It is said that selenite can be so effective at clearing negative energy that it even works on psychic vampires — meaning it will keep your mind free from being drained by others. No matter what your intentions when purchasing crystals, selenite should at least make the top five on your list.

Crystal System: Monoclinic

Colors: White, Pink, Blue

Energy: Loving, protective, comforting

Chakra: Heart, Throat

Helps to Achieve: Clear communication, healing of emotional trauma, emotional balance, releasing headaches and stress.

Placement: On the chakra where there are problems, it is said that selenite can help to soothe and neutralize the pain. Using selenite daily can help to create a stronger energetic shield around any chakra problem area.

Best Used With: Rose quartz, emerald, golden labradorite, chrysocolla, aquamarine

Fascinating Fact: Selenite is the only mineral on Earth with its own star, known as 34 Draconis.

Citrine

This beautiful yellow variety helps to bring positive energy and good luck. It is believed to lift your spirits, making you happier with life. The Citrine's power comes from the sun and is often known as the merchant's stone because it promotes business success. It assists in developing new skills and abilities, which is ideal for those just starting in their careers. The gentle energy of citrine can bring abundance into your life, giving you the peace of mind that allows you to relax, knowing everything is going according to plan. Citrine allows you to achieve inner peace and trust in the universe, making a serene feeling emerge within those who carry it. It is considered a stone of abundance and success, as it brings good health and fortune to those who wear it.

Crystal System: Trigonal

Colors: White, Yellow/Gold, Orange/Brown

Energy: Loving, grounding, strengthening

Chakra: Sacral (below the navel), Solar Plexus (stomach area)

Helps to Achieve: Acceptance of change, acceptance of yourself, helps to overcome fears, procrastination, and self-doubt – and helps by improving concentration.

Placement: Citrine should be used with the chakras affected by the problem, such as the stomach area, to overcome fears or below the navel to help with self-acceptance. Placement should be made into a grid pattern, drawn in lines of yellow.

Best Used With: Carnelian, black tourmaline, smoky quartz, angelite

Fascinating Fact: Citrine was considered a symbol of wealth and royalty in ancient civilizations.

Clear Quartz

Clear quartz is known to be the master healer of crystals, as it helps to amplify energy. It also brings clarity of mind and good luck to those who carry it. The energy of clear quartz is said to help remove old emotional wounds. It can also help you to understand what you are feeling on a deeper level, enabling you to become more self-aware. Many cultures have used this stone throughout history, including the ancient Egyptians and Native Americans. In the old days, people would use clear quartz as a conductor of lightning or electricity because it is known to help with nervous disorders and diseases that affect the heart, genitourinary system, kidneys, throat, muscles, and bladder. Clear quartz is also known to promote healing on a spiritual level, bringing good luck in all experiences — including those requiring patience.

Crystal System: Trigonal

Colors: Clear (colorless)

Energy: Open, cleansing, calming

Chakra: Throat, Third Eye (between your eyes), crown chakra (top of your head)

Helps to Achieve: More self-confidence, a rise in your vibration level, helps you to overcome jealousy, opening the mind and heart.

Placement: A fine grid of clear quartz should be used to electrify and clear any energy blockages in the physical and chakra bodies.

Best Used With: Rose quartz, lemon quartz

Fascinating Fact: Clear quartz was used by ancient Egyptians for writing hieroglyphics on the walls of their tombs.

Rose Quartz

This soft pink variety is known to be one of the most important stones for women. Rose quartz has a nurturing and calming energy, which makes it perfect for soothing any negative emotions and troubles that have been in the way of your happiness. It is often used when working with the heart chakra, as it helps to heal emotional wounds. Many women are drawn to rose quartz because its soft pink energy gives a feeling of love, peace, and hope, making it the perfect stone to enhance self-love and confidence.

It is believed that rose quartz can help create harmony between yourself and others, which will strengthen your relationships. The gentle energy of this stone can bring feelings of inner peace and love, which will lead to a higher vibration in your life. Rose quartz is typically used for self-acceptance purposes and gives you the courage to be yourself — even if others do not accept you. It can also help you overcome procrastination or the habit of putting things off until later. High vibrations of rose quartz symbolize a soft pink light that is calming and healing to your entire being.

Crystal System: Trigonal

Colors: Pink/White (pastel tint), Pink/Grey (gray shade)

Energy: Open, loving, soothing

Chakra: Heart Chakra (center of chest)

Helps to Achieve: Emotional growth, achieving balance in desires, greater self-love, and happiness.

Placement: Rose quartz should be used with the chakras affected by the problem, such as your heart chakra, to overcome jealousy. Placement should be made in a grid pattern, drawn in lines of pink.

Best Used With: Rutilated quartz, sunstone

Fascinating Fact: In 2009, a pink "super quartz" was discovered that was five times more powerful than the regular rose quartz.

Amethyst

This purple-blue stone has long been considered a powerful gemstone. It is believed to balance the emotions of both men and women. Its energy is said to help you to break through negative patterns in life, soothe anger and resentment, and reunite with your true self.

Amethyst.
https://pxhere.com/en/photo/1560451

Amethyst is known for its amazing healing qualities, as its power is strong enough to heal deep emotional wounds from past experiences. It is known to help you let go of old memories and experiences so that you can learn to live a more peaceful life. It's also said to help with balance and contentment, which can lead you down the path of self-love and happiness. There are many shades and varieties of amethyst, ranging from clear blue with white streaks to lavender-looking stones that look like pastel violet clouds.

Crystal System: Trigonal

Colors: Purple/Blue

Energy: Deep, grounding, uplifting

Chakra: Brow (between the eyes), Heart (center of chest)

Helps to Achieve: Overcoming negative past experiences, overcoming procrastination, supporting your true self.

Placement: Amethyst should be placed into a grid pattern, drawn in lines of purple. You should clean the amethyst crystal regularly, as it will hold negative energy and drain you if you do not cleanse it.

Best Used With: Personal talisman

Fascinating Fact: The ancients believed that amethyst would help those who drank from cups carved out of this stone not to become drunk.

Lapis Lazuli

The lapis lazuli, also known as the blue stone, is a semi-precious stone that is formed from a mixture of minerals from the Badakhshan region of Afghanistan. This stone has a beautiful color and luster and is said to help heal all illnesses. Lapis lazuli was used as a stone of healing by the ancient Egyptians, and, to this day, it is still known for its healing properties as it strengthens the mind and body and helps to calm emotional issues. Lapis' deep blue color gives off soothing energy that can help you regain your serenity. It has a spiritual energy that brings about wisdom and knowledge, which can help you overcome issues with intuition and the mind.

Crystal System: Cubic

Colors: Blue/Black, Blue/White, White/Black (tinted)

Energy: Deep, mystical, soothing

Chakra: Brow (between the eyes), Third Eye (in the center of your forehead)

Helps to Achieve: Inner peace, balance in emotions, and greater wisdom and knowledge.

Placement: Anywhere in your home or around your workspace will be beneficial, but be sure to keep one with you at all times and another in a crystal grid.

Best Used With: White pearl, turquoise.

Fascinating Fact: Ancient Egyptians believed that anyone who carried lapis lazuli would have the power to command spirits and bring them back from the dead.

Green Aventurine

This variety was named due to its similarity to the quartz family. However, aventurine has a distinct green color that differs from the other quartz. This stone is commonly known as the "stone of opportunity" and is often used to attract prosperity and good luck. It is believed that green aventurine helps bring abundance into your life by increasing your flow of money, success, and happiness. Green aventurine can help you overcome blockages in your life that may be holding you back. It is believed to increase intelligence or help develop your potential for intellectual growth. People often carry green aventurine as a talisman of protection and luck, as they believe this stone is the key to solving problems and overcoming adversities. The mystical energy of the stone has unique properties that can be used for spiritual training and development, in addition to helping you to achieve success and abundance in your life.

Crystal System: Trigonal

Colors: Green, Dark green

Energy: Energetic, uplifting

Chakra: Heart (center of chest)

Helps to Achieve: Success, prosperity, abundance, healing emotional issues, overcoming blockages in life.

Placement: Green aventurine can be placed anywhere in your home or office and carried with you as a talisman or amulet.

Best Used With: Jade, citrine

Fascinating Fact: In Ancient Greece, green aventurine was often used by Apollo, the sun god.

Moonstone

The moonstone is thought to have been sacred to the ancient Egyptians, Sumerians, and Greeks and revered as a symbol of the goddess Isis. It is also believed to symbolize hope, inner strength, and the renewal of life. This beautiful crystal helps you to overcome emotional and mental blocks that may be holding you back from happiness and success in your life.

Moonstone.
https://commons.wikimedia.org/wiki/File:Natural_Blue_Moonstone_loose_gemstone.jpg

It's said that moonstone can help you release emotional trauma from past experiences to heal yourself. It is also believed that moonstone can help with emotional stability and support you in overcoming the emotions of fear, anger, and insecurity. It can help overcome procrastination by giving you the confidence needed to fulfill your goals in life. Moonstone is an excellent stone that helps with emotional stability, security, and balance, which will give you the calmness and happiness you need to get through each day.

Crystal System: Monoclinic
Colors: Light-Green/White, White, Blue/White
Energy: Energetic, nurturing, balancing.
Chakra: Crown (top of the head)
Helps to Achieve: Greater emotional stability, overcoming fears, overcoming procrastination, overcoming blocks to achieving happiness and success.
Placement: Moonstones should be placed in a grid, in an area free of clutter and with good airflow.
Best Used With: Blue Topaz, Hematite
Fascinating Fact: In ancient cultures, it was believed that the moon's reflection on water would cause the moonstone to produce a glow.

Obsidian

Obsidian is black or volcanic glass formed millions of years ago. It has been used as a talisman and amulet for centuries due to its unique properties. Obsidian can help one overcome mental blocks and achieve mental clarity. It also helps overcome procrastination by encouraging complete attention and focus on the task at hand. It is said that obsidian can help bring balance into your life and to maintain peace in the face of adversity, which is essential for positive growth. Obsidian is an excellent stone that helps with success and prosperity by allowing you to overcome the fear of failure, which many people face. It can also help release feelings of guilt and shame caused by a traumatic experience. It's also thought that obsidian can help dispel negative thoughts and feelings and bring about a release from trauma from a difficult experience in the past.

Crystal System: Amorphous
Colors: Black, Brown
Energy: Protective, healing, grounding
Chakra: Root (base of the spine)
Helps to Achieve: Mental clarity, overcoming problems with procrastination, mental blocks, safety/protection from harm, and it helps release you from past traumas.

Placement: Any area in the home or office will be beneficial, but finding a place free of clutter and with good airflow is ideal. Placement can also be in a grid pattern for heightened benefits.

Best Used With: Amber, jasper.

Fascinating Fact: Obsidian was used by Aztecs and Mayans to make knives, razor blades, and arrowheads.

Tiger's Eye

Tiger's Eye is a beautiful golden-brown stone known for its bold stripes, resembling a tiger's eye. It's said that the tiger's eye can help you to activate your self-confidence and self-will. It's also said that this stone will bring clarity to your mind and help you see the truth. Tiger's Eye is believed to bring wealth and abundance into your life by helping to attract positive energy into your life. It can also help overcome melancholy, a state of hopelessness, or depression.

Crystal System: Trigonal

Colors: Golden, Red

Energy: Expansive, creative, healing.

Chakra: Heart (center of chest)

Helps to Achieve: Achieving success, overcoming procrastination, overcoming blocks to achieving happiness and success.

Placement: Tiger's Eye is a stone that should be kept in a positive environment with good airflow. It can also be placed in a grid pattern or worn as a necklace.

Best Used With: Gold, clear quartz

Fascinating Fact: In the early 1900s, it was believed that Tiger's Eye made the wearer invisible to their enemies.

Malachite

Malachite is a deep green stone known for its shiny, smooth surface. Since ancient times, it has been used as a stone to connect with the earth and nature. Malachite can help to heal deep-seated emotional issues and helps the user to find peace within themself. It can also help overcome procrastination by bringing positive change into their life, which will bring about success and abundance. Malachite is also said to be a great stone for meditation and can help concentration. It can help you move out of negative patterns and replace them with positive ones.

Crystal System: Monoclinic

Colors: Green, Brown

Energy: Supporting, cleansing, purifying.

Chakra: Heart (center of chest), Solar plexus (below the navel)

Helps to Achieve: Finding Peace within oneself, overcoming procrastination, success in life

Placement: Malachite should be placed in an area that has good airflow. It should also be placed in a grid pattern, if possible. It can also be placed on the solar plexus chakra or worn as a necklace.

Best Used With: Black tourmaline

Fascinating Fact: Malachite may have been used during the Egyptian era as a protective stone.

Hematite

Hematite is a red-brown stone that appears as a dull orange. It has been used as a talisman for centuries. Ancient cultures used hematite as a symbol of health and vitality, and, as a result, it is often associated with the heart chakra. It activates our dormant healing energies, which can be blocked by fears or issues surrounding self-esteem or being unworthy of love.

Hematite.
https://commons.wikimedia.org/wiki/File:WLA_hmns_Hematite.jpg

Hematite can help you snap out of your negative patterns and start anew. It can also help overcome procrastination by urging you to get started on an important task, which is a great way to clear the clutter from your mind and gain focus. Hematite will help you be optimistic and happy, which is essential for health and abundance.

Crystal System: Trigonal

Colors: Red-brown, Orange-brown

Energy: Empowering, protective, healing.

Chakra: Heart (center of chest)

Helps to Achieve: Being more optimistic and happy, overcoming procrastination, and removing blockages.

Placement: Hematite can be placed at the heart chakra or solar plexus for greater energy output. It can also be placed in a grid or worn as a necklace.

Best Used With: Tiger's Eye, Red Jasper, Red Garnet

Fascinating Fact: Hematite is found in the liver and spleen of animals. Also, the color of hematite can vary greatly depending on the mineral content. If you are concerned that your hematite stone may not be as rich in color as others, you can test it first with a piece of cloth soaked in vinegar and rub it over the stone. If it turns a vibrant red-orange, then it is clean enough to use.

Bloodstone

Bloodstone is a glossy black stone with red spots. It is also known as a "weather stone," meaning it is known to be dependable and bring good luck. This powerful stone can help you become more focused, find inner strength, and overcome procrastination. It can also help you solve problems and become a better communicator.

Crystal System: Trigonal

Colors: Green, Red

Energy: Enlivening, cleansing, protective.

Chakra: Heart (center of chest)

Helps to Achieve: Achieving success, overcoming procrastination, getting into a "flow" state.

Placement: Bloodstone must be placed in a grid pattern with red or green lines. It can also be worn as a necklace or amulet.

Best Used With: Carnelian, labradorite, tourmaline

Fascinating Fact: Bloodstones were important stones to ancient Egyptian culture. It was dyed red by the blood of sacrifices and then made into jewelry and other treasures of high value. The red color was believed to give it power, which would protect its wearer from harm. In Ancient Rome, it was used in a powdered form to stop bleeding and treat snake bites.

Chapter 5: 16 More-Advanced Crystals to Own

Some crystals can be more advanced than others because they have more sides with reflecting surfaces, making them more efficient electromagnetic radiation antennas than other crystals with fewer surfaces. So, you may not know it yet, but you're probably interacting with an advanced crystal every day. Advanced crystals can form more than one shape; they can curve, change color and texture, absorb light in different wavelengths from different sources, and reflect it in particular directions or bands. You could think of them as a sort of accident.

These are pieces of crystals that formed in a certain way or grew together to form a single large crystal with lots of surface area to reflect as many wavelengths of electromagnetic radiation as possible. Advanced crystals can absorb radiation from certain places and directions and may have the capacity to redirect it. They can also focus the radiation inward and take the energy for themselves. They can store it and release it later, or even take the energy from one source and transfer it to another. They can even use their energies to power other crystals" processes, like healing their owners or assisting in the owner's healing. They can produce a force of attraction more powerful than other crystals, enabling them to attract more than just light and electromagnetic radiation but emotions as well, making them useful in some therapeutic applications. These wonder crystals require a bit of experience, and of all the options available today, here are some must-haves to add to your crystal collection.

Moldavite

Moldavite is a green tektite, a glass that was created by the impact of meteorites or comets that crashed into the Earth. It was formed during the end of the Cretaceous period and is believed to be millions of years old. Moldavite was named after an area in the Czech Republic where they were first discovered in 1787 by a peasant who found them while plowing his field. Because of its mystique, this crystal is one of the more expensive crystals on the market today. It does not lose its potency and can be used for meditation, astral projection, and healing.

Crystal System: Amorphous

Colors: Green, white

Energy: Meditative, healing

Chakra: Heart, Third-eye

Helps to Achieve: Clarification, self-introspection, spiritual enlightenment

Placement: Moldavite should be placed around the neck or carried in a pouch to promote physical and emotional healing.

Best Used With: Aura Quartz, Petalite, Selenite, and Pink tourmaline.

Fascinating Fact: Moldavite was found to have healing properties in 1895 after researchers studied a Moldavian peasant's ability to recover from illness quickly.

Lemurian Quartz

Lemurian quartz was found in 1987 in Brazil. It is a crystal with a Lemurian theme and is believed to be connected to the Lemurian civilization, which existed from 3.9 million to around 13 thousand years ago. The crystal emits energy, which has been measured to be as powerful as the energy emitted by the sun.

Lemurian quartz can heal and balance all chakras and help bring harmony. Its energy is very strong and can sometimes be overwhelming, so it should be used with an advanced crystal to balance the energies. Although it was found to have highly powerful healing properties, Lemurian quartz is also a highly sensitive crystal and should be handled with care.

Crystal System: Hexagonal

Colors: Clear, blue, green

Energy: Healing, balancing, harmonizing

Chakra: All of them

Helps to Achieve: Clearing, manifestation, and transmutation of negative energy into positive. It can be used to regain balance by re-establishing the connection between the physical and spiritual planes and channeling soothing energy through its innovative vibrations.

Placement: Lemurian quartz should be placed on the heart, third eye, and crown chakras. It can also be worn on the body for protection and manifestation.

Best Used With: Lepidolite, celestite, kunzite and blue lace agate.

Fascinating Fact: The Lemurian civilization was a civilization that existed on Earth about 14 million years ago, just before the Great Deluge.

Sugilite

Sugilite is a crystal that has been found in Africa, also known as the "African Star of Living Water" or "African Buddha's Pebble." It is considered one of the major earth energy crystals. According to research and studies,

Sugilite.
https://commons.wikimedia.org/wiki/File:Royalazel_sugilite_smithsonianmuseum.jpg

Sugilite works on the root chakra. Since it's a very powerful crystal and has amplified or altered energies of other crystals, it's best used with other advanced crystals to balance the energies, although it does work well on its own. Sugilite can help us connect with the angelic realm, bringing messages to us from the angels. It can also help with past-life regression. Sugilite's connection to the root chakra increases self-love and compassion for yourself, others, and the world around you.

Crystal System: Hexagonal

Colors: Purple

Energy: Grounding, calming, healing

Chakra: Root

Helps to Achieve: Balance in life and spiritual enlightenment. It can be used to place a shield around your aura and balance the chakras, enhancing intuition, psychic abilities, and interdimensional traveling. It also improves creativity and self-expression, allowing you to speak your truth without bias.

Placement: Sugilite should be placed around the neck, in a pouch, or in the home. Placing sugilite under your pillow at night helps with foresight, intuition, and understanding of your dreams.

Best Used With: Celestite, rose quartz, malachite, and Dow quartz.

Fascinating Fact: Sugilite is a metaphysically charged crystal that can help awaken one's spirituality, open channels to psychic abilities, and enhance intuition. It has empathy in its energy, allowing it to recognize others" needs as well as one's own. Sugilite also acts as a psychic protector, blocking harmful energies from entering its space and keeping negativity at bay.

Shungite

Shungite is a mineral that has been found in the Georgia oblast of Russia. It is named after a town in Georgia after two miners found it while plowing their fields. It is believed that it was formed 2.6 million years ago. Like all the other crystals on this list, it emits very strong energies and can be used to heal and transmute negative energies (physical, emotional, or spiritual) into positive ones. It can also be used to help with heart and mind issues and is a very helpful crystal for all issues concerning mental health. Shungite is a stone of protection, giving the wearer strength, inner peace, courage, and self-confidence. It can also help to instill a feeling of goodness, generosity, and love into the bearer. Placed around the hips, Shungite can be used for protection from negative energies and worry.

Crystal System: Trigonal

Colors: Yellow, gray

Energy: Healing, cleansing, grounding, balancing

Chakra: Heart

Helps to Achieve: Clearing emotional issues and relieving mental stress.

Placement: Shungite should be placed on the heart, between the eyes, and over the crown chakra. It can also be added to waist beads.

Best Used With: Rose quartz, rose quartz, and petrified wood

Fascinating Fact: Shungite is a high-frequency crystal that channels light in healing many of the body's ailments, including joint pain.

Celestite

Celestite is a highly powerful crystal that has been found in the high deserts of California. It is known for its connection to the moon and does not respond to light from below a certain angle. It emits vibrant colors, which bring a sense of balance. Celestite is believed to be the only crystal that has been found in solids composed of pure iridescence. It is used to release negative energy, heal emotional and mental issues, and help with past-life regression. It can also be used to stabilize one's vibration, helping with an ascension process.

Crystal System: Orthorhombic

Colors: Blue/White, Green, Pink

Energy: Emotional healing, balancing, and purifying the aura

Chakra: Third-eye and crown

Helps to Achieve: Spiritual growth, bringing clarity of thought and emotion, cleansing of the chakras, past-life regression

Placement: Celestite should be placed on the third-eye chakra or in a crystal grid.

Best Used With: Rose quartz, citrine, blue lace agate, and green chalcedony.

Fascinating Fact: Placing a piece of celestite under your pillow at night helps you grasp the lessons you face in your dreams.

Labradorite

Labradorite is a feldspar mineral that has been found in Madagascar, China, and Canada. It is a stone of transformation and magic, helping the wearer become better in tune with their intuition.

Labradorite.
https://commons.wikimedia.org/wiki/File:Labradorite_Labrador_MNHN_Min%C3%A9r alogie.jpg

The iridescent qualities of Labradorite, also known as "flash stone," make it a wonderful piece for meditation. This stone draws off negative energies and helps to free you from emotional instabilities, making it helpful when dealing with depression. Labradorite is also called the Stone of Magic.

Crystal System: Triclinic

Colors: Grey, green, red, and white

Energy: Emotional healing, transmutation of negativity, and unblocking of the aura

Chakra: Throat

Helps to Achieve: Strengthening the throat chakra and clearing any blockages to one's aura.

Placement: Labradorite should be placed on the throat as it helps to open up communication channels.

Best Used With: Rose quartz, petrified wood, golden amber, and petrified wood.

Fascinating Fact: Labradorite has low iron content, so the crystal will not be affected by weathering.

Rutilated Quartz

Rutilated Quartz is a quartz crystal that has been filled with rutile (titanium dioxide). It was originally used to add iridescence to other stones, but it was discovered that it is an extremely powerful stone in its own right. This crystal aids in the ability to absorb strong emotions, such as jealousy, anger, and resentment. It helps one to relieve stress and unblock the heart chakra. Rutilated quartz also helps to develop spirituality in the wearer.

Crystal System: Trigonal

Colors: White, golden, sky blue, and red

Energy: Protection against negative energies, cleansing of the aura

Chakra: Heart and crown

Helps to Achieve: Stabilization of personal vibrations, calming the mind, and eliminating negativity within oneself.

Placement: Rutilated quartz should be placed on the heart chakra and crown.

Best Used With: Celestite, rose quartz, petrified wood, and pink tourmaline.

Fascinating Fact: Rutilated quartz is used in making infrared light to find counterfeit currency and driver's licenses.

Auralite

Auralite is a rare crystal that some believe came from an explosion of Atlantis, which destroyed the continent and sank it into the ocean. This mineral was found in a crater on the island of Mauritius by a French man called Bouvet in 1852, and he gave it its name. As with all crystals that have been related to Atlantis, it has been said to be highly powerful, emitting energies that can heal emotional wounds and imbalances within oneself. Auralite helps you to become more grounded and fearless in your life. It also helps you to become more aware of the spiritual world. Crystal healing guides note that Auralite can be used in clearing the chakras and connecting you with the spirit realm.

Crystal System: None, because it is made of 23 different minerals.

Colors: Red, Black/White, Purple

Energy: Healing and spiritual growth connection with the earth and other realms.

Chakra: Third eye

Helps to Achieve: Clearing of blockages, opening of the third-eye chakra to assist with meditation and spiritual exploration

Placement: Auralite should be placed on the third eye chakra.

Best Used With: Silver sage, rose quartz, and clear quartz.

Fascinating Fact: This crystal was believed by some to be the eye of God.

Libyan Desert Glass

Libyan Desert Glass is a type of lava glass that is made up of thousands of tiny bubbles of gas trapped in the lava. This glass is used in crystal healing because it helps clear energy blocks and removes stress from the body and mind. It can be used as a tool for meditation, as it enhances awareness during this time. This stone helps connect you with the energies of ascension and is said to meet your heart's desire if you meditate using it.

Crystal System: Amorphous

Colors: Clear, Yellow

Energy: Clearing negative energy, connecting with the earth and other realms, healing the aura

Chakra: Throat, third eye, and crown

Helps to Achieve: Clearing of blockages in the chakras, removing stress from the body and mind, and attaining enlightenment through meditation.

Placement: Libyan Desert glass should be placed on the throat, third eye, and crown chakras.

Best Used With: Moissanite, petrified wood, amethyst, and rose quartz.

Fascinating Fact: Libyan Desert glass was once known as "dragon's breath" as it was originally used as a tool by magicians.

Dow Quartz

Dow quartz is a form of quartz crystal that stretches out in long strands. It is named after its discoverer, Charles Dow, who found it in a mine in Brazil. Dow Quartz can be used for meditation and for clearing the mind. It is believed that this crystal can help the wearer let go of emotional baggage and heal emotional wounds or trauma from the past. It also helps to clear up negative energy and eliminate energetic blockages within the body. This crystal is good for those undergoing psychotherapy, as it helps the wearer understand their thoughts better. Crystal healing guides note that this crystal can be used in connecting with angels or other forms of spirit guides during meditation.

Crystal System: Trigonal

Colors: Clear

Energy: Connecting to earth and other realms, healing of the aura, emotional healing, meditation

Chakra: Crown and third-eye

Helps to Achieve: Clearing blockages in the chakras, eliminating negative energy from one's body and mind, and attaining enlightenment through meditation.

Placement: Dow quartz should be placed on the crown and third-eye chakras.

Best Used With: Amethyst, rose quartz, and clear quartz.

Fascinating Fact: Dow quartz was once used as an ingredient in toothpaste because of its ability to cleanse and strengthen teeth.

Herkimer Diamond

The Herkimer diamond is a type of quartz crystal that is translucent and has a hexagonal shape. It comes from Herkimer County in central New York, hence its name. This crystal is used to heal and protect the wearer from psychic attacks, negative energies, and spirits. It can also be used as a tool to channel positive energy. It is said to awaken one's psychic abilities by helping one gain clarity within one's mind. Crystal healing guides note that this crystal can be used to access the Akashic records.

Crystal System: Trigonal

Colors: Clear, White, Yellow

Energy: Protection from psychic attacks, healing of physical and emotional wounds, an awakening of psychic abilities

Chakra: Heart and crown

Helps to Achieve: Protection from negative energies and spirits, cleansing of the aura to release negativity within oneself, and attaining enlightenment through meditation.

Placement: The Herkimer diamond should be placed on the heart chakra and crown.

Best Used With: Clear quartz, amethyst rose quartz and clear quartz.

Fascinating Fact: In ancient times, Herkimer County was thought to be protected by a guardian angel named Herkimer, who protected the community from invaders. Legend has it that he would appear in the form of a gray horse when needed.

Astrophyllite

Astrophyllite is a type of plagioclase feldspar. It is named after its Greek name, a*stron phyllon*, which means "star leaf." Astrophyllite can be used to connect with the energies of the universe, helping you to experience the spiritual and creative forces within yourself. This crystal helps one to meditate easier by calming the mind in preparation for meditation. It is also believed to help with spiritual healing, which it can do by clearing the aura so that all negative blockages can be released from the body. It is a stone that can help you connect with your spirit guides and higher beings. This crystal holds energy from Mother Nature, Queen Gaia, and God's Voice.

Crystal System: Cubic

Colors: Brown, White, Yellow

Energy: Connecting with the universe, metaphysical healing, spiritual healing, imagination, meditation

Chakra: Heart and throat.

Helps to Achieve: Connecting with the cosmos, understanding one's place in the world, and attaining enlightenment through meditation.

Placement: Astrophyllite should be placed on the throat chakra and heart chakras.

Best Used With: Amethyst and clear quartz.

Fascinating Fact: The Milky Way has been said to hold astrophyllite within its core.

Azeztulite

Azeztulite is a type of felsic intrusive igneous rock with a light yellow to white color. It is named after the Azez tribe, who discovered it near Lake Van in eastern Turkey. Azeztulite is a hard stone that has been said to have miraculous healing properties. It is used to heal emotions and heal the spirit, releasing negative energies from within the body. This stone can also be used in crystal healing and to stimulate the growth of plants.

Crystal System: Hexagonal

Colors: White, Clear, Streaky Orange, Pale yellow

Energy: Emotional healing, releasing negativity from within the body, eye health and balance, meditation

Chakra: Third-eye, throat

Helps to Achieve: Healing emotions and releasing negative energy from within one's body through meditation.

Placement: Azeztulite should be placed on the third-eye chakra, throat chakra, and crown.

Best Used With: Black kyanite, clear quartz, lapis lazuli, and aquamarine.

Fascinating Fact: Azeztulite has been used to help cure eye problems such as macular degeneration, cataracts, and glaucoma.

Seraphinite

Seraphinite is a form of fibrous chlorite and is a type of mineral that looks like white cotton or as if it is spun from glass. First discovered near the town of Pennsylvania, it is named after the seraphim because of its silky texture, which resembles an angel's feather. It is used to heal the mind, body, and spirit through meditation and prayer. Seraphinite can also be used to channel energies from within the universe for healing purposes. This stone can also stimulate growth within plants.

Crystal System: Monoclinic

Colors: White, Deep Gray, Green

Energy: Healing of the mind, body, and spirit through meditation, attaining enlightenment through prayer.

Chakra: Third-eye and crown

Helps to Achieve: Healing of the mind, body, and spirit by prayer and meditation.

Placement: Seraphinite should be placed on the third-eye chakra and crown chakra.

Best Used With: Rose quartz, rainbow moonstone, and clear quartz.

Fascinating Fact: Native Americans used this stone to bind the spirit of the dead.

Kyanite

Kyanite is a type of feldspar that has a prismatic, transparent color. It is found in many regions of the world, including Madagascar, Australia, and the United States. Kyanite is also called "blue-tinted quartz" because it sometimes has blue/green or blue/white bands within it. It can heal numerous physical ailments and boost energy levels, helping one increase their psychic abilities by bringing forth intuition to their conscious mind. This stone can also increase awareness.

Crystal System: Monoclinic.

Colors: Gray, Green, Blue, White

Energy: Intuition and psychic abilities, healing of the aura and all physical ailments through energy manipulation and meditation.

Chakra: Third-eye and crown

Helps to Achieve: Increasing self-awareness by spiritual insight and attaining enlightenment through meditation and prayer.

Placement: Kyanite should be placed on the third-eye chakra and crown chakra.

Best Used With: Turquoise, moonstone, and clear quartz.

Fascinating Fact: Native Americans believed the Kyanite to be a lightning talisman.

Jasper

Jasper is a unique stone that is found in many areas of the world. The name "jasper" comes from the Greek word for "to heal." It is a very smooth, fine-grained stone that does especially well in projects made of gold, silver, or other soft metals such as brass. It has a shiny and slightly veiny texture due to the mica within it.

Jasper.
https://commons.wikimedia.org/wiki/File:2010_-_red_jasper.jpg

Jasper is widely known for its protective and healing properties. It can be used in healing rituals to cleanse the aura, increase one's psychic abilities, and help the user to connect with spirit guides. Jasper has been known to help encourage creative ideas, including creating new visions and plans in life. It is also known to stimulate the release of endorphins, the body's natural feel-good hormones, thus helping reduce stress and depression.

Crystal System: Trigonal

Colors: Green, Red, Orange, Yellow

Energy: Healing of the aura and physical ailments, connecting with spirit guides through meditation.

Chakra: Third-eye and heart

Helps to Achieve: The release of endorphins for a happy feeling and reduction of stress in one's life, spiritual guidance by connecting the conscious mind with the inner-self to achieve enlightenment through meditation.

Best Used With: Clear quartz, rose quartz, and hematite.

Fascinating Fact: Jasper was widely used by Native Americans in ancient times. It was believed that these stones would protect the holder from harm, and it is now thought to have granted the user luck while they played a game similar to modern American football.

Chapter 6: Using Crystals for Protection

One of the best uses for crystals is to protect you from negative energy. Negative energies can come from other people in your life; family, friends, and even strangers. The surrounding environment can even cause these negative energies. Crystals can be used to minimize or eliminate such energies and thereby protect you from any undesirable or even harmful consequences. There are two primary ways to use crystals for protection; by hanging them in your home and by carrying them with you. Both methods produce amazing results, so it really comes down to a matter of personal preference.

Hanging a crystal in your home is an excellent idea for those who need a visual reminder to stay protected. The crystal will act as a powerful ward against unwanted energies and influences that may enter the property through doors, windows, or other means of access. The most effective way to hang crystals for protection is by placing them at key points in the property, especially where there are no physical barriers. This can be done using wire, string, or twine to create a grid of points across the whole area.

If you have a basement that is accessible from outside the house, that would be a particularly good place for placing a crystal for this purpose. Don't forget the garage, attic, and outside areas vulnerable to neighbors" unwanted energies. Hanging a crystal on each side of the door is a good start. You can immediately hang crystals in the driveway and area around your home for an extra boost.

Another effective way to use crystals for protection is by wearing them yourself. This can be done in a variety of ways. If you need to carry your crystal around, you can wear it on a cord around your neck. Another good way is to tuck it into your pocket or under a shirt cuff. You could also stick it in a purse or bag. If you use crystals for protection during a trip, place the crystal inside a purse or bag you always carry so you don't forget it. It can also be placed under your seat or in the glove compartment of your car. You can place two crystals at home on each side of your bed. These will protect you from negative energies entering your space as you rest.

The Evil Eye

The evil eye is an ill will directed toward another person. It is usually given to someone else out of jealousy or envy. It is believed that if someone gives you the evil eye, they attempt to harm you somehow. This belief can be found in several cultures and religions, but it is most commonly associated with Greece, Macedonia, and Turkey.

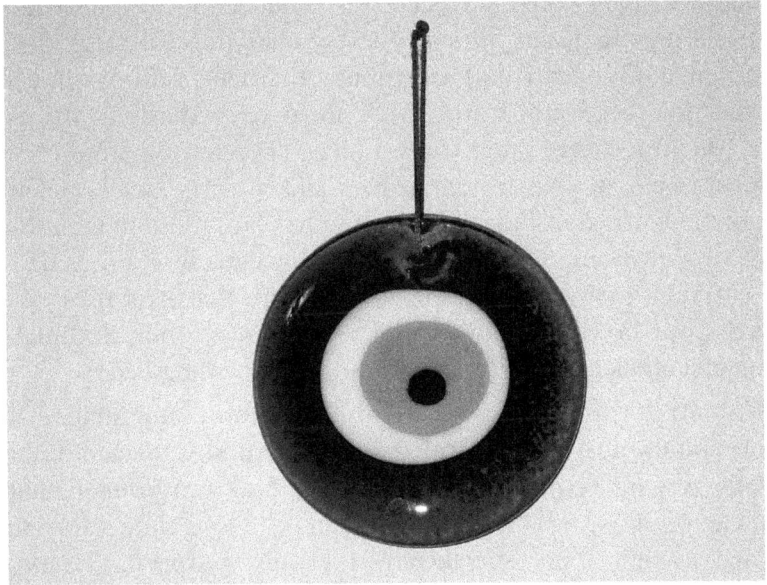

The Evil Eye.
https://commons.wikimedia.org/wiki/File:Cheshm-Nazar.JPG

The effects of the evil eye can vary according to the culture and can include anything from having a fever or headache to an ailment leading to death. Using crystals to protect against the evil eye is very common and effective. Numerous crystals can be used, but those that specifically relate to protecting against the negative effects of jealousy and envy are the best options. The use of crystals for protection against the evil eye is more effective than using just your own willpower to combat it. Crystals are designed to help you focus your thoughts on one thing and reduce confusion, which will act to counter the ill will and negative energy in your life. In fact, the more you concentrate on the feeling of protection, the stronger it becomes.

EMFs

Electromagnetic Frequencies (EMFs) are invisible fields of energy that surround all electrical devices, power lines, and appliances. Excessive exposure to EMFs can be harmful or even fatal to human beings. Crystals provide a natural barrier against electromagnetic frequencies and are highly effective when used to protect you from their negative effects. The vast majority of EMFs are produced by electronic devices such as mobile phones, computers, televisions, and stereos. While they may provide us with entertainment and time-saving benefits, these devices can be detrimental to health and contribute to many serious illnesses. Crystals for protection from EMFs are used similarly to the ones used for protection against the evil eye. You can use large crystals as focal points in your living environment or carry small ones with you on a necklace or bracelet. It is best to place these in high-traffic areas of your home and keep them within sight at all times. If you are carrying a crystal for protection, ensure that it is pressed up against your body (preferably under an item of your clothing) so that it can efficiently absorb and neutralize incoming EMFs.

Crystals for protection can come in almost any shape, size, color, and even material composition. The most important thing is that the crystal resonates positively with you and your situation. You can even use a crystal you have had for a long time rather than buying a new one specifically for this purpose. However, purchasing a protection crystal will help you to establish a clear intention for using it as a protective device. Some good protection crystals include:

Black Tourmaline

Physical Description: Black tourmaline has a rich, deep, and velvety black color. Its crystals are often found in combination with blue, green, or clear Quartz. Modern-day black tourmaline is usually the result of heat treatment during the smelting process.

Why It Is Used: Black tourmaline is a powerful stone, often used to stimulate the brain's higher spiritual and psychic centers. It can be used to protect from negative energy, as an antidepressant, and promote peacefulness and tranquility. It is one of the best stones to use if you are confused and cannot think clearly. It is thought to protect you from all kinds of negative energy, including that which is potentially dangerous or lethal.

How to Use It: It is used for protection by wrapping it in silk and putting it under your pillow at night. You can also place it on the bed close to where you sleep and put the bed sheets over it to prevent any negative energy from entering the room. Black Tourmaline with blue, green, or clear quartz is usually combined with a second crystal to form a grid-like formation of positive energy. This grid can be worn around your neck like a pendant or placed on the body where you feel you need more protection. You can also hang a piece on your wall or carry one. You can purchase and wear black tourmaline jewelry if you have enough money.

Botswana Agate

Physical Description: Botswana agate is a green-banded opal-colored stone that displays a variety of patterns. It usually has black and light brown or yellowish-brown bands, but some may display white or black stripes as well as orange and red stripes. Some may display various black patterns resembling ropes, spirals, or bars. Some displays will have alternating black and light-tan bands.

Botswana agate.
https://commons.wikimedia.org/wiki/File:Agate_18_(30746155537).jpg

Why It Is Used: Botswana agate is used to stabilize emotions and provide protection from negative energy. It can also help to protect against environmental pollution, such as electromagnetic frequencies, and other detrimental effects of modern technology, such as cell phones and power lines. Healers and mediums often use this to enhance their own ability to connect with the spirit world. It is sometimes referred to as the "stone of transformation" because of its ability to stimulate the higher spiritual centers in the brain.

How to Use It: Botswana agate is used for protection by placing it on a window sill or on top of or beside your bed or pillow. You can also carry a piece with you in the form of a pendant or bracelet to wear on your wrist or hang on your wall.

Onyx

Physical Description: Onyx is a rock that has bands of color, usually black, white, or brown. It may also display red or yellow shades.

Why It Is Used: Onyx is thought to be protective against negative energy and evil spirits and to provide relief from stress and anxiety. It is also used for protection from electromagnetic frequencies, radiation, and other evils that modern society has to offer.

How to Use It: Onyx is used for protection by carrying it in your pocket or wearing it as a piece of jewelry. It is also recommended that you place a piece in your bedroom, your work desk, or any other location where you spend a lot of time.

Lodestone

Physical Description: Lodestone is the magnetic form of iron oxide that is found in chunks of rock or as small, rounded stones. As its name suggests, it is a naturally magnetic substance that can often be attracted to certain objects.

Why It Is Used: Lodestone is used for protection against evil and negative energy, as well as to increase prosperity and defend against curses. It also enhances psychic powers and attracts love, friendship, and good luck.

How to Use It: Lodestone can be used in many ways. In the form of a pendant, it can be worn by those at risk of being cheated or as an amulet if you fear an evil eye is targeting you. It is also used to protect those who work with poison or chemicals, as well as by people who are involved in work that can cause them to suffer from radiation exposure. Lodestone, when placed on a window sill or under the pillow, can help to ward off negative energy and protect you from psychic attacks. It is also said to be effective protection against electromagnetic frequencies.

Hematite

Physical Description: Hematite is a shiny, reflective metallic mineral that is black. It is often found in combination with other minerals like iron ore and quartz.

Why It Is Used: Hematite is used to increase psychic powers and to provide protection against negative energy and spirits. In Ancient Egypt, it was used as an amulet to protect the pharaohs from harm during their journey into the afterlife. It is also commonly used by witches, shamans, and other people who work with the spirit world.

How to Use It: Hematite is used for protection by carrying a piece of it with you or by wearing it on your body as jewelry. It is also recommended that you place a piece in your bedroom, home, office, and in the windows and behind doors to prevent malevolent entities from entering your home.

Tiger's Eye

Physical Description: Tiger's eye is a stone that displays a golden color in shades of brown and yellow, as well as gold and white. Some stones may have black or gray stripes embedded in them, while others may be just black.

Why It Is Used: It is used to help boost personal willpower and to protect against negativity. It can be used to relieve depression, and it is thought that it can help alleviate grief. It is also used to attract good fortune, as well as to help the user to make decisions.

How to Use It: It is used for protection by carrying it around as an amulet in your pocket. You can also wear a piece on your wrist or neck by simply placing the stone in a piece of jewelry. It can also be placed under your pillow at night to keep you protected from negative energy.

Smoky Quartz

Physical Description: Smoky quartz is a variety of quartz that displays a gray color that may be sometimes darker or lighter. Some stones may display brown or black swirls, while others may have patches of gray or white.

Why It Is Used: Smoky quartz is used to increase psychic powers and to provide protection against negative energies. It can also be used to protect against electromagnetic radiation, such as the frequencies generated by cell phones, microwaves, and other devices. It is also used to keep your mind sharp and to improve your mental clarity.

How to Use It: Smoky quartz is used for protection by carrying it in your pocket or wearing it as a piece of jewelry. It can also be placed on your bedside table in a grid formation with other crystals like white topaz or blue lapis lazuli to protect you from psychic attacks while you sleep.

Black Jade

Physical Description: Black jade is a fine-grained variety of jade that is almost black. It may also be purple.

Why It Is Used: Black jade is often used to ward off negative energy and to protect against curses and black magic. It is also used to dispel evil spirits, as well as to increase physical and mental healing and promote longevity.

How to Use It: Black jade is used for protection by carrying a piece close to your heart. It is also recommended that you place it around your house and in your workplace to ward off evil spirits.

Pyrite

Physical Description: Pyrite, also called Fire Silver, is a black mineral with a metallic luster. It can also display gold or green colors and usually has a golden tint on the surface.

Why It Is Used: Pyrite can be used to protect yourself and loved ones against curses, malevolent entities, and evil forces. It is also used to safeguard those who work with precious metals and bring money into your life and increase prosperity.

How to Use It: Pyrite can be used for protection by carrying it on the body. It can also be placed in the four corners of your house, in your vehicle, office, or any other location where you spend a lot of your time.

Opal

Physical Description: Opal is a colorful variety of quartz that is transparent. It is often found to have a colorful array of bands, which are often referred to as "fire trails."

Why It Is Used: Opal is used as an extremely powerful protection stone and a stone of manifestation. It can be used to protect against negative energies, including those that are generated by electromagnetic waves and radiation. It is also used to reduce stress and increase intuition.

How to Use It: Opal is used for protection by wearing it on your body, particularly on the left side of your body. You can also place a piece in an empty picture frame and place such a picture frame over the entrance of each room in your house to protect you from negative energies within that room.

Smithsonite

Physical Description: Smithsonite is a type of Zinc ore that is often bluish or greenish. It most commonly appears as a silvery-white mineral with a metallic sheen.

Why It Is Used: Smithsonite is used to help ease emotional stress and trauma. It protects you from the negative energies generated by your mind, and it is used to help release energy blocks within the body, restoring your physical and emotional health.

How to Use It: Smithsonite is used for protection by placing it on your third eye chakra or on your solar plexus chakra. It can also be placed in the four corners of your house. It is recommended that you carry a piece of Smithsonite with you whenever you leave the house to protect yourself from negative energies.

Jet

Physical Description: Jet is a type of mineral that displays primarily black or gray colors. It is most often used to make jewelry, as well as for decorative purposes.

Why It Is Used: Jet increases your awareness, helping you see things for what they really are. It can also be used to enhance communication with other people and spirits.

How to Use It: Jet can be used for protection by wearing it as a ring or pendant and placing it in a grid formation with other stones such as lapis lazuli or rose quartz. You can also place a piece of Jet under your pillow or beneath your mattress to protect you while you sleep.

Clear Quartz

Physical Description: Clear quartz is a variety of quartz that shows a bright, transparent quality. It may even show a rainbow halo of color if it is very pure.

Why It Is Used: Clear quartz is an energy amplifier that raises your vibrational rate to help you connect with higher chakras and make more positive changes in your life. It is also used to clear the mind, helping you to make decisions and respond appropriately to new developments. It protects you from any negativity that may be present in the environment and also shields you from electromagnetic pollution and radio waves.

How to Use It: Clear quartz is used for protection by wearing it on your body and placing it in a grid formation with other stones such as rose quartz or amethyst. It is also recommended that you carry a piece of Clear Quartz in your purse at all times to help purify negative influences aimed at you.

Amazonite

Physical Description: Amazonite is a green variety of quartz often found with blue or brown inclusions. It is usually a light color but may display darker shades under certain lighting conditions.

Amazonite.
https://commons.wikimedia.org/wiki/File:Amazonite_3.jpg

Why It Is Used: Amazonite can absorb negative energy and facilitate its release from the body. It can also help you overcome anxiety, reduce stress, and improve your overall energy level.

How to Use It: This stone can be worn as an amulet or placed in a grid formation with other crystals such as turquoise. Amazonite should also be used while meditating, as it can offer protection well beyond the physical realm.

While the list above is by no means exhaustive, it does cover some of the most popular stones that are used for protection. Each of these crystals provides you with useful levels of positive energy and can help to block out any negative energies that may be aimed at you. Using these stones is not just a good idea for yourself but also for everyone around you, including your furry friends. They serve as protection to those who enter your space and allow you to focus on the positive energy within.

Chapter 7: Crystal Cleansing and Maintenance

If you've been around crystals for a while, chances are you've heard about the need for proper crystal cleansing. This is necessary because healing stones store and accumulate negative energy from those who have worked with them. Over time this can cause problems such as the crystals feeling dull and lifeless despite being charged in the sun or moonlight, crystals feeling heavy and drawing your thoughts down into sadness, or other physical changes to the crystal such as color changes or cracking surfaces.

Most people think that crystals must be cleansed once a month or every year, but this is not very inaccurate. Crystals need to be cleansed on an as-needed basis, depending on what you've put them through. When you're learning to use crystals in spell work or energy healing, it's good to cleanse them regularly because they're so sensitive and will pick up on every energy you expose them to, even by accident. Once you've learned how to use crystals properly, it's best to only cleanse them before and after specific spells or healing.

Things to Note about Crystals

Crystals can be destroyed from prolonged use by negative entities who know how to harness crystal healing energy for their own illogical purposes. Some crystals are more susceptible to this than others, so it's best to never keep the same crystals in use for more than a month at a time. So how do we cleanse crystals properly? Before we begin, you must know the following:

- Crystals like to be touched or exposed to movement or friction. This can be done by handling them by wearing gloves while clearing your crystals or rubbing them with a loofah or cleansing cloth.

- Crystals must be cleaned frequently, at least once a day if possible. Concentration crystals have more cleansing needs than regular stones because they are extra sensitive to energy from you and your surroundings, so cleaning them regularly is important.

- Negative energy from other people, spirits, and animals can be driven out of the crystal through contact with water.

- You don't need to use specific types of water to cleanse crystals. Tap water or water in a swimming pool (although chlorine may affect crystal energy) will work fine. If you are cleansing your crystals in a stream or other natural body of water, such as a river or lake, check the water for stagnant areas, such as bird droppings and animal scat beforehand.

- If you use self-cleansing crystals like Selenite, they don't need to be cleansed regularly. They are designed to balance their own properties, and any negative energy is immediately discarded through a special energy vortex in the crystal.

- Crystals that have been cleared of negative energy can be re-programmed by holding them under running water for about fifteen minutes. This will refresh your crystals and make them more receptive to your intentions, allowing you more control over how they work in your life.

Cleansing Techniques

Smudging: Smudging involves burning a small bundle of herbs to remove negative energy from the area. You can smudge your crystals and other objects throughout your home or location while they are not in use. Burning herb bundles is especially useful if you are using the crystals in spell work. By offering the smudged bundle to the crystal, you offer your desire into its energy field, and they will magnify and strengthen this intention for you. It's not advisable to smudge a crystal to take away negative energy all the time, but it is most helpful at the start and end of a spell when you are bringing in positive energy; it should not be used constantly, or it will drive the positive energy out as well.

Smudge sticks are easy to make yourself with dried herbs, roots, and flowers. Always test an herb or flower before you use it as a smudge because you may have an allergy to it, or it may be toxic in large doses. To make a smudge stick, simply bundle the herbs together tightly and tie them with string. If you are using flowers or skewers, try to use plant material that is already dried out and brittle rather than fresh or living. You don't have to be specific about which kinds of herbs you use, but it is best to avoid using anything toxic. Good examples include sage, cedar, lavender, rosemary, cinnamon, and patchouli. Crystals that are best cleansed with this method include aventurine, modalite, emerald, garnet, malachite, or any deep green or brown crystal.

Saltwater Rinse: Another way to cleanse your crystals is to use a saltwater rinse. This is especially helpful for clearing away the negative energy in the morning when you are beginning your day. Simply place the crystal in a small dish of purified saltwater and leave for fifteen minutes. You can substitute seawater for this method if you feel so inclined. After fifteen minutes, rinse the crystal off under running water and leave it on the windowsill or any other place where it will receive direct sunlight. This will encourage its healing. Soft textured crystals should not be exposed to water because it will cause physical damage to their structure. Crystals best cleansed with saltwater include jasper, obsidian, amethyst, agate, labradorite, rose quartz, and any other hard crystal.

Moonlight Cleansing: There is a very strong connection between the moon and magic because it is the one constant in our lives, every single day of every single month. The moon is a great way to help balance energies and remove negative energy that has built up in your life or on your crystals. You can cleanse crystals by placing them outside while the moon is full on a night where there is no chance of rain or other elements that might damage the crystals or soil, such as wind. You can even place one or more of your crystals in a moon bowl and leave it out at night. Crystals that are best cleansed with this method include aventurine, amber, chrysoprase, emerald, jade, and rose quartz.

Sunlight Cleansing: This is a very effective method that you can use if you find yourself needing to cleanse your crystals regularly. Sunlight is the most powerful and available form of energy in the world. It is, in a way, pure magic and can have a great effect on your crystals. You can take any crystals you feel may need cleansing out into the sun and let them sit there all day while charging their energy with the sun's energy, but make sure that no one but you touches the crystal after it has been exposed to sunlight. The sun is the best natural energy cleaner there is and will naturally repel any negative energy from your crystals. Crystals that are best cleansed with this method include amber, tiger's eye, smoky quartz, peridot, and aquamarine.

Water Cleansing: This is one of the easiest ways to cleanse your crystals. It only takes a few seconds, but you should never leave crystals in water for longer than fifteen minutes, no matter how clean you think the water is or how hard the stone is. Water can seep into small cracks and damage the crystal's structure. Place your crystals under a faucet and leave them there for about fifteen minutes or less. This will wash off any negative energy from them and freshen them up for another day. Crystals best cleansed with water include agate, amethyst, aqua aura, and other hard stone.

Burying Them in Soil: If you have many crystals, it may be useful to bury them in the ground for a few days. Simply dig a hole in your garden or somewhere where you can bury them and leave them undisturbed. It's important to place something on top of the buried crystals so that they aren't disturbed by animals digging or other elements, like the wind. You can bury them while they are in a smudge bundle, using two purification methods at once. This is a great way to cleanse your crystals, but be careful not to bury any crystals with a hole in them or markings because this will cause unnecessary damage. Crystals best cleansed with this method include any Black or white crystal, blue crystal, or brown crystal.

Using Reiki to Cleanse Your Crystals: Reiki is an ancient healing art that is used by many people all over the world. It involves sending your intention into an object or person to heal and purify that energy field. You can use Reiki to cleanse your crystals by simply holding them in your hands or letting your hand hover above them and sending your energy into the crystals. You can do this for as long as you want and anywhere that you are. However, ensure that you are vibrating at a high frequency and radiating only positive energy before you do this because your crystals will take any energy you give, so it's wise to ensure it is positive. You can also cleanse crystals in this way if you are out of town or on vacation. Crystals best cleansed with Reiki include amethyst, emerald, jade, quartz, and any opaque-colored stone.

Cleansing with a Generator Crystal: If you are working with a very large quantity of crystals, it can be difficult to cleanse them one by one. In this case, using a generator crystal is a good idea. What this means is that you find a special crystal that will act as a central focus for all the other crystals in your collection. Each time you cleanse this generator crystal, you will be cleansing the rest of your crystals and not having to cleanse them individually. Crystals that are best cleansed with generators include any clear crystal and labradorite.

Cleansing with Essential Oils: Many essential oils are powerful cleansers on their own and will naturally repel negative energy. Some oils you can use for cleansing crystals include Lemon, Bergamot, Sandalwood, Palo Santo, rosemary, patchouli, and frankincense. You can cleanse your crystals by putting a few drops on your fingers and rubbing them over the crystal. You can also place a few drops in a dish with saltwater and allow the crystal to rest overnight before rinsing it in the morning. You can even rub a few drops of essential oil directly onto the top of your crystal. Either way, this will be a very powerful cleansing and should be done regularly. Crystals that are best cleansed with essential oils include aventurine, amethyst, sodalite, and quartz.

Cleansing with Magnets: Magnets are very useful to cleanse your crystals, as they help to repel the negative energy that comes into contact with them. There are many ways to do this, but all involve using magnets to protect the other crystals in your collection. You can place your crystal on a piece of paper, take a magnet and swipe it across the crystal, or you can place your crystal in a box with the magnet and shake it around. Another effective way to do this is to have a large magnet resting on a stand and have your crystals placed on top of it. This will protect all the crystals in your collection and will also work to cleanse them. You can cleanse your crystals using a magnet anytime you feel they need some cleansing, but it is best if you do it regularly. Crystals best cleansed with a magnet include amethyst, clear quartz, blue crystals, and metallic crystals.

Cleansing with Selenite: Selenite is a special kind of crystal that has the power to protect your crystals and keep them clean. It works as a protective shield around all the other stones in your collection and will help keep them clean and pure – and positive. The great thing about Selenite is that it will work consistently with your other crystals and will do all the work for you. You can use Selenite as a central focus of your cleansing efforts, or you can simply have it in your collection and let it do the work for you. Crystals that are best cleansed with Selenite include any clear crystal, blue crystal, black crystal, and brown crystal.

Self-Cleansing Crystals: Some crystals are especially effective at cleansing other crystals, but they can also be used to cleanse themselves without your help. They do this by emitting their own positive energy and purifying their energetic field. Self-cleansing crystals are especially useful for keeping high-energy stones clean and protected. They are also useful for cleansing stones with high iron content from any negative energy that their iron may have attracted. Self-cleansing crystals can also be used to cleanse a smudge bundle because they work as a filter to get rid of all the harmful energies in the bundle and bring out its positive energy. Common self-cleansing crystals include Blue kyanite, black tourmaline, carnelian, selenite, and citrine.

What Is Crystal Programming?

Crystal Programming is a collection of techniques you can use to program your crystals with your intentions to amplify their energy. It's a way to give the crystals a specific purpose. You can program your crystals to carry different energy frequencies, magnify your intentions, or help with anything else that you need. You can also program them with information about yourself and re-program them if you need to later on. This is also called charging or activating your crystal. To program your crystals, you need to know the following:

1. **Choosing a Base Frequency:** This is the frequency or energy you want to give your crystal. When choosing this frequency, keep in mind that vibrations thin out as they get further away from their source. This means that the energy and effects of your crystal will be stronger if it is physically close to you when you program it, so it is best to keep it in your hands during programming.

2. **Choosing an Intent:** An intent is a direction that this new programmable energy will take. The goal you are trying to achieve with the crystal can be anything from healing yourself to attracting money. To choose an intent, you should take into consideration what it is that you want from your crystal.

3. **Choosing a Symbol:** When charging your crystal with intent, it's not only important to choose this intent but also a symbol for the crystal. A symbol is a specific object or item that can help your mind focus on this new frequency or intention. It's important to choose something with personal meaning and energy, such as an object that means a lot to you or something that represents your intent. You can also use things like letters or shapes rather than objects. When choosing a symbol for your crystal, it's important to remember that it should make sense according to the intent.

4. **Cleansing the Crystal:** This is important when programming crystals. This is because you want to ensure that your crystal is as clean as possible before giving it a

new purpose.

How to Program a Crystal

After choosing your base frequency, intent, and symbol, it's time to program. You can do this by following these steps:

Step 1: Visualize the Crystal: Start by looking at the crystal in your mind's eye and imagining that there is an energy flowing from it. Now make sure that you imagine this energy going into every fiber of your being until all the energy has been absorbed.

Step 2: Program the Crystal: You now want to open up a channel between yourself and the crystal. To do this, you will be using the intent that you have chosen. You can either say the intent out loud or inside your head. It's important to put as much energy into it as possible and visualize the crystal absorbing this energy.

Step 3: Say Thank You: When programming a crystal, it's always good to say thank you. This helps close the channel between yourself and the crystal, so your energy doesn't continually flow into it.

Step 4: Repeat This Process Every Day: If you want your programmed crystal to stay with these intentions, then you will have to repeat this process every day or as often as you remember until you decide to change them. If you ever want to change the intention, you can simply re-program the crystal. This will make the crystal react to a new frequency and emit new energies according to your needs. You will need to cleanse the crystal before re-programming to get rid of negative or old energies in preparation for the new intention.

TO RECAP: Crystal maintenance is important for all crystals, regardless of the frequency or intent you have given them. This is because they are energy, and energy needs to be recharged periodically. To keep your crystals working in their optimal condition and make sure their vibrations remain where you want them, you will need to cleanse them regularly. This will also keep them free from any foreign vibrations or negative energy that could be trapped in their energetic field. It's up to you what method you choose to cleanse your crystals, and more than one method can be used at the same time if you like. It's also up to you to decide how often you do it, but, as a general rule, cleansing your crystals every week is a good idea. The quality of your crystals is important to the outcome of their energies and purposes, so having higher quality crystals that are properly maintained will lead to better results.

Section Two: Crystals and the Zodiac Signs

Chapter 8: Crystals for Earth Signs

Earth signs are grounded, practical, ambitious, and usually have a strong sense of self-preservation. They are also natural leaders, which is one of the reasons why they're drawn to entrepreneurship. The basic thing all members of this group have in common is that they prefer stability in life and work. A job title isn't what defines them. It's about the work they produce.

Earth signs strive to achieve stability because it will be their constant during times of change — which means being able to provide for themselves and those they love. They also tend to be very grounded individuals with a practical thinking approach and like getting straight down to business without getting caught up in feelings or worrying about what others think. This can sometimes mean that earth sign people aren't very social, but this is not personal and is simply a natural trait. Due to their groundedness, earth signs tend to be very practical and realistic, something that's often reflected in their work. The four earth signs are Capricorn, Taurus, and Virgo.

Capricorn (Dec 22-Jan 19)

Capricorn is ruled by the planet Saturn and is symbolized by a goat. Capricorn is someone who will be very focused on the job at hand and will excel in the workplace. They're also someone who will be incredibly dedicated to their work and strive to reach the very top of their game, which is a trait that's typically very attractive to employers. As someone who enjoys working hard, Capricorn people also tend to be quite ambitious and determined. They also tend to be rather private, so don't expect them to talk about sensitive matters or emotions easily.

Capricorns excel in practical situations and are usually very good at focusing their energy and directing it toward productive activities. They also tend to be quite reserved. This is because they're very careful about building new relationships and opening up to others, which sometimes makes them appear aloof. They're not always the best at picking up social cues, especially when they come from other earth signs. Their greatest strength is being able to work alone, but this can also be seen as a weakness because they might come off as cold and distant.

The Capricorn person is very good at motivating and inspiring others. They are definitely the best at leading and managing others. People tend to trust them implicitly with their money and their careers. They love to plan ahead, which makes it really easy for them to see holes in other people's plans and rectify the situation. This is why they generally make very good managers, able to prevent problems before they arise. The only thing that can slow down a Capricorn is getting caught up in details or waiting for everything to be perfect before taking action. For example, they can often become paralyzed in the face of criticism, worrying that they've made a mistake. They also tend to be workaholics like other earth signs and can never get enough work, making them quite miserable at times.

Their greatest weakness would have to be tardiness and procrastination. When developing a detailed plan for an activity, a Capricorn needs to ensure that everything's up-to-date and there aren't any gaps in the plan. If they can't see this, they may do things last minute or rush through something. This can result in frustration from the other people involved in the activity or the Capricorn person themselves, which can sometimes cause them to avoid activities entirely.

Capricorns tend to be very loyal and protective of their partners in intimate relationships. They're very supportive and sincere lovers who are always attentive to their loved ones. They tend to be very guarded and careful when looking for a relationship and dating. They definitely don't jump into things lightly. When they meet someone who catches their eye, they'll keep it at the back of their mind, wondering how to approach them. They'll pay attention to everything their potential partner says and does in an attempt to figure out what kind of person they are.

Earth signs aren't usually very easy on the eyes. There's a natural seriousness to them that can sometimes be off-putting. Capricorns are no exception. Despite this fact, many Capricorns tend to be incredibly charming. People tend to like them because of the way they carry themselves. All things considered, Capricorn is an excellent employee and an even better leader. They're also very present, able to see the big picture, and will do everything they can to ensure things go smoothly. Their search for stability means they're willing to work hard and not complain about their life. Instead, they happily do what's needed to make things easier for others.

Crystals for the Capricorn

Red Garnet: As the birthstone for this zodiac, the red garnet stone is a must-have for Capricorns. Red garnets are associated with passion and destruction, which the Capricorn needs to be especially careful with. Red garnets should be placed upon the area of the body prone to accidents and injuries, such as the upper arms, elbows, and knees.

This is the colored stone of courage and devotion, two traits that are necessary for leadership, a position perfectly embodied by the Capricorn. The garnet stone is also a perfect item for this sign as it helps regulate emotions, particularly those relating to self-control or self-discipline. Garnet inspires inner calmness by helping those who wear them stay focused on their goals and ambitions no matter what kind of external pressures are thrown at them.

Ocean Jasper: Ocean Jasper is something that any Capricorn should have in their possession, especially if it's a Capricorn male. Ocean jasper is a stone that helps those who wear it find the inner strength to face their fears head-on. This is perfect for the Capricorn, who tends to be quite insecure at times and has an unpleasant tendency to overthink every little decision they make.

Ocean Jasper also helps those who wear it face their sorrows and learn from them instead of writing them off as mistakes or reasons for shame and embarrassment. This is perfect for the Capricorn male, who tends to judge himself harshly and whose fears often lead them to make ill-advised decisions that ultimately end up leaving them feeling worse than when they began. By learning from past mistakes, Capricorn can develop self-confidence that helps bring out the best in themselves and others.

Sunstone: This is another crystal that any Capricorn should definitely have in their possession. It is a wonderful stone for those who wear it, as it enhances happiness and confidence.

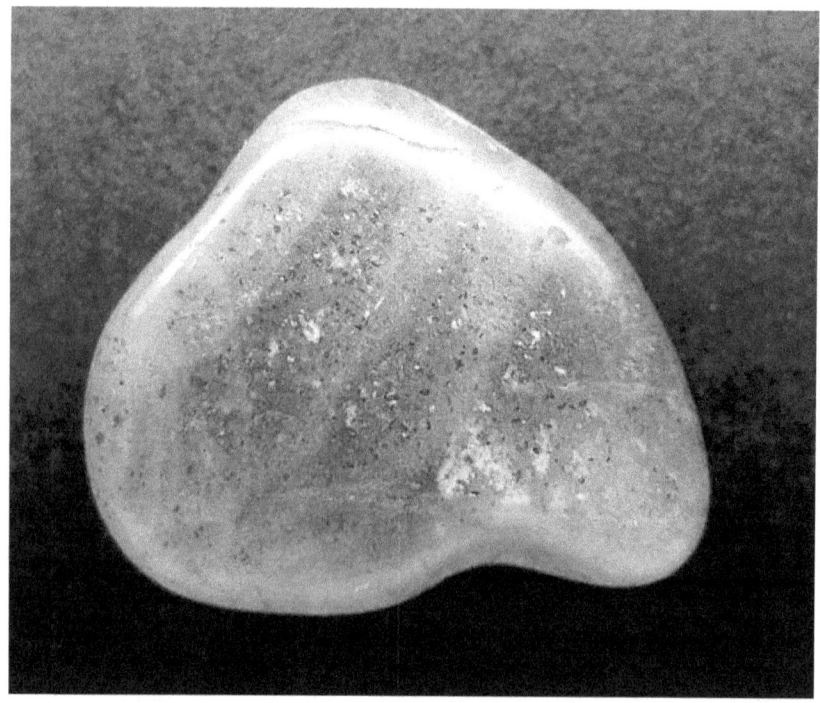

Sunstone.
https://commons.wikimedia.org/wiki/File:Oligoclase-Sunstone_from_India2.jpg

This is perfect for the Capricorn, whose tendency toward shyness can sometimes cause them to doubt their own capabilities, leading to mistakes and missed opportunities. Sunstone helps prevent this by creating an atmosphere of warmth and affection that makes others feel comfortable and confident, no matter what kind of situation they find themselves in. The Capricorn also tends to be very negative at times, often worrying about things before they even happen. Sunstone helps Capricorns overcome their fears and be more positive about themselves.

Apulian Quartz: For the Capricorn, Apulian Quartz is a stone that can be of great assistance. This quartz can bring a sense of wisdom to a person, helping them obtain self-knowledge and an understanding of the relationships between people and things. This is essential for the Capricorn, who has such a keen interest in anything that relates to the world. They are very curious by nature and want to learn about everything available to them. Apulian Quartz can help Capricorn understand their own strengths and weaknesses, allowing them to be more compassionate towards others and even the people they may otherwise have trouble forgiving.

Taurus (April 20-May 20)

Taurus is ruled by the planet Venus and symbolized by the Bull, representing strength and perseverance. The Taurus is generally even-tempered. They are trustworthy people who never let their emotions get the best of them, except during a rare period when they become overly stubborn. The Taurus is a very thoughtful person. They love to talk about things that have happened in the past or situations that may happen in the future rather than being in the moment

When it comes to friendships, Taurus people aren't exactly the most loyal sign in the zodiac. They do tend to play favorites and hold grudges as well. Sometimes, they may seem cold and distant, but this is only because they don't want others to get too close. They enjoy having friends around them and are very social creatures, but their moodiness can sometimes make it difficult for others to maintain a friendship with them.

Mostly, they like to keep things at a reasonable distance from friends and family. If you're someone who likes to be close and intimate with everyone you meet, you may struggle to connect with a Taurus. They won't always make it clear when they don't want your company but instead will wait for you to just assume that they don't want to see you. Don't take it personally, though. They can get very moody when they're not in their comfort zone. They do tend to hold grudges from time to time as well. This is something that definitely needs work on their part. They can be very difficult to deal with during these times, so it's important to know what sort of buttons to avoid.

They also tend to be a little materialistic, which isn't exactly surprising given that their ruling planet is Venus. They do like to surround themselves with beauty and luxury. Although, for the most part, this isn't done offensively. It's just something that they're accustomed to from birth. Don't let it offend you if they ask you for something too extravagant. If you really care about them in the first place, some things are worth splurging for.

Taurus people are known for being very sensual and passionate lovers. They're the sort of people who need to feel comfortable with someone before they even begin to open up. They prefer to take their time before expressing their love physically, making them a bit of an old-fashioned romantic at times. They don't rush into relationships but instead choose the right person over time and let their feelings develop naturally. Once they truly fall in love with someone, it's hard for them to see anyone else as more beautiful or charming than the one who has captured their heart. Most of them have an eye for beauty, so this isn't really that surprising.

They're generally very confident people, even though they tend to hide their emotions behind a curtain of reservations. However, once they feel completely comfortable with someone, they will open up and reveal the depth of their feelings. They aren't one-sided, either. They appreciate someone who can be romantic and thoughtful, so as a Taurus, make sure that whoever you look for is willing to turn up the heat in the bedroom too.

Crystals for the Taurus

Blue Topaz: Blue Topaz is a stone that can help Taurus to be better-rounded in the emotional department. It can give them more empathy for other people, helping them to understand that not everyone is as fortunate as they are. It's also very helpful for those who wear it, as it helps them stay grounded in their personal goals and ambitions. Topaz keeps a person focused on what is important and rationalizes why things are happening as they do. This is perfect for the Taurus, who tends to wallow in their own troubles and problems at times, making it difficult for them to see how others cope with similar setbacks. Topaz helps them to take control of their feelings and emotions, becoming able to see things from a different perspective.

Ammonite: The Ammonite is a wonderful stone for the Taurus. This crystal can help them to smash the mental barriers that may have hindered their progress in the past. It's a stone that allows the Taurus to overcome their fears by banishing all doubts from their mind. It also helps them cope with any emotional issues they may be experiencing. The Taurus tends to feel overwhelmed and uncertain when they're feeling particularly vulnerable, so Ammonite is excellent at helping them pull together when they are daunted.

Kunzite: Kunzite is a very calming crystal, which can be wonderfully helpful for those who wear it. It's known for bringing peace to the spirit and is an excellent stone for those who find themselves highly stressed.

Kunzite.
https://commons.wikimedia.org/wiki/File:Kunzite-Hiddenite.jpg

Kunzite can help a Taurus find their center again when feeling a bit off or out of balance. It has a very gentle energy that is noticeable the moment that it enters your space, and this energy will help any Taurus who requires a bit of peace and quiet.

Goldstone: Goldstone is a wonderful stone that can help a Taurus feel the earth's passion and energy. It's very helpful when they need to get their juices flowing and feel quite dull. It can help them to be more active, even if they're stuck sitting down. Goldstone is a stone that anyone can appreciate, no matter their occupation. If you're someone with a creative side, it's a great stone for you. The gold stone is also perfect for you if you're an accountant or a banker.

Virgo (Aug 23-Sept 22)

Virgo is ruled by the planet Mercury and symbolized by the Virgin, representing purity and health. The Virgo is someone who is a perfectionist. They are always striving to be their absolute best to impress others. They are extremely analytical people, meaning that they tend to think things through before making a decision. Thanks to this quality, many of them make excellent doctors and surgeons. They have the attention to detail that helps them identify when something just isn't right. No matter what field a Virgo ends up in, you can rest assured that they'll do their job perfectly.

Virgos are known to be very cautious. They almost always think about the worst-case scenario, which means they're probably constantly worrying about everything. This can likely be traced back to their childhood. Virgos, on the whole, tend to have a bit of a hard time growing up. Many of them have complicated families, so they learn very early on in life that they have to be careful with how they deal with people to survive.

On the outside, Virgos can come across as cold and distant. They don't usually like to open up too much beyond their inner circle and tend to trust very few people throughout their lives. They are usually very hard workers, so you might never see a Virgo sitting around doing nothing. They tend to take on a lot of jobs and have to be perfectionists about everything they do. This can lead to burnout for some Virgos since they are juggling so many projects at once. Those who don't push themselves too hard will find their lives becoming more balanced and manageable with time. It just takes a little experience to figure out how much is too much.

Every Virgo has one requirement when it comes to love and romance: They must be with someone who sees them for who they truly are. They will not tolerate someone who doesn't see them for what they are, so be sure to be open and honest with your Virgo lover. You don't want to lie to them because you'll only end up hurting each other in the long run. They are very straightforward individuals and will not tolerate lies. This is something that you should take into account when dealing with a Virgo lover. When it comes to commitment, the Virgo is cautious but loyal. This means that they are usually very difficult for anyone to break away from once they're tied down.

Crystals for the Virgo

Sapphire: The Virgo can benefit from the use of sapphire crystals for a variety of different reasons. Sapphire is known to ward off stress, which is something that a Virgo feels on an almost constant basis. There are many ways to use this crystal. You can place it in your wardrobe or in your purse, carrying it with you at all times. For an even stronger effect, place a sapphire under your pillow while you try to sleep. The results will become apparent within days.

Sardonyx: Sardonyx is known to bring in new energy, so it's a great stone for someone who is looking to revamp their life. They need to clear out the negative items that may be weighing them down. Sardonyx can help them in this regard. It will remove all the negative energies from their life and change them to something better, something that a Virgo needs in their life.

Moss Agate: Moss Agate is an excellent stone for the Virgo. It helps them to be very honest with themselves. They tend to be very guarded, so they need to learn to open up and trust people. Moss Agate is a stone that will help them become aware of their deep emotions and allow them to feel things they've repressed. It will help them connect with their inner-self in a safe place where they won't feel self-conscious about what they're feeling.

Unakite: For the person who is a little indecisive, unakite is a great stone to use. It helps them see the bigger picture and makes them feel more at peace. The Virgo is often very analytical, meaning that they like to break things down and analyze them. If something is bothering them, they'll usually figure out a way to fix it. This often comes at the expense of their emotional side. Unakite can help Virgo realize that it's okay for them to depend on others for support when dealing with difficult situations. It will help them know when it's time for someone else to step in and deal with the problem.

Chapter 9: Crystals for Air Signs

Air signs are best known for their intellect and creativity. They have an appetite for knowledge and the flexibility to take on many tasks. They are good at communicating and enjoy working in groups or with others equally much as they enjoy working alone. They are optimistic, intellectual, imaginative, friendly, flexible, and adaptable people. They love change and being stimulated by new ideas, which often results in their curiosity about the world around them. As a result, they can be very inconsistent individuals as they do not like to work on one task too long but rather focus on many things at once, with the goal that everything will work out for the best. They have a tendency to be quite idealistic, as they are willing to imagine the best qualities in people and situations.

Air sign natives are restless and can be quite unpredictable, which makes them exciting and entertaining to be around. In general, they do not like routines or being stuck in a single place for too long a period. They can also be very impressionable, leading them to have difficulty making decisions without the support or assistance of others. On the other hand, they readily offer their support, insight, guidance, and encouragement when another person is stuck on a particular problem or task.

Air signs are very much involved with the society and environment in which they live. They often like to study other people's ways of doing things and will try to apply their creativity, intellect, and imagination to make the best use of social situations. This often leads them to try out different activities such as life coaching or artistic endeavors such as painting, poetry, or writing. They enjoy being surrounded by people and thrive on working with other individuals or groups, as they share a great sense of adventure and love for new ideas. Belonging to this group are Libra, Aquarius, and Gemini.

Libra (Sept 21-Oct 23)

Libra is ruled by the planet Venus and is symbolized by the scales. The Libra is known to be a very complex individual. They are incredibly sensitive and feel things on a deeper level than anyone else. They often feel they need to express themselves through art or poetry, making them very artistic individuals. They have a bit of a mysterious aura about them, which stems from their ability to manipulate the emotions of others.

Libra people are typically very caring individuals with hearts that can be easily broken. This is because they tend to put their own feelings aside to help someone else who may need it far more than they do. However, they are sometimes very manipulative and use their charm and allure to get away with things. They are very good at putting on a front, so they need to make sure that they're emotionally balanced to avoid letting the Libra side of them become too much for other people to handle.

Libra is a sign that has many personalities. Some have extremely powerful and manipulative sides, while others have much more do-gooder energy. The Libra is a very committed sign and doesn't like to break promises or stray outside their boundaries. This can sometimes result in conflict with other signs because they don't tend to change as easily as the other signs.

They are very romantic and passionate lovers who tend to put so much passion into everything they do. They are very emotionally driven and have trouble separating their feelings from the world around them. Because of this, the Libra is often guarded, but once you figure out how to get beyond this, things become more interesting. They tend to be attracted to those who appear confident and outgoing. Those who lack those qualities will not appeal to Libra in any way.

Libra children will often find themselves very emotional from a very young age. They want to be noticed and loved for who they are, which can end up being difficult for them if they don't receive the attention they desire. They tend to become dependent on their parents early on, which can make it hard for them to deal with adulthood. As adults, they may have a hard time with their emotions. They may even have difficulty separating themselves from the emotions of others.

Libra people struggle to keep both aspects of themselves in balance. They do not like when one side dominates or overpowers the other. When this happens, they may find themselves losing control of their emotions and feel like they're no longer in the driver's seat. This can cause them to feel intense anger and frustration. Hence the importance for them to keep both sides in check.

All in all, Libra is a very charming individual with a lot of charisma. They're able to get almost anyone's attention simply by walking into a room. This can be a great thing for them when they're trying to get something done, but sometimes it becomes a bit overwhelming. They tend to be very social and like to surround themselves with others who are just as extroverted as they are. When they feel alone, they may find themselves becoming restless and unfocused. This is usually the time when Libra will feel most vulnerable and may start getting into trouble.

Libra is easily able to spot whether someone has ulterior motives. While other signs may trust someone simply because their personality pulls at their heartstrings, Libra does not like being tricked in any way. They are very cautious and will not allow themselves to be taken advantage of.

Crystals for the Libra

Turquoise: For the Libra that needs a little more grounding, Turquoise is the perfect stone for them to connect with. It will help them to get in touch with their emotions and bring them back to a place of balance. This can be extremely helpful for those who fall into destructive behaviors. Turquoise will help them to understand other people's feelings and what it's like for others to be in the same situation as they are. It can also help those who are suffering from self-esteem issues. It will give them a little boost when they feel they aren't good enough or don't deserve anything better than what they already have.

Pink Tourmaline: For the Libra who has had a hard time letting go of the past, Pink Tourmaline is a great stone for them to work with. It's very good at healing emotional wounds and can help those who are suffering from depression to feel more at peace. It has a calming energy that helps clear out old issues and bring forward new thoughts and emotions. This can be incredibly helpful for those who find themselves overwhelmed by the world around them. They will be able to find a moment of peace with this stone in their hands.

Fire Agate: For the Libra that's struggling with making decisions, Fire Agate is the perfect stone for them. It will help them to be decisive and allow them to set boundaries. It can also help get their feelings out of the way when it's time for them to make a decision. For those who are having a hard time coping with life situations, this stone can help to turn things around and give them some clarity about the choices that they have made.

Pyrite: For a Libra that's becoming increasingly paranoid about the people around them, Pyrite can help them be less wary of their surroundings and trust the people in their lives. It helps them find inner peace and can even lead to protecting themselves from other people's negative intentions. It's perfect for those who are too trusting of others and who tend to get hurt by this. It will shield them from their overly suspicious nature and help them to have a more reasonable outlook on life.

Pyrite.
https://commons.wikimedia.org/wiki/File:Pyrite_(18858891699).jpg

Aquarius (Jan 20-Feb 18)

Aquarius is ruled by the planet Uranus and symbolized by the water container. The Aquarius is not only very loyal to their friends but also to their causes. They tend to be extremely intelligent individuals with many opinions about almost every topic in life. They don't like being told what they should think or how they should feel. This can sometimes cause a bit of friction between them and other signs because they're much more independent than other signs tend to be.

The Aquarius can see both sides of an issue, making them very good at finding solutions to problems. They're also able to grasp concepts and ideas that seem completely foreign to others; they simply have a different way of looking at things than everyone else does. This can make Aquarians appear as though they're a bit disconnected from reality, but they are some of the most intelligent individuals you'll ever meet.

The Aquarius has one problem that may prevent them from living out their full potential: impatience. They don't like being told that something is going to take some time or that there is a chance of failure during something. This is because Aquarius has an extremely optimistic view of life. They believe that if something can be imagined, then it should be possible to achieve. This can make them disappointed easily when things do not turn out how they thought they would. Because of this, they prefer focusing on the positive aspects of their lives rather than the negative ones.

The Aquarius tends to come across as a reserved individual who likes to keep people at arm's length. They like having plenty of space around them and dislike feeling crowded or trapped. They crave adventure and excitement to help keep their sparks alive. This is why some of them choose careers where they travel all over the world. Although they tend to be very positive people with a great outlook on life, they become extremely cynical when they lose faith in humanity.

The Aquarius is incredibly loyal and committed to those they care about. They like to feel as though they are making an impact on the world around them and will put others before themselves every time. Aquarius doesn't believe that you should take things for granted, which is why they give everything that they have to make a difference in the lives of others. This is one of the main reasons for their popularity amongst those who know them well.

Crystals for the Aquarius

Morganite: This is a stone that will help the Aquarius to understand their own feelings. It will help them find a healthy emotional balance, which will aid them greatly in making decisions in their everyday lives. Morganite also has a huge impact on an individual's mental energy and can be used to help lift the spirits of those severely depressed. It allows them to see past their own problems and the world around them.

Pink Halite: This crystal is a great choice for the Aquarius who's having a hard time dealing with the emotions of others. It's very good at keeping feelings in check and will help them to be aware of when they're becoming too involved in situations that don't concern them. Halite is also a stone that helps heal emotional wounds and can give the Aquarius much-needed support when they struggle with their own life issues.

Ruby: For the Aquarius who feel as though they don't have the right to feel angry, Ruby is a great choice. They will be able to better handle their own emotions toward people, which will help them become more in tune with how they're feeling and what they're going through. It's a calming stone and will be helpful for those who are struggling with too much stress in their lives. It helps them to relax and take things one day at a time.

Cinnabar: Cinnabar is a stone that can help the Aquarius to tap into their potential. It's a great stone for those trying to make their dreams come true and can give them the motivation they need to reach the top of the mountain. This stone will stop them from giving up on things before they've even begun and can help them to stay focused on their goals in life.

Gemini (May 21-June 21)

Gemini is ruled by the planet Mercury and symbolized by the Twins. The Gemini tends to be an extremely social sign who loves having intellectual conversations with those around them. They are very curious individuals who always ask questions about everything they hear or see. They'll often find themselves distracted because they want more information about things.

The Gemini has a huge abundance of personality traits that makes it very difficult for others to get to know them on a personal level. This is why very few people can ever tell what type of Gemini they're dealing with. They can be as emotional, witty, and creative as they are intelligent. This can certainly lead to some confusion within their own lives.

The Gemini tends to have a short attention span and often lose interest in things when they get bored. This often leads to making poor decisions, which can cause them much frustration. They're also highly impulsive individuals who tend to test the waters before they go in with their next move. Because of this, they're not always able to build up the trust of others around them. The Gemini can understand all sides of an argument, but they don't always take the time to truly listen to what others are saying. Because of this, they often find themselves getting stuck in arguments with their loved ones.

The Gemini is definitely an impressionable sign and will have an incredibly difficult time when it comes to making hard and fast decisions. It's almost as though their minds are split into two halves, which causes them to be very indecisive. This can cause great frustration for the Gemini because they're very anxious about making the wrong decision. They try to avoid making up their minds as often as possible.

Gemini is a very playful sign who loves to flirt with the people they're romantically interested in. They tend to love having fun and will often say whatever they need to get someone of interest on their side. They also tend to test the waters when it comes to approaching others, which can lead them to get frustrated when turned down. The great thing about the Gemini is that they can be completely honest and open with their significant other. They have no problem telling anyone how they feel. They aren't afraid to tell their loved ones EXACTLY how they feel and will often share too many details of how they're feeling with their prospective partner.

The Gemini is a very fun-loving sign who will always want to be around others. They'll even find themselves jumping into relationships without thinking things through first. This is because of their need to know that the world around them is safe and that no one will hurt them. They're also very self-sufficient individuals who enjoy spending time on their own, which can lead to relationship problems when it comes to feeling a sense of togetherness.

They are a very lively sign and will keep things fun and exciting all the time. They'll often find themselves enjoying what they're doing without even realizing it. These individuals have a huge desire to be able to make an immediate difference within the world around them and will set out in good faith with the hope that something good will come from it. The Gemini can understand how others are feeling and know exactly what to say or do to help them feel better.

Crystals for the Gemini

Blue Apatite: This crystal is a great choice for the Gemini who's having a very hard time understanding how other people are feeling. They will be able to feel when someone is truly upset and will be able to help them find a calmer, more peaceful place in their mind. Apatite that can increase confidence in those who are living their lives in fear. It is very effective at reducing feelings of stress and anxiety.

Iolite: This crystal can help the Gemini when experiencing deep emotional turmoil. It is very good at helping them calm down and get back into balance, which will allow them to move on from what's bothering them emotionally. Iolite is also great at helping them become more aware of what is affecting them and will help them finally understand where their feelings are coming from.

Lemon Quartz: This crystal is great for the Gemini, who tend to doubt themselves even when they're approaching something they truly enjoy. It can help them build their self-esteem and feel more confident in their abilities. Lemon Quartz is also effective at helping those who feel out of control about their lives. It can help them to step back and see the bigger picture.

Leopardskin Jasper: This is a great crystal for the Gemini, who tends to jump right into things without thinking them through first. This crystal will help them slow down and think over their decisions before they finalize anything. It will also be able to keep them grounded and make sure that they can see how their choices affect their surroundings.

Chapter 10: Crystals for Fire Signs

Some people say that the fire signs are born leaders with an innate ability to command attention just by standing in a room. Others say that fire signs possess exceptional leadership skills but find themselves at odds with those who want power for its own sake. All of them agree on the powerful magnetism they exude and the way their presence can make anyone feel like they're floating above everything else. They tend to be independent, preferring to handle problems and challenges on their own.

Fire signs possess a profound artistic and creative sensitivity, often manifesting as an unusual talent for music and dance. Some have described a deep emotional connection with their art and the world around them. The rosiness of their emotions is something that no one can resist falling into, and it's also what makes them so attractive as friends and lovers. Even though it could be said that fire signs go to extremes in both drama and passion, they always succeed at bringing out the best in themselves and others.

Although fire signs can be great leaders, the true power in their lives lies in their family relationships. They always find themselves making family a priority and living for the good of their loved ones. In fact, fire signs are so good at making life better for the ones they love that sometimes they forget to tend to their own needs.

Everyone should try what it's like to be on the receiving end of a fire sign's love and care. However, this comes with a warning. Once a fire sign chooses you as their friend or partner, they will protect you and fight for you with the same passion that they fight for themselves. It means that there will be consequences if you hurt them in any way, no matter how unintentionally. And those consequences are not forgiving in the least. The fire signs are represented by Sagittarius, Leo, and Aries.

Sagittarius (Nov 22-Dec 21)

Sagittarius, represented by the archer, is ready to shoot down anything that stands in their way of doing what they want. They can make great leaders because they can stand up for what they believe in and look at things from a very broad perspective, which can help others figure out what's really important when making a decision. The Sagittarius is someone who enjoys learning new things and will make sure that they have all the facts before making any decisions about their lives. This also helps them to avoid making snap judgments about people or situations, although they fall prey to this sometimes.

Sagittarius is a self-motivated sign which has a very hard time letting others tell them how to do things. They like to take the reins when it comes to their lives, which can sometimes cause them to act out of character and step over the line. The Sagittarius can become so entangled in making decisions that it starts to interfere with their personal relationships. They'll often start making quick judgments about people and will focus on the negative aspects of other people. They like to be right, which can cause them to get very upset and angry when they're proven wrong.

They are very open-minded individuals who thrive when they have a lot of freedom to make their own decisions. They enjoy their daily lives and will always find something they want to do. They're never ones to settle for the same thing over and over again. The Sagittarius is someone who doesn't mind spending time alone once in a while and will often seek out opportunities to spend time in nature. They also enjoy spending time at home with their family, being able to be completely honest with them, and discussing things that are bothering them. This can really help them deal with their emotions.

Sagittarius are very passionate individuals when they fall in love. They're willing to do whatever it takes to make their relationship last. They're capable of falling in love with almost anyone, which can cause them to get into relationships quickly and often leave them with a broken heart later on. They are very good at reading the emotions of others and will be able to tell when someone is lying or exaggerating things; this can cause them to feel a great deal of angst when they don't see eye-to-eye with someone else who's involved in their life. This can cause problems within certain relationships and cause the Sagittarius to act out. They are capable of getting very jealous when they feel that someone else is taking their partner away and will often try to make the other person jealous as well.

Sagittarius is a very social person and enjoys the company of others. They're always looking for new friends to enjoy their time with and often have many friends they spend time with in unequal amounts. They're very honest people who are going to be upfront with their friends about how they feel. They're not afraid to speak their mind and will always be willing to point out any flaws that they see within themselves or others.

The Sagittarius is also very curious about everything in life, which can cause them to become so engrossed in a subject that they forget to pay attention to the bigger picture. They'll often get in over their heads, which will cause them to have trouble seeing where they are going and what they need to do next. They have a hard time making up their mind about things because of the many options available. This could lead them into situations that they may not otherwise have landed in if they had made better choices.

Crystals for the Sagittarius

Yellow Topaz: This is a great crystal to have for the Sagittarius, who tends to jump into things without thinking them through first. This crystal will help them slow down and think things over before they get out of control. They'll also be able to see a bit more clearly about other people's motives and will quickly be able to spot when someone is up to no good.

Azurite: This is a great stone for the Sagittarius, who finds it hard to get rid of their negative emotions. It will help them process things without being caught up in the moment's emotion. It is also very good at helping them to move on from a relationship that isn't making them feel good about themselves.

Hematite: This is one of the best stones for this individual because it's going to help them see their surroundings much more clearly. They'll be able to see when someone is doing something out of character and won't judge them for it so harshly. They'll also be able to recognize when someone else has been hurt or upset by something they said or did. If a situation isn't handled the way it should, a Sagittarius needs to let others know there is likely to be a problem.

Leo (July 23-Aug 22)

The first thing you notice when meeting someone in the Leo community is that they have a big, loud personality. They are very social and outgoing people who like to make a good impression on others. They tend to be very expressive individuals who like to let everyone know how they feel about them. They are born leaders. Those in their lives will often look up to them for guidance and know they are there for them at any time.

Leo is someone who looks at the world around them and decides what needs to be improved. They like to make sure that they are making everyone's day better, which can make them a great leader. They can be overly enthusiastic about their work and tend to go all out when they're doing it. They are very social in nature and like to have a good time at the weekend. They'll often go out and get drunk to forget about their problems.

Leo is a very intelligent and high-powered individual who is always looking for ways to better their situation. They can be very competitive and would love to show others that they're better than them in some way or another. They will often compare themselves to others to feel superior in some aspect of their lives.

If you ever encounter someone who acts one way in public and another way in private, they likely have Leo as their Sun sign. They can be very hard on themselves and tend to fall into the trap of trying to please others. They need to learn how to be more honest with themselves and how they feel about everything. They will find it easier to become the individuals they want to be in the long run if they work on accepting themselves for who they are rather than who someone else wants them to be.

Leo tends to be very honest with everyone else but themselves and won't hold back on the things on their mind. They are someone who will speak freely about topics that other people find uncomfortable, which is why many people admire them for their honesty in communication. You'll also notice that they always have a very happy outlook on life and love to be the center of attention.

Leos are leaders who have a hard time accepting criticism. They're very hard on themselves and can let people's words get to them. They'll often take what has been said as an insult or something they shouldn't have done. You'll find that Leo is someone who will try to confront anyone who is criticizing them, which can make it hard for them to move forward and make any real changes in their lives.

They are very expressive individuals who love being around people and don't mind a loud personality to get others" attention. They're passionate about whatever it is that they do and will speak candidly about their feelings. However, you'll find that they are quite sensitive, which can cause them to become over-emotional about situations. All of this is fine for someone who has a Leo as their Sun sign, but those who aren't born with one have a bit of a hard time understanding this individual. All things considered, Leo will always try their hardest to make sure that they are doing the right thing, bringing the most positive energy into their life.

Crystals for the Leo

Peridot: This is a great crystal for a Leo who tends to get wrapped up in their work and forget to enjoy life. It will help them slow down and spend more time with people they love. It is also great for helping them find their center and will help them to feel relaxed and confident.

Red Spinel: This is a great crystal for Leo, who can be overly sensitive to other people's words. They're going to find that they can process things much better when they're around this crystal. It will help them to see that other people are just trying to be nice and that there is no one out there with ill-will toward them.

Crimson Cuprite: This is another great crystal for those who have a tough time letting go of negative energy or criticism. It will help them to process things much better and will help them to move on from situations that don't make them feel good about themselves.

Tiger Iron: This is a great crystal for Leo, who isn't getting the right kind of attention. They aren't going to be as concerned with people's opinions and will find that they can go after the things they want. They'll also have a much easier time handling their responsibilities and won't let others get in their way.

Aries (April 20-May 21)

Aries are go-getters who have a unique and outgoing personality that attracts other people to them because of their energy and enthusiasm. They're very spontaneous and love to take chances, often coming up with the best ideas for new projects.

They can be a bit brash in nature, with the tendency to speak their mind without concern for how that may affect others. They don't like to keep their opinions about people to themselves and will often speak about how they feel about someone even when they're in public. They are also very competitive. If there's something that they want, they aren't going to take no for an answer.

Aries people are natural leaders. They are very confident in the things that they say and do. They like to be in a position where people look to them for guidance because it makes them feel good about themselves. They have very expressive personalities and will easily tell people what's on their minds. Their biggest flaw is that they can be too impulsive at times, and this often leads to situations where they aren't aware of how their actions will affect others.

They are very sensitive in nature and have a very hard time when it comes to dealing with criticism from others. They can take things very personally and will sometimes avoid situations because they don't want to be told what they are doing wrong. They are very ambitious and like to prove themselves to everyone around them. If you ever find yourself with a struggling Aries, you'll usually know about it. They tend to express their inner voice quite easily.

Aries is a person who wants to be in charge of things. They aren't going to let anyone else have control over them, no matter what it takes. Oddly, they can also be very trusting of others and will tend to trust people too easily. This can cause them to get into some bad situations that they may not be able to get out of until they learn that things are usually not what they seem.

Aries is definitely a person who believes in working hard and playing harder. The first thing you should know about these romantics is that they are very passionate about the ones they love, which can sometimes get them into trouble. They will do anything but hold back to show their passion. Aries is looking for someone who can be a team player. They will want to feel like they are working toward a mutual goal.

They are very straightforward and honest, which is something that most people crave on a personal level, so they aren't going to take too kindly to you being dishonest with them. They like things around them to be real. If you're not interested in being serious with someone, this isn't your person.

They tend to be a bit immature in their actions and sometimes get into trouble. This can be difficult for them to overcome unless they're willing to learn from their mistakes, which isn't something they are too keen on doing. They will have many people tell them that they need to grow up at one point or another throughout their life and will often take this as a direct attack on who they are and how they feel about the world around them, even though most of it comes from their own actions. They aren't willing to overlook something just because you tell them it's a bad idea. They will argue with you until they prove themselves right.

If you find yourself with a man or woman born under this sign, you will want to realize one thing. They are looking for someone as confident in their actions as they are. They will also want someone who can handle their desire for adventure and excitement, so don't try and keep them cooped up inside your house all day because it won't end well.

Aries will have a very hard time getting over a bad breakup, as they tend to hold grudges for a long time. This can cause them to be very lonely for some time because they don't want to get involved with the wrong person, which is often their biggest fear.

They are looking for someone who has the same qualities that they do and can keep up with them during their adventures.

Generally, Aries is very friendly and will often be found talking with others. They have a unique personality that draws many people to them for their warmth and honesty. They are also very good at building relationships with others, as they have a genuine desire to see people do well.

Crystals for the Aries

Vesuvianite: You will find that this is the stone for Aries, as it brings them a sense of calmness during times of stress. This is a stone that you can use to help bring your body and mind back into balance when you feel like everything in your life is getting away from you. Wear this stone when you need to relieve stress. It will provide you with the serenity that you are looking for.

Zircon: This is a stone that you can use to help clear negativity from your life. If you're feeling a bit down and have noticed some changes in your life that are not an improvement, this is the stone for you. Wearing this will bring you a sense of positivity and balance. It will give you an idea of what's going on around you and help get it back into focus.

Emerald: This green stone helps with the hard task of balancing other people's energies around you. This is the stone for you if you find yourself surrounded by people who are all about themselves. The energy will clear the area and make sure that everyone is on the same page.

Zoisite: This stone will bring you a sense of relaxation and balance. If you are having trouble falling asleep, this is the one for you. It will provide a calming effect that will allow you to get your rest so that you can begin your day feeling rejuvenated and ready to tackle anything that comes your way.

Chapter 11: Crystals for Water Signs

The water signs are the polar opposite of fire signs. Think of them as the calm, cool, and collected ones who like to stay out of trouble whenever possible. They prefer to deal with their problems privately. If they need help, they'll ask for it, but they do a good job taking care of themselves independently.

They don't particularly enjoy the spotlight and don't especially like the idea of being in charge or at the head of something. They're perfectly happy sitting on the sidelines and letting others take care of everything. This can lead them to a life of self-absorption, but they make up for it by being loving and loyal in their friendships and partners.

They are very good listeners, and they make excellent counselors. They're often compassionate in their dealings with others and can be very caring and understanding, especially when it comes to those they love.

Although water signs exhibit many of the same psychological characteristics as earth signs, they are fundamentally different in that there is more room for the internal self within their emotional makeup. Unlike earth signs, they can honestly express themselves, who tend to keep their feelings bottled up inside. Water signs allow themselves to feel whatever emotions come up without inhibitions or restrictions. This openness seems to give them a better understanding of other people's feelings and a greater ability to make meaningful relationships with others.

They are the psychics of the zodiac, hence their uncanny ability to understand what's going on with other people and in other situations. They are naturally mysterious, and their reserved and quiet nature does nothing to dispel this mystery.

They are the most intuitive of all the signs and can often sense what's going on in the hearts and minds of others without needing to be told. They have a unique way of looking at the world and can easily put themselves into other people's shoes because they're so good at imagining how they would feel if they were in someone else's circumstances. This can make them seem psychologically "in tune" with people and makes them very effective at helping others. They are sensitive to the mood of their environment and respond appropriately to it. They're good at maintaining their equilibrium in stressful circumstances, but they can sometimes be too passive and self-sacrificing and need to learn to let go more often.

Although they are naturally friendly, they tend to be a bit shy, especially with strangers. They learn early on through experience that it's best not to open up too much or reveal too much about themselves because people will only use that information against them one way or another. The members of this group are Pisces, Scorpio, and Cancer.

Pisces (Feb 19-Mar 20)

Pisces are tender and sensitive souls who like to avoid conflict wherever possible. Their thoughts are usually focused on the past, causing them to be emotionally driven people. They are kind and considerate in nature and love to nurture those that they feel close to.

This sign is an overall dreamer and loves nature, although this can make it difficult for them to finish their schoolwork, as they will spend a lot of time daydreaming and envisioning their life laid out before them. Pisces can be very creative people who want the world around them to be perfect. They don't like anything that is messy or requires a lot of action or physical labor.

They are often known for being very indecisive due to their sensitive nature. They may have a hard time making decisions and always looking at other people's points of view. Pisces need to find someone who can stand up for them and push them out into the world. They also need to find someone that can be sensitive and understanding when they get hurt.

When it comes to relationships, Pisces will want someone who understands that these things take time. They know they are a bit scattered at times and will want someone who is there to pick up the pieces when they fall apart. They generally don't like conflict or confrontation and will try to avoid it at all costs.

One of the best things you can do for this sign of the zodiac is direct with them. Pisces doesn't respond well to beating around the bush, so you'll want to get right down to it when you have something that needs to be said. They tend to look past things that are wrong due to their naivety and can be hurt by others without even realizing it. Be sure to be honest with them, as they need guidance in their lives to grow as a person.

Pisces will make a great romantic partner. They will happily do all they can to please the one they love and are very good at showing their feelings when they are in love. It's important to them that the other person knows how they feel, so don't be shy about expressing your feelings to them. Pisces has a soft spot for those who are sweet and kind, which is why you might want to look for someone who can be both caring and selfish at the same time.

They are very affectionate and love to cuddle up to their loved ones. They will be willing to put all they have into the relationship, as they don't have many friends that they can rely on when they have problems. Pisces will not leave a relationship easily, which is why you must stick around when things start getting a little rough. Make sure you give them plenty of positive attention, though, as Pisces do like having people love them, and this can make them seem clingy at times. This sign likes to be romanced, so if you want to stand out, you'll want to make sure you lavish them with attention and gifts.

Crystals for the Pisces

Chlorite Phantom Crystals: You will find that this crystal is directly connected to the element of water. It will bring you the calmness and serenity that you are looking for. If you want to feel like everything around you is okay, this stone can provide that for you. It's a calming force that anyone can notice when they are around it. It will bring the inner peace and tranquility that most Pisces need in their lives.

Larimar: This is a crystal that helps with opening the heart chakra. This is the stone for you if you feel like you've closed yourself off from the world. It will help bring balance to your life and allow you to become more patient and open with those around you.

Zebra Stone: This stone is wonderful for Pisces, as it helps you to get in touch with your inner power. It will give you the strength and resolve you need to carry out your dreams. This stone is perfect for people who have a strong desire to go after something but don't know how to begin. It will give them the energy and strength that they need to make those dreams a reality. This is a great gift for the Pisces in your life.

Variscite: This is a stone that you can use to help raise your consciousness. If you find yourself stuck in a rut, unable to move forward, and unsure of what's going on around you, this is the one for you. It will give you the insight you need to get yourself out of the situation. It will help bring your inner light out, so you can see what's really going on in your life.

Scorpio (Oct 23-Nov 21)

Scorpio is an intense and passionate sign who will do almost anything to achieve its goals. They can be a bit impulsive and hot-tempered, but that's just how this sign likes things. They are sensual and loving people who will do whatever it takes to get what they want.

Their biggest issue is that they tend to get caught up in the materialistic things in life, which can make them seem shallow. They are not. They enjoy the finer things than anyone else, but it's definitely not their main focus. They would rather spend their money on things that will help them live better lives and create long-lasting memories.

Scorpios are known for being quite aggressive with whatever they are doing. They don't like to wait for things to happen; they want to make them happen now. This can cause some issues with those around them, but if you want results, you should give them space to do their thing. Scorpios are passionate about everything that they do and will do whatever it takes to get what they need when they need it.

One of the biggest things that Scorpios need to work on is their trust issues. They tend to get jealous of those they are close to and want to make sure that no one is trying to move in on their territory. They may even set up ground rules and boundaries for this purpose, but this can cause issues with their relationships as they can come off as too controlling. This sign needs to learn how to trust others, especially those they love and care about the most.

Scorpios want someone who will challenge them as well as accept them for who they are. They will want someone who is loving and caring, with a personality that can stand up for itself. This sign likes to be around people who can stand their ground. They don't like to walk on eggshells around their significant other.

One of the most important things that you can do for this sign is to be *honest with them at all times.* They will have no problem telling others what they think and how they feel and want the same in return. Scorpio doesn't like being around people who are fake or full of lies, so if you want to be a part of their life, you will need to lay it all out on the table.

This sign is a very passionate one. They are confident and direct in their feelings, which is something that they will definitely want to present to their lover. Scorpio is a very sexual sign that wants to be able to experience all the wonderful parts of life, including having a loving partner. They need their lovers to be strong and proactive. They don't like weak people or those who would be too passive in their actions. They need to be able to trust that their partner isn't going anywhere and would never be a threat to them.

Crystals for the Scorpio

Red Zoisite: This rare stone was created when molten rock cooled inside an extinct volcano in Tanzania. It is said to have mystical healing powers. It will help you to gain more focus and put your mind into action. You will be able to accomplish anything that you set your mind to using this stone.

Apache Tears: This stone can help you take the negative energy and resentment you've carried inside you for years. It will help to clear out old wounds and allow you to let go of harmful emotions like anger. You will have more peace in your life as a result of using this crystal.

Blue Lace Agate: This stone can bring out your fears, thus allowing you to face and heal them once and for all. When you can deal with the issues holding you back from moving forward, this is a stone that you should use. It will help release your fears when it comes to making decisions or going after what you want in life.

Rhodonite: This stone will help you ground yourself, stabilize your life and keep things moving in the right direction. If you feel like nothing is going right, this stone can be used to help you find your way back to safety and comfort. It is a good calming stone that can be used when stress seems like it cannot be overcome.

Cancer (June 22-July 22)

Cancer is a very emotional and sensitive sign that can be prone to mood swings. They can become quite defensive when they feel like they are being attacked or criticized in any way. When they are feeling down, they tend to throw themselves into their work and focus on building something of their own.

Cancer is a very nurturing and caring sign that wants to feel needed in the lives of others. They want to be a part of something bigger than themselves and make others feel like they are valuable, something that they didn't get when they were younger. They are survivors who will do whatever it takes to ensure that their family and loved ones will always be taken care of. This can cause them to become martyrs on occasion and put too much pressure on themselves to provide for everyone else. This is only an issue when they are dealing with people who do not appreciate their actions, taking them for granted.

They like to be in relationships that are full of romance and passion. It helps them to get the attention they need to feel alive and loved. They like to feel safe and secure with the person they are with and want that person to offer them support during their low points.

They tend to be very indecisive about their lives, especially when it comes to making major decisions about their personal life. They often tend to second-guess themselves and end up pushing those they love away. They want someone who can help them see when they are being silly or indecisive about a situation, but this can also be difficult for their partner.

Cancer needs to learn how to deal with their emotions, especially when it comes to dealing with their anger. They tend to hold onto things that frustrate them before they explode and lash out at others in the process. This is not healthy for anyone involved, so as a Cancer, you'll need to work on showing your emotions and standing up for yourself without being aggressive.

This sign needs to learn how to talk about their feelings and be able to listen when others are sharing their ideas as well. They will want someone who can help them express their views and opinions without feeling judged. They also want to know that they are seen and loved for who they are when it comes to the people who matter in their lives.

This sign is a lover at heart, so if you want something amazing, then this is a sign that you should go after. You will need to be able to let go of your fears as well as make some hard decisions for this sign to be happy with you. They will have no problem letting you know just how much they love you and what it is that you mean to them. Just be sure to show them the same thing.

They are very emotional people who are often lost in their own thoughts, so they need to be able to open up their feelings and share them with their partners. They need someone strong enough to listen when they want to talk about any heady subjects and who can show them the same amount of enthusiasm that they give.

They are often perfectionists when it comes to their work. They will tend to push themselves very hard to achieve the best possible results that they can find. They tend to feel stressed by the pressure they put on themselves and their partner. You will need to help them relax and get some good rest at the end of the day. They love being able to work on their projects from home and will want you there when they are working on their own things. You can encourage them to take on new projects and find their own way to express their unique way of thinking.

Patience will be the most important thing you need to have when dealing with your Cancer. They will tend to spend an awful lot of time thinking about something before they make a decision, which can help them to deal with their indecisiveness, but if someone pushes them too hard, then they will go into their shell and simply be unable to deal with certain situations.

If you want to show your Cancer that you are serious about spending the rest of your life together, you need to partner with them as friends and lovers. Spend time getting to know them and do not push them into doing anything that they are not comfortable doing. Listen when they have something important to say or have an idea. This will help you figure out how they like to work through the things that frustrate them and give them the patience they need when making a decision. Work with their emotions so they can feel safe in your presence - loved and truly cherished.

Crystals for the Cancer

Pearl: This stone symbolizes nurture and motherhood. It will help provide you with healing, inner peace, beauty, and happiness. This is also a stone that helps to build strong family values, so it's important for people who want to strengthen their families. The energy of this stone encourages wisdom and patience in those who use it.

Moon Quartz: This stone will help connect you with the feminine energy and bring balance to your life. Working with this stone makes you feel more connected to the world around you. It will also help with your personal happiness and help you be more focused. This stone can be used by those who do not only want to improve their appearance but also boost their physical self-confidence as well. Use it for its strength and healing powers or for its feminine energy and connection to Mother Earth.

Serpentine: This stone is powerful and comes from Mother Earth herself. It is one of the oldest stones known to man and will help open you up to the world around you and connect more closely with nature. This stone will help you channel your inner feelings and improve how you connect with all things in the universe. It is a good stone for those who are interested in metaphysical healing as well.

Orgonite: This stone will help you to harness your own energy and use it to connect with the universe positively. This stone can be used for healing purposes as well as to improve the flow of energy in your life. It can also be used for the protection of your home, business, or personal space.

Section Three: Using Crystal Grids

Chapter 12: Understanding Crystal Grids

A crystal grid is an organized layout of crystals or stones set in some sort of design to create a single, focused healing space. Most crystal grids are created with a specific purpose in mind, such as removing negative energy, attracting abundance, or making an area safer. The stones and crystals used in these grids can vary greatly depending on the type of energy you want to infuse your space with.

Crystal grids work with the natural properties of crystals and shapes to create healing spaces. The power created from the grid can aid in finding a true sense of purpose when added to your spiritual or wellness practices. Crystal grids are not just for spiritual healing. They are also an exercise in geometry. Normally when you think about crystals, it's the energy and properties that come to mind, but the geometry of a crystal forms its structure and, in turn, shapes its natural energy. A sacred geometry pattern is a way of organizing objects based on the inherent properties of geometric shapes and figures. Crystal grids take this idea one step further by using crystals with specific healing properties to create a variety of different grid patterns. To understand crystal grids, it's important to know the meaning of sacred geometry and what these patterns mean to the grid.

What Is Sacred Geometry?

Sacred Geometry, also known as the divine proportion, is a form of geometry that works with the properties of nature and divine entities. It can be seen throughout the art and architecture of ancient cultures, in everything from the Great Pyramid at Giza in Egypt to medieval cathedrals. Geometric shapes can also be found in natural objects like crystals and flowers. The idea behind sacred geometry is that these geometric figures are more than just shapes; they represent ideas, patterns, and numbers. Their relationship holds cosmic significance because they're said to reflect the actions of divine powers at work in nature. They're used to depict religious ideas and spiritual truths through mathematical equations found within nature and built into shape-based forms. Sacred geometry is used in crystal grids because each geometric shape represents a different kind of energy. When placed together, these shapes create a unique energy that combines the powers of each individual stone or crystal, creating larger energy than one could have imagined on its own.

The Power of Geometry

Geometric figures have been used in art and design for as long as humans can record their history. The meanings behind geometric figures can vary greatly depending on the culture they originate from, but there are certain universal concepts most cultures share. The most common geometric figure you can find in sacred spaces is the triangle. Other figures include squares, circles, crosses, and spirals. Each of these shapes represents a different meaning, depending on the culture, time, and the way they're used. Triangles are considered a feminine shape in art. Ancient Egyptians believed triangles represented the spirit or breath of life moving through their pharaohs and queens. In modern times, triangles also represent power and truth because when they're connected, they form a pyramid, which is often used as a symbol of divine strength.

Another familiar shape found in sacred spaces: the circle. This figure represents either wholeness or unity between people or ideas. It can also represent the sun or moon since both celestial bodies are round. Circles are often used as a symbol of protection, guidance, or healing.

The cross is another typical figure that can be seen in sacred spaces and is commonly represented by symbols of light at night, such as the cross on Christmas trees or illuminated buildings at night. The cross has even been used as a symbol of both salvation and death. Some people also associate crosses with humanity and its connection to the divine.

Sacred Geometry in Nature

Geometry is found in almost every natural form, such as flowers, crystals, and trees. Plants, for example, naturally grow in a circular pattern. This geometry helps them collect and direct sunlight to reach their deepest root systems. This circle is called the golden ratio, or phi (1.618) because it's found naturally and can be recreated through complex calculations. The golden ratio is also found in hurricanes, pine cones, spiral galaxies, and even insects. Crystals are another example of sacred geometry occurring naturally. When a crystal is cut, the way it breaks is based on mathematical calculations that look at how the crystals reflect light and how its cut interacts with surrounding faces. The golden ratio significantly affects materials like glass and stone, which is why so many look great when arranged in shape-based patterns. The human body itself is based on geometric shapes as well. Our fingers and toes each curve in a way that follows these shapes – and this geometry is found throughout the body's organs, muscles, bones, and nerves.

Sacred Geometry and Philosophy

Geometry has been used to measure and study the universe since ancient times. In fact, many early civilizations started out as math-based cultures. Geometry was a way to study the universe because it had a natural connection to the divine. Geometry is used in sacred spaces because it's used to understand how to better connect with the divine and harmonize with their actions. Plato, for example, believed that the universe had been created out of a single geometric form called the perfect cube. He believed that the perfect cube was the mold into which all other objects were cast and was used as a template through which physical reality was formed. This idea likely stems from ancient Egyptian beliefs that the universe was created out of one single geometric shape called the Great Crystal. The Great Crystal is even said to be a direct representation of human consciousness.

The findings of mathematician Johannes Kepler also support the idea of geometry playing a role in the characteristics of the universe. However, instead of applying geometry to explain human consciousness or the structure of galaxies, Kepler went one step further and applied geometric calculations to a relationship between planetary movement and ratios. Kepler found that rotational movement on Earth is mathematically linked to movements within a single star, according to a 2009 article published by BBC Science. This means that planets are being accelerated in certain patterns based on certain mathematical ratios. Because current laws of physics can't explain these ratios, they suggest something has created them from within the nature of space itself. These shapes have even been found in the paintings of historical artists like Leonardo da Vinci, whose work has been recently compared to that of cosmic spiritualists like Pythagoras and Kepler.

Many people believe that modern science has separated humans from the divine, which is why sacred geometry is often used in sacred spaces to reconnect. Sacred geometry is used in crystal grids and mandala art to help bring back human connection to the divine. This is also why sacred geometry is sometimes used in meditation. The belief behind this process is that if you can get in tune with the geometric shapes around you, you can become more in tune with the divine and better understand humanity's place within nature. Sacred geometry for meditation can be very helpful to those who are trying to feel closer to their deity or their own spiritual side.

Crystal grids are often used to create sacred space within a room, home, or backyard. They are made by understanding the properties of geometric shapes and then placing crystals in specific locations so that the energy field of the crystals can amplify each other. Sacred geometry plays an important role in crystal grids because it organizes where crystals should be placed. Therefore, determining how energy flows through the grid and how powerful it will be in influencing its surroundings.

Common Sacred Geometry Shapes for Crystal Grids

Crystal grids are made up of geometric shapes and are most effective when they're organized properly based on the shapes they contain. The following shapes are the most commonly used in crystal grids:

The Seed of Life

The seed of life is arguably the most important shape for crystal grids because it's a symbol of creation. It's made up of seven circles inscribed inside a larger circle. The seven circles represent the seven days of creation, and the larger circle represents the eternal nature of time and space. The seed of life is a symbol of the universe and all things within it and is usually found at the center of sacred geometry patterns. When used in a crystal grid, this shape helps bring a person into closer contact with their deity or higher power. It can also help them draw in positive energy and power from the universe and use it to purify their soul.

The Vesica Piscis

The Vesica Piscis is the shape formed by two overlapping circles that create an oval-shaped space between them. This is a very important shape because it represents two people coming together in harmony and the unification of male and female characteristics within nature. In sacred geometry, this form represents wholeness and purity. The middle portion of the shape (the oval) has been associated with God's womb, while the two circles represent God's penis. Together, they represent the divine union. This shape can be found in many places in space and is often found surrounding the seed of life. It's often used in crystal grids because it keeps the energy out of two areas while they are still connected to each other.

The Flower of Life

The flower of life is also made up of circles, but they're organized differently on each side. Each side has eight small circles and one larger one in the middle. The eight small circles have been subdivided into more circles that are evenly divided. The larger circle at the center represents unity, while each smaller circle divided into four separate parts represents nature's ability to transform matter into energy over time through a process called the law of cycles. When used in a crystal grid, the flower of life helps the person using it become more at one with nature and their own divinity. It's often used with other geometrical shapes because it's a symbol for creation and has been compared to the "superstring theory" of physics, which holds that all matter is made up of vibrating energy. These theories give insight into how different elements and atoms are formed in the universe and why they exist in the way that they do.

The Star of Ishtar

This shape is made up of 12 equally proportioned triangles. According to ancient myth, Ishtar was the goddess of love and warfare, who was said to have created social order through war. The star of Ishtar represents order, strength, and constancy, as well as divine energy contained within the universe itself. It can help you open up to your true feelings about something or someone and encourage you to overcome obstacles as a way to learn more about yourself through your life experiences. This shape can be found in many sacred spaces, such as monuments and buildings of the ancient world, as well as in the Hebrew Bible itself.

The Tetrahedron

The Tetrahedron is a three-dimensional shape that represents the triangle, the square, and the pentagon. It's believed to be one of the oldest geometrical symbols and was said to have been found in Roman ruins. Just as there are three sides of a triangle and four sides of a square, there are also three sides of this shape and four sides of a pentagon, which each connected to one another. These figures also represent spiritual strength as well as eternal cycles (or time). This shape can be used in meditation to help you understand yourself more and your place within the universe.

Metatron's Cube

Metatron's Cube is a geometrical shape created by using a square, pentagon, and hexagram. It contains six points, each of which represents an element of human nature; the head (fire), the heart (water), the stomach (earth), the womb (air), and the bones and marrow (heaven) of humankind.

Metatron's cube.
https://pixabay.com/cs/photos/metatronov%C3%A1-kostka-geometrick%C3%BD-6096685/

The cube affects all of these elements to help you become more harmonized within yourself. It also helps you become more in-tune with the energy of the universe, making it easier to recognize and connect with your own feelings.

The Lemniscate

This shape has two loops that intersect at a single point that is inside an oval shape. It's often called "the infinity symbol" because it represents eternal change, combining different forces together in a way that allows them to transform into something new. There are many symbolic components of this shape, including intention, communication, unity, and truth, which can help anyone using it to understand their own feelings better. It's also been said to represent the nature of love in that it has no beginning and no end.

The Hexagram

The Hexagram is a Star of David drawn in 3 dimensions. There are two intersecting triangles, one small and one large. The intersection of these triangles represents a large circle that contains smaller circles with six points. These smaller circles represent the six places in the universe where heaven and earth come into contact with each other and are called the "Places of God." The hexagram is also known as "the seal of Solomon" and represents divine order and spiritual truth. This shape can be used to help you better understand the spiritual nature of humankind and how it compares with the physical laws that govern the universe.

The Square

This shape is often used in meditation to help you become more grounded within yourself because it represents the four elements within a person: earth, water, fire, and air. It helps you see your own place within creation and the nature of your emotions. The square also has its own geometric structure, which creates a balance between its four sides. This can be useful when trying to meditate on the senses because the square is used in many ways to make people aware of their surroundings and how they function on a physical level. Many sacred spaces are often contained within squares so that they can surround individuals with peace and protection while they commune with nature's energy.

The Triskelion

The triskelion shape is made up of three spirals that come together at a point. The center spiral represents the cycle of life, and the two smaller spirals represent the cycles of death and rebirth. These cycles are part of the same process that ensures nature continues to exist. This shape can be used in meditation to help you balance your emotions while striving to find new ways to improve your life. It's also been said to be used by shamans during rituals and spiritual ceremonies as a way to gain insight into the past, present, and future.

The Tesseract

A tesseract is a four-dimensional object formed by eight cubes that are connected at their center. It's part of what's known as hypercube theory, which states that four dimensions can be seen on the surface of each cube. As a result, you can look at any point on the tesseract and get a 360-degree view of everything within the surrounding area. Sacred geometry often uses cubical shapes in its designs because they represent physical strength, stability, weakness, and immaturity. This shape is often used in crystal grids because it allows you to boost the stability of your energy field and that of other people and objects in its space.

The Spiral

This shape is a symbol of infinity and a tool many people use for meditation. The spiral is often depicted as having no beginning and no end, which can help crystallographers visualize the center of their own existence. The spiral is one of the oldest symbols in the world because it's been found in ancient texts and artifacts from much farther back than written historical records exist. Spirals represent life itself, or the cycle through which all things move towards completion. This shape is often used in crystal grids to help you see your own life as part of a universal energy flow, symbolizing your oneness with everything that exists within it.

The Circle

A circle is a type of shape that's both a simple geometric shape and a symbol for the center of life. While it looks like a simple circle, it contains many points and shapes, including triangles, squares, pentagons, and other geometrical forms. The circle represents protection, which makes it a popular symbol in sacred spaces to express the importance of protecting nature and the environment from harm. The circle is also a symbol of unity because it can be used to connect people together and to the center of their own existence.

The Sunburst

The Sunburst is a shape used to represent the center of your own existence. Many people use it in crystal grids because it represents the source of life, the connection between everything in the universe, and a reminder that you're not alone on your journey through life. The heart and the center represent your personal power and strength, while the rays are symbols of your ability to create a life rich with love and compassion. The Sunburst can be used to help you understand how energy flows through your own body and throughout creation, which is useful knowledge for anyone who uses crystals for personal healing.

Whether you choose to meditate, pray, or perform any other spiritual activity in accordance with the teachings of sacred geometry or not, it's important to remember that the concepts of sacred geometry are not just a trend that started with today's popular spiritual movements. The history of sacred geometry stretches back into antiquity, and many cultures have used it throughout history to approach issues related to spirituality. It can be seen as a suggestion for dealing with day-to-day living, whether you're trying to use it for basic tasks like balancing your hormones and general physical health or are more focused on the metaphysical aspects of life. Sacred geometry is a great addition to any spiritual practice because of its ability to change your internal attitudes and mental outlook on your own experiences. Once you become more in tune with your own mind, your life will open up to new possibilities. Trying out some of these shapes and symbols can be fun to learn about different techniques and concepts related to the geometrical world, so feel free to experiment.

Chapter 13: Crystal Grids and the Stars

Ever watch the sky at night and wonder about how the different patterns of stars are placed overhead? The whole premise is quite fascinating but in a very abstract sense. If you dig deeper, however, you may uncover some clues as to why star patterns behave the way they do. From a scientific perspective, there is a correlation between crystal grids and the constellations in the night sky. It has been known for millennia that some of these same patterns can be seen in natural crystals. However, this connection is not so easily made and is usually dismissed as a coincidence. Over the past few years, some have uncovered information proving these patterns are extremely effective at healing and can be used to enhance our experiences with crystals during meditation and other relaxing or healing practices. In this chapter, you will learn how to create your own world of crystal grids that are based on the star map or grid of the night sky. You can use these grids for meditation and other crystal healing practices, as well as for visualizations and creative sessions.

Crystal Grids and Constellations

In the sky, various star patterns are aligned in a grid or constellation. The idea behind these grids is simple. Each planet has stars that are related to its location in the galaxy and its movement inside it. Because of this, one can use what one learns about each planet relative to the others – along with how they rise, set, and move through their own zodiac sign – to help create a comprehensive mental map of energies that works well with a variety of crystals and crystal grids. Most star maps or grids are based on the idea of the fixed nature of stars. This nature of stars suggests that each star will always be in its place, even as it moves further away from or closer to other constellations. So far, however, no one has been able to show that a specific star pattern is actually "fixed" and unchangeable.

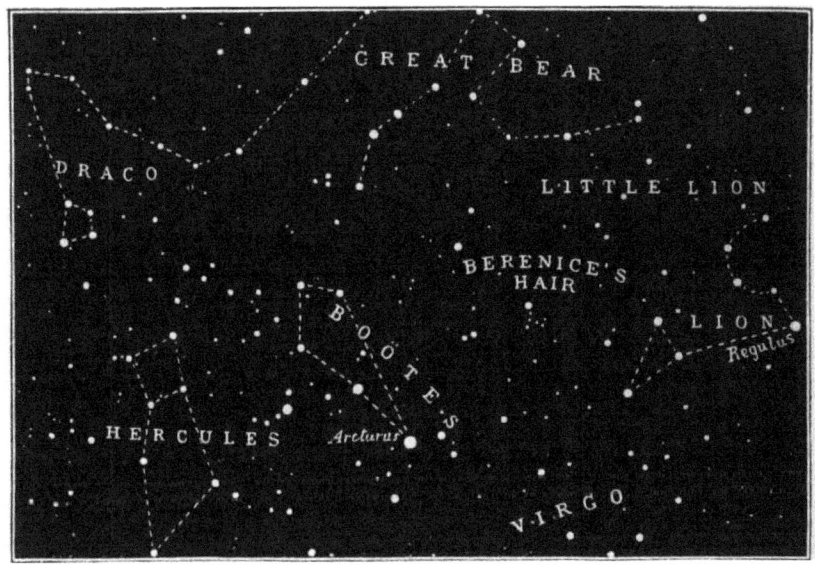

Constellations.
https://www.publicdomainpictures.net/en/free-download.php?image=astronomy-constellation-vintage&id=391934

Of course, you may be wondering how exactly a fixed pattern of stars could be aligned in the first place. According to medieval philosophers who thought about the same subject, the stars are, in fact, attached to one another by "beams of light." This is important because it tells us that if one star moves away or another moves towards it, they would still be attached through these beams of light. As such, there may not necessarily be a fixed alignment but rather a changing alignment. The real mystery here is why the universe seems to have chosen this particular structure for its organization.

Another possible way to find out if there is a fixed pattern would be to take a survey of where the stars are located relative to one another. You will quickly see that their positions do not stay in their expected places, as many stars appear to be moving in ways that are unlike those of a fixed pattern. In fact, you can think of most star patterns as being subject to constant change as they interact with other planetary energies and move according to natural laws. The point is that you cannot use any particular star pattern or grid as an accurate template for your own personal grids because they are constantly changing. That is not to say that we will never find patterns in the stars. The point is that if we do, the patterns will most likely be fixed in relation to the movement of other stars, not due to some cosmic law that says, "This is where the stars will always be." So, you cannot always go by what you see at any given moment but rather by a more general principle; the Hermetic Principle of Correspondence.

The Hermetic Principle of Correspondence

The Law of Correspondence has been used for thousands of years by philosophers, alchemists, artists, and theosophists to help find ways that the Earth mirrors what is happening in the heavens. The most obvious example of this principle is in astrology, an art that uses a map or grid of the stars (the zodiac) to forecast all kinds of events that happen on Earth. In fact, some people use crystals based on their astrological signs to enhance their energy flow and better digest information. It should come as no surprise then that the stars also have their own energy fields, just like crystals do. The inclusion of star patterns into the practice of crystal healing has been viewed with skepticism in the past due to a lack of information and evidence. However, in recent years, this type of knowledge has been expanded upon, and we now know that natural crystals mirror certain star patterns.

Zodiac Signs and Crystal Grids

Ancient mystics knew about the correspondence between the zodiac sign and the crystal grid. They were taught how to align their crystals' energy fields with Earth's own energy grid to absorb cosmic energies from surrounding stars. They would then use this energy to enhance their healing abilities, and many types of crystal grids can be used for this healing. A good example is the Aquarius crystal grid.

The Earth's grid is divided into twelve sections, marked by a circle of twelve constellations which are the signs of the zodiac. More than 2000 years ago, Greek astronomer Ptolemy introduced this system to describe Earth's natural cycles and explain why certain aspects of human existence, such as emotions and sexuality, occur in pairs or in a group for one year. Optimal times for these things are marked by their corresponding signs of the zodiac. Thus, you can use the signs of the zodiac to mark a standard time when you will be better able to work with the energy of specific crystals. This is a very convenient way to work with crystals during meditation because they only align with specific energies while you are in the zone.

As you can see, the Law of Correspondence suggests that we should use the starry sky as a template for creating our own grids. Each star pattern or constellation can be paired with one or more crystals depending on their unique vibrational frequencies and corresponding energies. What follows are explanations of different star patterns and what types of healing properties each one offers you. Some patterns are still under study, but there is very little doubt that these patterns exist in reality.

The Pisces Constellation

The striking feature of this star pattern is its distinctive shape, which looks something like a fish, or two fishes joined together by a line. It is one of the largest constellations, covering about 20% of the entire sky, and yet it does not contain any bright stars. A good place to find it is in the western sky just before sunset. If you can locate the Great Square of Pegasus, you can spot this constellation easily because it lies above or below this square.

The Pisces constellation is known for being the "followers" of the fish constellation, which is where its name comes from. This could be because stars associated with Pisces are also connected to spiritual aspects such as intuition and meditation, as well as consciousness and psychic awareness. The main star in this pattern is called Denebola, which means "tail of the fish" in Latin. This star sits about three-quarters of the way from where the fishes join together to form this shape. It has a very strong magnetic energy due to its position close to Earth's magnetic pole. This star has a vibrational frequency that is important to unite your body with the Earth's energy field and cosmic energies.

The crystal associated with Denebola is the moonstone, which is said to be beneficial for those who wish to make contact with the energies of other dimensions. Moonstone can also be used to enhance intuition and psychic awareness and protect energies from outside influences. There are several ways to display the star pattern of Pisces on a crystal grid, such as by using the zodiac sign or a specific combination of Pisces-affiliated stones to create a crystal grid. The combination of moonstone and malachite would make a very strong gemstone grid, while if you add carnelian, jasper, and lapis lazuli to the grid of moonstone and malachite, you have a crystal grid that is used to connect with the Sun. You could also use this same pattern with an aquamarine crystal grid to increase your connection with the Father-Mother Godhead. It will start you off in conversation with the Earth's solar system.

The Aries Constellation

The Aries constellation consists of two main stars, Hamal and Sheratan, plus a third star called Mesarthim (which lies in between these two). The main feature of this constellation is its distinctive shape, which looks like an astrolabe or an armillary sphere. Aries is separated from the groups of stars by four bright stars called the Great Square of Pegasus. The Aries star pattern is associated with the Air and Fire elements. Stars in this constellation are also connected with vibrational frequencies that enhance communication, mental sharpness, and inner vision and encourage memory and learning. If you wish to enhance your physical healing capabilities, then this constellation's crystal would be a good choice because of its ability to balance autonomic nervous system functions while helping you deal with therapy issues more maturely. The crystal that works especially well with this pattern is aquamarine. Aquamarine balances the whole of your nervous system so that you won't lose control over your emotions. Aquamarine is also a good choice for those whose tasks require them to make quick decisions. It will sharpen your mental focus, improve memory, and improve your communication skills – an essential asset in today's society.

The Gemini Constellation

This constellation can be found in the eastern sky in the early evening. It is shaped like a pair of twins, and when you look at it, you can easily see why it's called Gemini. This constellation is one of the 48 Ptolemy group constellations. Its stars are associated with various energies, including intellectual skills and memory, as well as communication skills, movement, and coordination. In addition to these healing properties, Gemini's energy can also be used to clear negative energy from your aura so that you will become more energetic. You can use the energy of a star associated with Gemini to help you accomplish this, such as Sirius, the brightest star in this constellation, whose vibrational frequency can be used to help you balance your emotions while assisting you in dealing with any problems brought on by other people. Using this star's energy is more beneficial if you pair it with a crystal that can be used for healing, such as a quartz crystal.

The Cancer Constellation

The most important feature of this constellation is its shape; it's like half a crab (or not a crab. It could be some other shape) with one claw facing upwards and the other towards the ground. It cannot be seen on very clear nights because it doesn't cover very much area in the sky. If you can spot it, then it is located between the wings of Pegasus. The Cancer Constellation represents the Water element and may be good for those who want to use their healing powers to help with issues relating to their emotions. This constellation's crystal could be used for both emotional balance and also for healing emotional issues such as anger. It can also help you understand others better and learn about human nature in general if you choose Agate as your crystal, which is strongly associated with all emotions. This will help you empathize with other people's feelings.

The Leo Constellation

This constellation can be found in the southeastern sky, just before sunset. It is shaped like an arrow, and when you look at it, you can easily see why it is called Leo. Stars in this constellation are connected to the fire element and to abilities such as thinking, planning, and communication. This is why many people believe that stars associated with Leo will enhance logic skills. They are also said to enhance mental awareness and psychic abilities. If you are interested in meditation or spiritual practices such as lucid dreaming, then this constellation's crystal would be a good choice because of its ability to help you connect with your inner self. If you use the crystal associated with this constellation, it is best if you pair it up with a green or turquoise crystal. This choice will help you balance the Fire energy with the Water energy to gain better control over your emotions.

The Virgo Constellation

The Virgo Constellation is shaped like a woman who is holding a sheaf of wheat, with her hands and arms bent in half and pointed at the sky. Its shape is like this because the stars associated with it are connected with the Water element, related to nurturing, caring for others, and intuition. Some people believe that stars in this constellation can help you become more intuitive and psychic. Others say that the energy of Virgo can help you to locate things easily. If you choose to use a crystal from this constellation, then you may want to pick Obsidian because it is highly effective at enhancing intuition and psychic capacities.

The Libra Constellation

The stars in the Libra Constellation can be found halfway between Orion and Gemini within the Milky Way. It is shaped like a pair of scales, with one indicating weight and the other indicating value. This constellation is associated with the Air element, as well as with balance and harmony. The Libra Constellation's crystal has properties that can help you find balance easily, especially in your life. However, it also enhances abilities such as creativity and artistic skills. Its energy can be used to help you create the perfect balance in your life to bring it into harmony with both your inner and outer selves. If you are interested in this star patterns crystal, then you might want to consider Citrine because it is believed to be one of the best crystals for creating balance within yourself - and peace around you. If your life is currently not in perfect balance, but you have a desire to bring it into harmony, then this crystal's energy may be able to help you.

The Scorpio Constellation

Scorpio is one of the 48 Ptolemy group constellations that can be found in the zodiac. Its shape resembles a scorpion, although some say it looks more like a lizard or spider. This constellation is associated with the Earth and Water element and power and regeneration. Stars in this constellation are associated with an increase in vitality and your ability to use your energies to rejuvenate yourself. There is a lot of variety in terms of crystals you could use from this star pattern, but Cassiterite is one of the most common. It's a stone of healing that can help you regain vigor and energy and invigorate your mind so that you can focus more on your healing tasks.

The Sagittarius Constellation

This constellation is well known for its shape; it looks like an archer with his bow held up to the sky. It is associated with the Fire element, as well as with health, healing, and your ability to take action. If you want to use a crystal from this constellation, then you should probably pick Turquoise. This is believed to be good for healing physical ailments and helping you get rid of mental issues. If you are suffering from any kind of injury or illness, as well as inflammation in your body parts, then this crystal's energy could be used to help alleviate pain and promote healing. Many people also use it to fight infections because of its antibacterial energies. It can also help relieve stress and anxiety because of its ability to strengthen the immune system.

The Aquarius Constellation

The stars in this constellation can be found between Gemini and Pisces, towards the southwest. Its shape is like a man with his arms up wide while carrying a staff. Its name comes from the fact that it represents the Water element, which is one of its main properties. This constellation is associated with being a visionary, which means that it can help you assess situations clearly and make good judgments in preparation for action. It is also said to enhance your intuitive powers and be good for communication because it allows you to understand some of the things that are going on around you. Stars associated with the Aquarius Constellation can be used to increase your ability to make wise decisions and to think clearly, and also to enhance your psychic awareness. If you want to use a crystal from this star pattern, then you may want to go for Rose Quartz because it is often said to be a very good crystal for communication. It is also good for healing and energy work because it is considered one of the most powerful crystals available.

The Taurus Constellation

This constellation resembles a bull reclining on the ground, facing the south. It is associated with the Earth element and represents something strong and solid. It has also been associated with fertility, conception, growth, and energy. Crystals from this constellation are quite common in jewelry because they enhance your beauty, improve your appearance and protect you from negative energy and illness. If you want to use any of these crystals, then Opal would be the best choice because it can do most of these things exceptionally well. It is also good for healing and enhancing your psychic abilities.

The Capricorn Constellation

The Capricorn Constellation is often represented by a goat that holds an inverted half-moon on its head. It is associated with the Earth element, as well as with fertility, abundance, and growth. This constellation is also sometimes associated with the Water element because of its watery stars and associations. Also, this constellation has been related to the idea of being wise or having good judgment. If you want to use a crystal from this star pattern, then you may choose Amethyst because it is thought to be a good crystal to enhance your beauty and charm. You may also want to go for Malachite because of its earthy properties and its ability to heal physical ailments and enhance your psychic abilities.

So far, you have been informed about the star patterns of 12 different constellations. For instance, you may wonder which star pattern should be placed where on a crystal grid, like the Seed of Life. The answer to this question depends on you, your preferences, and the kind of connections you want to make with the crystals. Perhaps it could be interesting for you to arrange crystals from different constellations in a way that creates an image of each constellation, like a picture in your mind's eye. This could be an experiment to see if you can imagine the energy of each crystal without physically arranging them on a chart. It could also be interesting to group crystals that are connected by their energetic properties or by color and then arrange them again into a pattern that creates the shape of the star pattern associated with each constellation.

The stars used in the star patterns are symbolic and not representative of a particular stone you could use. However, these star patterns are very useful in identifying which crystals are most useful for healing certain conditions and ailments. This can help you decide which crystals to bring into your life, how best to use them, and when to use them. If you or someone you know has any questions about how best to use particular stones, then I recommend reading up on the characteristics of a crystal before using it (Refer to chapters 4, 5, & 6). They can help you make good decisions regarding your health and well-being and identify what problems a particular stone would be good for.

Chapter 14: Activating Your Crystal Grid

Activating your crystal grid is the first step toward making it work for you. Your intention sets the tone for how energy flows through the grid. A grid can provide grounding, calming, and uplifting energy in various ways, depending on what you set as your intention. This is similar to the way your body responds to emotion. It can be calming, soothing, or simply energizing. For example, if you set an intention to be productive or creative, that intention will manifest differently than if your intention is to relax and enjoy the moment. You must give insight into what you intend to do with your grid, *so your intentions are clear.* Activating a crystal grid can take a few days to manifest with most grid designs. This process works by establishing a connection between your mind and the crystal grid by repeating affirmations and sending energy down into it with your intention.

Setting Your Intentions

It is wise to use positively phrased rather than wishful. For example, instead of saying, "I want to be productive," you could say, "I am productive." Instead of saying, "I want more energy," you could say, "I am full of life and energy." Your thought forms can either reflect positive or negative energy, so be careful with this step. Setting intentions with a positive tone will help the energy flow in the direction intended. While there are many things you can set your intention to do, it is best to do something that is in alignment with your goals and desires. What you set as your intention will activate and manifest in accordance with your own energy. If you are looking for more insight into what you want to accomplish, think about what makes you happy and results in success. You can also think about any challenges or problems you currently face.

When setting your intention, be sure to state it in a positive, affirming tone with no fear of failure. Connecting with your intent and giving it all the energy it deserves is important. If you have an intention that is not working out as planned, don't beat yourself up about it. Instead, set another intention and release the one that didn't work. Eventually, you will find one that does. There are two you can do this:

- **Set an Intention to Manifest a Specific Item:** Think about what you need and state it out loud or write it down. If you need money, write down "I am financially successful." If you want a new house, state, "I have a new house." This can be done using different languages or symbols. The point is to focus on the item you want and release anything that would get in the way of the completion. This is the process of using your purpose as your intent.

- **Set an Intention to Manifest a Certain Experience:** Think of something new and exciting or something you would like to experience. You can list this as well or state it out loud while visualizing the experience in your mind. This will give you insight into what brings joy to your life and keeps you from experiencing your full potential. By asking yourself these questions and listening for answers, you will gain insight into what might be lacking in your life.

Affirmations

Affirmations can be used to communicate your intentions, crafted to bring you what you want and need. Affirmations are those words, phrases, or sentences that you use to tell yourself a certain story. You can create affirmations by writing them down or by visualizing or drawing a picture of the outcome in your mind. A powerful affirmation demonstrates how beneficial it would be for you to have the thing you desire, how happy and fulfilled it will make you, and how much more success and meaning you will experience once it manifests. Affirmations should be heartfelt and about your intention rather than just something being done for you. You can choose words that excite you, express your desires, and make you feel good. If you do not have a full affirmation written yet, don't worry - *you can create one while focusing on your intention*. When you are finished creating the affirmation, repeat it to permit yourself to put it into action.

Drawing the positive outcome on paper or in your mind is a simple visualization technique that can be added to any intention for quick results. If you have a lot of energy and motivation for what you are working on, draw or visualize yourself experiencing it. This will help boost your enthusiasm and put all the pieces into place for manifesting.

When setting your intentions, it is wise to choose one which is specific and sparks a passion for yourself. If you have more than one intention at a time, some may not manifest while others do. For example, if you set an intention to become rich and successful, then an intention to find love and be happy together, only the one that aligns with your true purpose will manifest. The ones that don't align will turn up in a different form, so it is best to focus on one intention at a time to avoid confusion.

Setting your intention and focusing on it without fail is important. You can do this by visualizing the outcome and writing down a few affirmations each day, depending on your available time. If people, places, or situations in your life are preventing you from getting what you want, you can use your intention to help resolve the problem. Doing this can help to relieve stress, which is often caused by excessive thinking or worrying. Using crystal grids to set an intention may be intense at first, but it gets easier as time goes on. When using a crystal grid to set an intention, you can place your affirmation at the center of your grid after constructing it or simply repeat it like a chant during crystal placement. You can tell yourself that you have set your intention and are willing to accept what comes. You can also pick up the crystal from the grid, hold it close to your heart and tell yourself that you are manifesting what is in alignment with your purpose.

Your goal should be to focus on your intention and be grateful for whatever happens. If it seems like nothing is happening, don't worry about it; stay focused. If you find yourself doubting and worrying, just change your focus to something else that will bring peace and love instead of stress. When focusing is difficult, take a break and do something else to distract and calm you. This can range from dancing to engaging in creative activities like writing or drawing. These things can trigger creativity and inspiration.

As you set your intention, you can use certain affirmations to help manifest the goal faster. You mustn't doubt the process or let your own thoughts get in the way of what you are trying to do. This is because your thoughts have energy, and energy is vibration. Your intention must be followed by action, and one of those actions should be acting as if it has already manifested to create a stronger connection between where you are now and where you want to go, especially if this is a new area for you. Your affirmations can range from anything to everything, but here's a quick list to get you started:

- I am vibrating in harmony with my desire and manifesting my purpose
- I am in perfect alignment with what I want in life, and nothing is standing between me and my manifestation
- I am mentally ready to receive what I want
- I am committed to my purpose in life
- I am loving unconditionally
- I am open and receptive to all opportunities
- I am worthy
- I love myself
- I am grateful for what I have in life
- My energy is aligned with my intention
- I am creative and inspired
- I am confident and powerful
- I have faith that my desires will be fulfilled
- I am joyous, happy, and free

- I am in the flow of life
- I can step into my power and create my desired reality
- I am in acceptance of what is occurring in my life

Choosing the Right Crystals for Your Grid

There are many types of crystals, and each one has a unique vibration as well as unique properties that can help manifest your intention. You should choose crystals that are special to you, have meaning for you, resonate with a feeling or emotion that is important to you and match the other crystals in your grid.

When choosing crystals to put into a grid, you should feel the energy coming from them. This can be done by holding the stone in your hand and feeling the energy within the crystal. If it is not emanating energy, it may need to be cleansed or recharged before you begin working with it. Crystals come from all over the world, and each has something special that makes them unique from the rest. You must be familiar with certain crystals and what they represent from the previous chapters. For example, turquoise is an earth element stone that represents grounding and is associated with protection. Lithium is a metal element stone that represents the sky and is associated with expansion and abundance. Fluorite also has an association with expansion but also brings in knowledge and wisdom. So, when choosing crystals for your grid, you must consciously consider your intentions.

Also, when determining which crystals to place in your grid, use color as a guiding factor to help connect them to a feeling or emotion you wish for - and to resonate with other crystals in your grid. For example, if turquoise is your intended color, you can use it to surround whatever other turquoise stones are in your grid and any other stones that you feel bring harmony to the surrounding energy.

If you want a more specific way of knowing which crystals can be used for your grid, you can refer to the previous chapters or several websites that provide lists of crystals compiled by others. These are good resources if you want to know which crystals have been used for different purposes such as healing, love, money, and protection, but ultimately, you decide what will work best for you.

When you have determined which crystal or crystals will work well with your intention, it is time to place them into your grid.

Choosing the Right Shape for Your Grid

Several shapes can be used for your grid. You can choose one depending on your intention, or you can use two or more shapes to amplify the power and strength of your intentions. Choosing a certain shape or pattern that has meaning to you will help concentrate your intentions and powers into something specific. Your sacred geometrical shape also represents certain energy, vibration, or spiritual element that must be considered when choosing which one to use. This is because each shape has its own unique properties and uses, as well as representing an aspect of the divine source. If you want, you can even make your grid with a shape with no known spiritual meaning, but sometimes, this can take away from your intention's purpose. If you want to know the different properties and associations with each sacred geometry shape, check out chapters 12 and 13.

Crystal Placement

Once you have decided which crystals and shapes will work best for your grid, placing them onto the grid pattern is time. You can place the crystals in any pattern that you want, but for the purpose of this book, we will be creating a grid with the Seed of Life layout.

Step One: The first stones to be placed are the outermost stones, also called the Desire stones. They sit around the perimeter of the grid, just touching it and holding the shape in place. These stones represent the manifestation of your intention and will direct energy into your grid. You can choose one type of stone or different ones to represent and create the energy needed for manifestation. These stones must be placed first because they represent where the grid will begin.

Step Two: The second stones that you place onto your grid are called the Way stones. They surround the center where the focus stone will be placed. They are the power and strength of the grid, as well as its guidance. They can be any shape and size but must be at least one inch in diameter to make them functional. The way stones can move energy and amplify vibrations.

Step Three: The last piece you place into your grid pattern is called The Focus stone or Anchor stone. The stone is placed in the center of your grid to diffuse and direct energy. It is used to maintain the energy of your intention. You must place the stone in a location that you feel represents your intention and a location that you are comfortable with, but it must be at the center of all the other stones. The focus stone represents the main intention of your grid pattern and is made up of a stone that resonates with your intention. This stone must be at least 3 inches in diameter and enshrined so it cannot move.

Step Four: The last step is to "connect the dots," so to speak. This is where you use a pen or pencil to connect the edges of the stones around your grid pattern. You can use different colors or different ways of connecting the dots depending on what you want to represent with your grid. Many people choose to connect their grid pattern using one color only and a specific technique that emphasizes one color over the others. These lines are also called Paths. They are the routes that travel through the center of your grid, connecting the stones to one another. The vibrational energy of the grid flows through these lines from one crystal to another. They are also considered to be the pathway between physical and divine reality. Either way, these lines can be drawn over or below the stones, but it is best to make sure that the line is directly touching the stone it connects to. This way, it creates a visual connection between the two pieces of energy.

Chapter 15: Caring for Your Crystal Grid

It can be a very rewarding experience to use a crystal grid. Allowing the energy of your crystals to flow into one another helps create a powerful, receptive energy that can stimulate the chakras and bring balance into your home. Most importantly, your crystal grid offers a positive, beautiful focal point that helps pull you and your family into a deeper state of relaxation and contentment. However, as you attend to your grid daily, there are certain things you will want to keep in mind to maintain the effectiveness of your grid.

Crystal Grid Maintenance 101

A quality crystal grid can be an investment that will last for many years. It is important to be gentle and patient when caring for your grid. Be sure to treat your grid with respect, not damaging its crystals or stones. You will also want to ensure your crystals are stored away from direct sunlight when they are not being charged because this can fade the bright, beautiful color of your crystals over time.

If you find that your crystal grid has become dusty, you can use a soft, dry silk cloth to wipe away the dust. Do not use a damp cloth or water to clean your crystal grid because this can damage the softer crystals. When cleaning your grid, try to keep as much of the grid's shape and layout intact as possible. It is recommended that you place the crystals in their original positions after cleaning so they can restore the intended flow of energy.

To avoid stressing your crystal grid out, it is a good idea to keep your grid on display only when you desire to draw energy from it. Place your crystal grid where you can see it, but make sure not to place it in very high-traffic areas of your home where lots of people will be walking through. Remember that altering or changing the shape or layout of a crystal grid can have unintended consequences, so if you decide to alter your grid layout, consider leaving the original layout intact for some time before making any changes.

Charging Your Crystal Grid

While the best way to keep your crystal grid in good shape is by taking care of it, you should also be sure to charge and revive your crystals regularly. Crystals will eventually lose their power, just like anything else made from earth energy. When this happens, you should consider recharging them, so they can continue to bring balance into your life. Remember that each crystal in your grid will hold different energy; therefore, each will have its unique way of absorbing and holding the energy given to them.

To recharge your crystals, you will want to fill the crystals with the energy they need by placing them in a bowl or some other sort of container that can hold them. Next, you will want to use your intent to send energy through your body down into your hands and into the crystal. You can also use a pendulum to help direct the flow of energy from your body and into the crystals. Keep in mind that this process will require practice, so you should not be frustrated if you do not receive immediate results. There are several techniques to help you concentrate your energy and ensure that the energy does indeed reach the crystals.

One simple method is placing one or more of your crystals (only the hard ones) into a bowl with a glass of water, which will help direct the energy you want to send. Utilizing this technique requires no special setup, just a bowl to hold your crystals and a glass of water. Once you have placed your crystal in the bowl of water, it is important to sit quietly and think about what you would like the energy to achieve. It is also helpful to think about the crystal and what it means to you so you can amplify your energy and send the crystal a clear message. Then, you should place your hands gently on the bowl without touching the crystal and try to feel a warmth flow through your hands and into the bowl. You will want to repeat this exercise as often as needed until you are confident that the crystals in your grid have been recharged with the appropriate energy.

Another way to charge your crystals is by using a pendulum. A pendulum can be set to vibrate at certain energetic frequencies, which will help the energy move from your body and into the crystal. You should set the pendulum at an approximately one-inch distance from your crystal and allow it to swing back and forth between you every time you repeat an affirmation. Then, after each swing back and forth, hold the pendulum motionless for a few moments to calm down before continuing with the next swing. You should do this for about ten minutes every day, using different affirmations each time.

Once you have recharged your crystals, you will need to place them in their original positions. Try not to move the crystals around too much. However, if you do, simply take a moment to let the energy be aware of their new location. You would want to ensure that the crystals are placed as close to their original positions as possible unless you created a new layout entirely. This will help ensure that the crystals can effectively redirect the energy sent to them.

Remember that everything has its own unique way of absorbing energy, animate and inanimate things alike. Do not be alarmed if your crystals take a while to absorb or hold the energy you are sending to them. Simply keep at it and remember that it takes practice to become skilled at charging crystals.

Crystal Grid Deactivation

If you have decided that you would like to deactivate your crystal grid, there are a couple of steps that you will need to follow. First, you should remember that if the grid has been up for a long time, deactivating it may cause the energy stored in the crystals to leak out into your environment. Therefore, if your crystal grid has been up for a while, you should make sure you reset it before removing any of the crystals to avoid damage to the energy field of the crystals themselves.

To deactivate your crystal grid, begin by collecting up all the crystals. A crystal grid is made up of many pieces, so if you decide to remove some crystals, you must begin with the piece that is highest in vibration. In addition, once you have removed some crystals from your grid, it is helpful to wear a piece of jewelry with protective energy to help restore your balance during this period. Now place the crystals in a bowl or some other container that is clean and preferably plastic. You can then submerge the crystals in salt or dirt and bury them somewhere outside so that they can return their energies to the earth. Leave them buried for at least two weeks, but longer is even better. After the crystals have been properly discharged, remove them from the ground, wipe them with a dry cloth and store them away from direct sunlight.

Long-Term Grid Maintenance

It is important to remember that crystals are, in a sense, alive. They have their own individual personalities and therefore may react in a variety of ways when they are near one another. In addition, sometimes, you may notice that the crystals in your grid seem to be "talking to each other." In these instances, try not to get nervous or upset. Instead, utilize this as an opportunity to communicate with them through meditation or some other means. Crystal grids are meant to feel organic. They should grow and change over time like any other living being, so try not to get too attached to your grid, as it will no doubt change over time.

Crystal grids can provide a wealth of insight into how we interact with the world around us. For example, if you are having trouble in a certain area of your life, adding crystals related to the problem into your grid is a good idea to find out what they have to tell you. Of course, keep in mind that sometimes it is difficult to understand what a crystal is trying to tell you, so make sure to pay careful attention and look beyond the surface of things. It is also a good idea to keep a journal to get the most out of your crystal grid. This can help you pinpoint where your energy leaks are and what areas of your life need the most attention.

Having a crystal grid active for a long time can breed some fascinating attachments. If you are interested in exploring how crystals attach themselves to people and events in their surroundings, sit down and look at your grid from a holistic perspective. You may be surprised to notice that the energy of your crystal grid is, in many ways, tied to the energy of the people who share your space. Crystal grids can also help us better understand our personal energy fields. By creating a grid of crystals around ourselves, we can be more empowered to reach out into other people's fields and effectively connect with them through the power of the crystals.

A crystal grid that has been up for some time creates a possibility for the energy to leak out into your surroundings. If this is the case, you may find that some crystals in your grid are not glowing as brightly as they once did. You may also receive unexpected phone calls or emails and even feel intense emotions or sudden feelings of euphoria. These are all signs of energy leaking out into the world and communicating with you on a spiritual level. When this happens, it is important to remember that the crystals are not reacting to you. Instead, they are communicating with your environment. Do not feel intimidated by this; rather, take a moment to remind yourself how connected you truly are to everything around you through your grid.

Finally, if you have been working with a specific crystal grid for some time and have noticed that the results seem to be less dramatic than they once were, this may be a sign that it is time to create a new crystal grid altogether. Remember, crystals are not stagnant energies, and so you may need to create a new grid if your current one is no longer working for you. A good way to discover whether this is the case is by using your intuition. If you are feeling tired and drained for no particular reason, start to note the activities you have been engaging in lately. Try to identify the energy that is being drained from you and determine whether it has anything to do with your current grid. If this is the case, you may want to investigate why it is no longer helping you and then decide whether it's time for a new one. Remember, you are the most important factor in the success of your crystal grid, so if you feel that things have changed, make sure to investigate and take appropriate action.

Now, while crystal grids are a powerful tool for manifestation and self-development, it is important to remember that they are not magic wands. They can help clarify your intentions and provide you with the necessary energy to follow through with them, but it is still up to you to ensure that your goals are aligned with your higher self. Even more importantly, if you want to experience a true transformation, take the time to be with yourself and really nurture your spiritual side. Remember, a crystal grid is your connection to the universe's energy, so it is your responsibility to cultivate this connection to receive the fullest benefit.

Getting the Most out of Your Crystal Grid

Once you have created a crystal grid, there are various things that you can do to maximize the positive effects of the crystals that you have placed in it. The first of these is to shift your focus away from negativity and instead spend more time focusing on the positive aspects of your life. Do this by going through the affirmations you created for your crystal grid, following them as though you were actually talking to a loved one about your life. You will eventually find this process habit-forming, and you will find yourself wanting to talk to your crystal grid as though it were a family member having a casual conversation.

Another way to ensure the effectiveness of a crystal grid is to take the time to look at the crystals while talking to them. While doing this, make sure you visualize everything you would like to improve about your life, and then imagine the crystals are sending out the energy to accomplish these things. In addition, when you have finished putting your crystal grid together, make sure that you go through some of the things you are grateful for. This will help keep your focus on the positive aspects of your life, which will, in turn, increase their vibrancy in reality.

Finally, it is important to note that a crystal grid should never be used as a substitute for medication. If you feel overwhelmed by too much stress or negativity in your life and simply need a break from it all, make sure you seek out professional help instead of relying on crystal therapy alone. It is important to remember that the best crystal grids make use of the power of positive thinking and action. Therefore, ensure that you are not relying too heavily on your crystals to make your problems disappear. If you need to take medication, as a result, do not feel afraid to do so. Instead, think about your crystal grid as a tool for maximizing the positive effects of your medication.

While the healing powers of crystals are undeniable, it is important to remember that you still have to take care of yourself physically. You will notice that your crystal grid can greatly improve how you feel, but your thoughts and actions will determine whether your life will be transformed into the reality you wish to create. Remember, a crystal grid is an opportunity for you to start thinking about what constitutes a truly meaningful and fulfilling life. When you approach this from the standpoint of true passion and clarity, you will notice that your life will start to change in dramatic ways.

Conclusion

Crystal healing is a New Age practice that is often seen as a magical form of treatment for physical and mental illnesses. This new perspective on healing can be both a blessing and a curse to those who are exploring their wellness in this way.

There are many kinds of crystals and stones, some of which may have different effects on the body depending on the person's intention when using them. Many people are using crystals and stones in conjunction with their daily wellness practice by incorporating them into meditation, healing baths, or wearing them as part of crystal jewelry. Others use them to create jewelry or other forms of amulets to carry around with them, while some use them as a means to promote self-love or as a way to heal from the past. Crystals and stones can be used in a variety of ways, both physically and emotionally. They are one way to balance your chakras and promote relaxation, clarity, and healing.

With the many ways to incorporate crystals and stones into your practice, they have increasingly become a unique form of healing. By understanding the different types of crystals and what they can do for your health, you can learn how to implement them into your self-care routine in a new way. By learning how to use them holistically, you can help your body heal itself, return to its natural state of balance, and bring peace to your mind and soul. The future of crystal healing looks bright for those who are dedicated to the practice and feel positive about the results. I hope this book makes you one of them.

Part 2: Crystal Grids

Unlocking the Secret Power of Crystals and Sacred Geometry

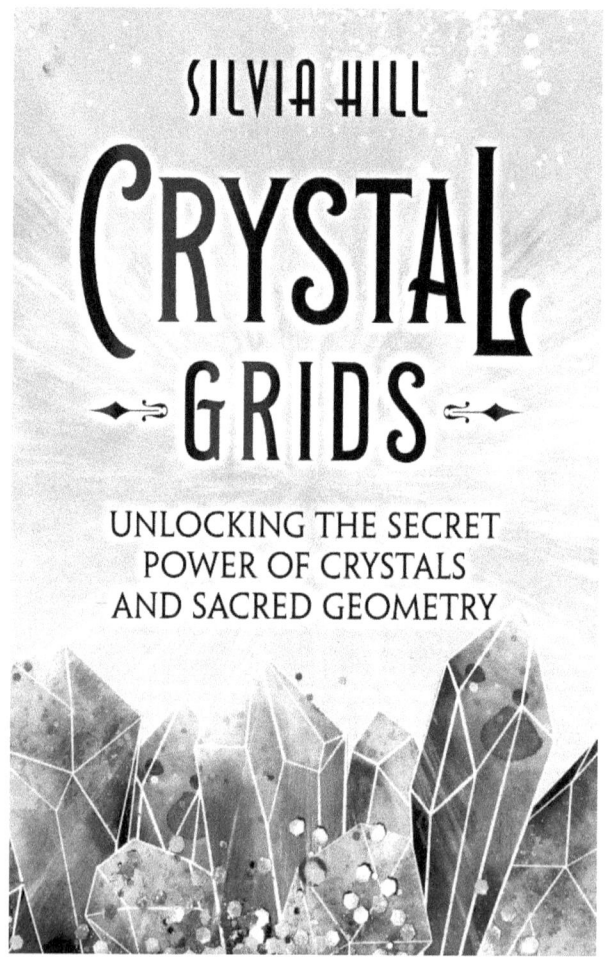

Introduction

The use of crystal grids for the purpose of healing was first introduced during the 1980s. This practice is rooted in beliefs, traditions, and studies dating back several centuries. Numerous majestic monuments from all over the world have influenced today's holistic healing practices. The masterminds behind these megalithic structures undoubtedly knew of the power healing stones possess. Ancient philosophers recognized the significance of stone placement and how this was linked to the Sun, the Moon, and the Stars.

Modern-day researchers suggest these monuments were used for rituals and other spiritual and healing practices. It was believed that, by using these stones, one could connect with the core energy of the Earth. It is also said that the ancients used crystals to tap into the universe's energies. Not only did they pay attention to the placement of the crystals, but they were also attentive to the locations of the monuments themselves. They made complex calculations and considered Vortex Points, which link ancient architecture to Sacred Geometry. This book covers the concept of Sacred Geometry in depth. Upon reading the first few chapters, you'll understand how Sacred Geometry played a key role in the creation of the universe and how it is related to the basic patterns of life. You will find out how you can benefit from this concept and use it to your advantage.

The following chapters also illustrate the connection between Sacred Geometry and crystal grids. You will understand how arranging healing stones in a specific symbolic pattern can help you enhance the four main aspects of your well-being and improve the quality of your life. Crystal grids are a development originating from the ancient megalithic monuments we mentioned above. Drawing on the traditions of Sacred Geometry and the metaphysical properties of crystals, this spiritual practice has greatly evolved over the centuries. You probably already know that each healing stone has its powerful properties. Now, imagine how combining the power of several healing crystals with the potency of Sacred Geometry can transform your life. The power of a single healing stone is amplified within the context of a grid. This simple practice can allow you to manifest your desires and create the reality you have dreamed of.

While there are simpler ways to use healing stones, crystal grids can help you obtain the desired results and achieve your intentions. Typically, the complexity of the practice depends on the grid itself and how the crystals are arranged on it. It also depends on whether you use a pre-printed geometrical shape or crystal grid card to guide you through the process. Fortunately, this book is perfect for beginners because it includes step-by-step instructions on creating a crystal grid. You'll understand which crystals you should use based on your intentions and desired outcome. From love, relationships, wealth, and success, to psychic development and spirit communication, you'll find hands-on methods to create a crystal grid for each purpose. Let's jump right into the enigmatic world of crystal grids without further ado!

Chapter 1: Crystal Healing Explained

Crystals have been used since the dawn of time for multiple purposes. Our ancient civilizations recognized the value of these naturally occurring rock formations and incorporated them into their lives. They used crystals for ceremonies, beauty-enhancing rituals, and healing purposes. After several industrial revolutions, the focus shifted to the aesthetic and material value of the stones. Recently, however, many people have started rediscovering the spiritual properties of crystals. This chapter will reveal how crystal healing works and the benefits you can gain from these stones. It will also lay the foundation for the information about gridwork that you'll receive in the subsequent chapters.

The Energy of Crystals

Energy surrounds us from every side, and crystals are the perfect tool for connecting with the purest form of energy. This power comes from nature, which can cleanse and rebalance your spirit. Crystal energy can be used in various ways on your mind, body, and soul. Should you choose to share this gift with others, you can also implement their powers into your healing practices. Crystals can help you understand your own energetic makeup and what it takes to heal your energy system. They store energy in their symmetrical structures, made of minerals. In their purest form (as they should be used in energy healing), crystals are composed of only one mineral. This purity allows their structure to remain constant and maintains the stability of the energy they hold as well. This steadiness comes from the unique energy field and vibrations that resonate on particular levels.

Due to their stability, crystals enable you to tune in to anyone's energy system, no matter how unstable it is. In fact, the more imbalanced someone's energy system is, the easier it will get picked up by the crystals, and the sooner you will have the solution to the problem. Apart from helping you identify issues, prized stones can also channel the vital life force toward a targeted subject. Crystals naturally mirror a person's innate power and show where the energy is needed, making them an extremely dynamic manifestation tool. By infusing a crystal with spiritual intention, you can create a firmer bond with it.

Crystals allow you to tune in to anyone's energy system.
https://unsplash.com/photos/YRrj9QMbv9o?utm_source=unsplash&utm_medium=referral&utm_content=creditShareLink

Charged with the vital life force, any crystal can transform your energetic makeup and the system of anyone else you treat. However, as mentioned earlier, crystals already hold a considerable amount of valuable energy. After all, they result from accumulated organic matter over thousands of years, and each layer adds more power to its structure. This enables them to connect with natural elements and even the vital life force. The purity of crystals also allows them to resonate on higher levels, which is another reason to use stones made of only one mineral in your healing practice. After all, connecting to someone else's energy is difficult enough. To access their problematic areas, you'll need the most help you can get from your crystals, which entails finding the correct vibrational frequency.

When using the right combination of pure crystals, their combined effect will be even more potent. This is because aligning crystals along a geometric shape allows the individual stones to connect to each other's energy, raising the collective vibrations of every crystal on the grid. The power of the individual crystals flows through the geometry of their mineral layers, putting pressure on their mineral composition and creating different healing energies. Their structure is under even more pressure than usual when used in a grid. This leads to a significant amount of energy being created and the possibility of performing crystal healing without placing the stone directly onto the chakra points in the body.

As you'll see later in this chapter, the secret to using crystals to map and heal energy systems lies in the makeup of these systems. Whether you have experience using crystals in spiritual practices or are a complete novice, using them for healing will be a whole new experience. It's one of the easiest ways to access your energy system and balance your vibrations, so you don't have much to lose by trying. Unlike other energy healing techniques, the crystals method doesn't require much attention to your vibrations, as the crystals will automatically do that for you.

The Flow of Subtle Energy

The subtle body represents the essence of the spiritual composition, known as qi or vital life force. Since this matter creates a link between living entities and inert objects, it can bring forward every physical stimulus you receive to your consciousness and process it there. When interacting with living entities, you can harness the life forces and gain the ability to grow, heal and move forward in life.

Subtle energy conducts information through a particular frequency in your body, just as sound waves do when traveling through the air or the vibrations a computer network makes when processing data. The life force can also manifest outside your body, allowing you to connect with different objects that emit vibrations and transmit vital information.

Physical sensations and emotions are all sources of information you take in and either hold inside or emit back when needed. Going too long without processing any stimuli has a negative impact on your subtle energy system. In most cases, this only leaves more information for you to process later. However, it can sometimes have more substantial consequences. Subtle energy is the medium that supports your mind, body, spirit, and everything around you. It interacts with vibrations coming from any direction. The energy source can also come from the inside, including your thoughts, beliefs, creative nature, speech, and physical actions. People have always been interested in subtle energy. Using the wisdom they've gathered during their observations, ancient cultures have even created several maps of energy pathways inside the body, including the chakra system.

The subtle energy has three main segments. The first ones are the meridians or nadis, which represent the path followed by the vital life force when traveling along the side of your body. There are 12 main meridians, divided into two equal sections. The nadis on either side of your body mirror each other, creating the perfect equilibrium. They are also linked to an internal organ, which can be affected when the two sides are out of balance. Energy flows through the meridians, keeping your body healthy. If the meridians are blocked, this manifests as the inability to regulate many functions in your body. Besides physical symptoms, meridian issues can manifest as psychological impairments. In turn, symptoms of stress and anxiety can obstruct the meridians, causing the rest of the symptoms.

The second component of the subtle energetic system is the aura. An aura is an image you project about yourself to the outside world. It's usually described as a veil of colored light developing the person's body. Although a person's aura can shine in several colors simultaneously, one color typically overpowers all the others. The aura is affected by your vibrations. Depending on your thoughts, emotions, and health, the color of the light projected by your aura can change drastically.

It's important to note that the aura is connected to the third component of the subtle energy, the chakras. When these are blocked, the light will appear dull or, in severe cases, even black. While you can't actually see the color of a person's aura with your eyes, you can visualize it to reveal potential issues with your energetic system. Crystals can help you uncover nuance changes and resolve them by cleansing your aura.

Crystals and the Seven Chakras

To understand how crystals channel the subtle energy through your body, you must first learn about the chakras and the part these energy centers play in your well-being. You can visualize chakras as spinning energy balls concentrating the vital force into several areas of your body. They are embedded in your core and are placed along a central energy axis. There are seven main chakras, all interconnected in a complex energetic system, which means that every other chakra influences each chakra. Each chakra can receive energy and channel it in the direction of another energetic center or an organ. They also project the vital force into the corresponding layer of the aura and open them outside the body. By receiving energy, the chakras carry messages through your body. When a message reaches its destination, it's converted into emotions and physical sensations. This is how your chakra system informs you about what's happening in your immediate external and internal environment. Crystals are natural aides for your chakras to harness energy from outside.

The seven chakras are aligned from the base of the spine to the top of your head, which is also called the crown. The positions of each chakra are associated with certain metaphysical aspects, different body parts, organs, or organ systems. You nurture a healing stone with a vital life force by placing a healing stone on a particular chakra. This renewed vitality benefits all parts of your body to which the chakra is linked. When your chakras are balanced and fully open, you feel relaxed, and grounded, can communicate your needs, express your individuality, and establish healthy relationships. By contrast, when these centers are blocked, you feel low and incapable of expressing your desires. By providing a positive energy flow, crystals can help you to avoid this.

Here's an overview of each chakra and its role in your body and mind:

- *The root chakra, or Muladhara*, is associated with the color red and is located at the bottom of your spine. When it's open, it has a grounding effect and provides a sense of security and self-confidence. Its imbalance manifests in symptoms that indicate the lack of these functions or physical symptoms at the chakra's location.

- *The sacral chakra, or Svadhisthana*, is represented by the color orange and reigns over creativity, sexuality, and relationships. It is located beneath your navel and affects the energetic flow in your lower abdomen. Its blockage or imbalance causes issues that either appear in this area or affect the energy flow toward your upper chakras.

- *The solar plexus chakra, or Manipura*, is linked to the color yellow. Its location in the upper abdominal area makes it the center of your gut feelings, self-esteem, trust, and the ability to form an intention and act on it. Its imbalance can manifest as a physical issue originating from beneath the sternum to the navel, lack of self-confidence, detachment from your instincts, or the inability of energy to rise to the upper chakras.

- *The heart chakra, or Anahata*, is associated with the color green. Its location near your heart links it to love, a strong sense of compassion, and the desire to provide and obtain forgiveness. Its abnormal functions lead to the lack of these emotions and the appearance of opposite ones. Physical symptoms involving the pulmonary and circulation systems can also occur.

- *The throat chakra, or Vishudda,* is typically represented by the color blue and is located in your throat area. Its healthy functions allow you to communicate your thoughts and emotions to your inner self and the outside environment. When blocked, this center causes physical symptoms manifesting in this area, communication issues, and an inability to channel the vital force to and through this chakra.

- *The third eye chakra, or Ajna*, is linked to the color indigo. Its physical focal point sits right between your eyebrows. It is universally associated with intuition, psychic abilities, open-mindedness, wisdom, and the ability to differentiate truth from falsity. Its blockage causes issues involving these functions and physical symptoms affecting your central nervous system and your entire chakra system.

- *The crown chakra or Sahasrara* is associated with the colors purple and white, which is the universal color for the entire chakra system. This and its location on top of the head indicate that its function involves providing guidance for spirituality, absorbing and channeling the vital force, and groundedness. While most issues associated with this chakra affect either the nervous system or mental health, they can also manifest as disrupting any other chakra.

Each chakra is associated with a particular color because it harnesses energy from elements that possess this color. Crystal healing uses this ability of your chakras. By connecting them using a stone in the color they are linked to, you are giving your chakras access to the purest form of natural energy.

Benefits of Crystal Healing

While crystals can't cure any condition or mend injuries, they facilitate the healing process by empowering your energetic system. They boost your immunity, help with pain relief, improve cognitive function, and alleviate the physical symptoms of stress. And although these effects can bring enormous relief to those suffering from physical illnesses, the popularity of crystal healing is mainly owed to the psychological benefits. Managing the physical symptoms alone can boost your mood and improve your overall well-being if you suffer from a physical illness. Those battling chronic mental conditions can also benefit from the positive energy of crystals, which acts as a balancing agent for realigning the energy system. The root of mental illnesses often lies in an imbalanced or blocked chakra, depending on the severity of the symptoms.

You don't necessarily have to suffer from a debilitating condition to receive a crystal healing treatment. Due to our busy schedules and the often unrealistic expectations of society, stress and anxiety can become our everyday companions. This makes it too easy to lose sight of our inner needs. When you feel disconnected from your spiritual self, the only way to repair this is by grounding yourself with a healing method that relies on natural energy manipulation, like crystal gridwork.

Crystal healing can help you eliminate disruptive behavior, including addictions and dependence on unhealthy or toxic relationships. Whether it's a substance, digital gadgets, or a person you want to break away from, you'll need your chakra system to be as balanced as possible. By raising your energy to healthy levels, crystals will help you accept that your actions should come from your innermost desires. It will make you realize that you don't need to use disruptive behavior or unhealthy relationships as a crutch and that you can be happier by listening to your gut feeling.

Crystals can help you even if your only goal is to connect with nature, transfer its vital energy through your body, and elevate it to your upper chakras. This is typically pursued by those aiming toward higher spiritual development. The stones will help you unplug your mind from the constant outlet of worry about the past and future and focus on the present. Here, you set your intention for spiritual development or any other self-care goal that you might have.

As you will learn in the following chapters, the best way to choose your crystals is to sense which stones' energy can connect to your energy. Your body is naturally drawn to the type of energy it needs, so you can actually subconsciously find the perfect healing method. This is perhaps one of the crystals' greatest advantages over other alternative therapies.

Another benefit of crystal healing is that it typically uses several different crystals. Moreover, practitioners often place the stones into a geometric pattern. Individual crystals possess unique powers, but when connected in a grid, the strength is multiplied far beyond what they can do for you on their own. This means less time waiting for them to take effect and a much shorter recuperation period.

Disclaimer

Crystals can be a wonderful source of empowerment when dealing with physical, mental, or spiritual issues. However, they should never be your *only* healing tool, but only a complementary one. If you regularly experience symptoms of any physical or mental condition, consult a medical professional before seeking alternative treatment options. Once a doctor has established the proper course of treatment for you, ask for their advice on using crystal healing. While the number of contraindications for this type of therapy is low, certain conditions - such as epilepsy - will make it impossible for you to receive any treatment involving vibrations.

Even with your physician's approval to use crystal healing, you shouldn't take the same approach as you would with traditional medicine. This means you can't enter into a session to alleviate particular symptoms. Unlike traditional medications designed to combat one or more symptoms or causes of disease, healing energy certainly doesn't work in that way. It simply channels the vital force to where it's most needed in your body, allowing it to heal you. This is also why much of the skepticism around the effects of crystals on hormonal balance is unfounded. However, having unrealistic expectations or misconceptions about crystal healing can do more harm than good, particularly in the mental health department. So, the sooner you strip away these beliefs, the sooner the crystals will be activated and raise your vibrations to cleanse your mind, body, and spirit.

Chapter 2: What Is a Crystal Grid?

Before we delve into what a crystal grid is, we first need to explore the concept of Sacred Geometry, which is typically integrated into holistic practices. Sacred geometry is all around us. It is the core of all the patterns we see, meaning that it's the essence of the structure and framework of everything in the universe. Like other geometric shapes, these patterns can be reduced to mathematical concepts, particularly ones that govern the physical and spiritual realms.

There are different archetypes of sacred geometry, providing insight into each geometric form and its vibrational frequencies. If you're familiar with the chakra system, you probably understand that every entity, whether an object or a living being, is indefinitely tied to everything around us. These geometrical archetypes ultimately symbolize this relationship. It is the epitome of unity and oneness.

Many schools of thought think of Sacred Geometry as the genesis of the universe or the template of all creation. This science, which has been practiced for millennia, examines the energy patterns that govern those concepts that transcend human understanding. Besides ideas like creation and unification, numerous natural patterns in life, such as movement, development, and growth, can all be traced back to at least one geometric shape.

The eye's cornea, leaves, flower petals, DNA molecules, galaxies, and, of course, crystals are all geometric patterns. Even elements essential to life, such as air and water, are made of geometric molecules and ciphers.

Why It Matters

You're probably wondering how all of this information can help you transform your life. Besides using crystal grids (more on that later), the simple act of observation can help you enhance the quality of your life. Take note of the various geometric patterns, codes, and shapes you come across daily. While we may not be aware of it, contemplating and acknowledging their presence can allow you to unlock a higher state of consciousness that connects you to the heart of creation and opens you up to the secrets of the universe. The divine, nature, and our physical beings are all connected by geometric patterns, making this practice a great starting point for your spiritual, emotional, and physical healing journey.

Ancient practitioners strongly believed that opening yourself up to the power of sacred geometry is vital when it comes to educating or nourishing your soul. They realized these shapes symbolized our inner soul or the worlds within us, which is why they played a huge role in shaping a person's self-awareness and level of consciousness. Learning how to use sacred geometry can help you strengthen your relationship with the spiritual realm and achieve inner balance and peace. You can also use this doctrine to harmonize with the external world. Many believe that the term sacred geometry doesn't do this doctrine justice, considering that it is the quintessence of all creation. This is why the term sacred architecture is perhaps more fitting.

Besides the world of the physical, sacred geometry and light come together to create a grid that unites our physical, mental, emotional, energetic, and spiritual beings. Since these are the four aspects of health, this healing practice is considered holistic. This grid emits light energy, connecting your physical and spiritual self to the infinitely vast universe.

Sacred geometry comprises high energetic and light frequencies that can help us awaken our chakras, heal, and ultimately transform. These symbols guide us throughout our life journeys, although we may not even realize it. However, using them consciously (crystal grids are one way to do so) can help you trigger a deep awakening of the soul.

In this chapter, we'll explore how Plato believed mathematics and geometry played a huge role in the creation of the universe. We'll also delve deep into the relationship between sacred geometry and healing. Finally, you'll learn everything you need to know about crystal grids and their uses.

Plato and Sacred Geometry

Three-dimensional shapes, or solids, are quite relevant to sacred geometry. However, the most notable solids regarding this doctrine are known as the Platonic Solids. Even though Plato was not the one who created these shapes, they were named after him because he mentioned them in his works. He explained that five different types of solids, namely the tetrahedron, octahedron, dodecahedron, and icosahedron, are the building blocks of the entire universe. Plato associated these solids with the four basic elements: fire, earth, air, and water. The four-sided tetrahedron corresponds to fire. The six-sided hexahedron is associated with the Earth. The octahedron (eight-sided) is linked to air, and the icosahedron (twelve-sided) is assigned to the water element. Finally, the twenty-faceted dodecahedron is relevant to the heavens. Plato described the universe's makeup in his work, establishing a theory using only five solids. His theory was generally discarded for centuries until it was brought back to life by Johannes Kepler in the 16th century.

Ever since their revival, the significance of the Platonic Solids has been widely acknowledged. This theory has been associated with the chakra system. For example, it is said that the root chakra corresponds to the hexahedron, while the sacral chakra is associated with the icosahedron. Exploring the concept of the Platonic Solids reminds us that we are merely a portion of the larger picture: The universe.

Sacred Geometry and Healing

Creating crystal grids is one way to use sacred geometry in your healing efforts. Since we've already established the idea that sacred geometry can help you raise your consciousness and unlock higher self-awareness, you probably realize that using crystals to create certain shapes and patterns can help you achieve this. Meditating with certain geometric symbols, which we will cover in more depth throughout the following chapters, and using crystal grids, can notably help you heal your inner child and overcome childhood trauma.

This is because sacred geometric patterns can enable you to return to your authentic self. They encourage the cultivation of inner and external harmony and allow you to grow on numerous levels. It encourages a rooted, grounded, and humble connection with yourself and your surroundings. Each geometric shape, whether it's a Platonic Solid or another symbol, carries its own energetic vibration. The shape you use to set up your crystal grid or incorporate into your meditative practices (whether through yoga postures or visualization techniques) comes down to your intention. To offset the healing process, you need to shift your awareness to how you feel the energy within you.

When using sacred geometry for healing purposes, an overall energetic shift is triggered. This change in consciousness and energy causes re-balancing and promotes healing. As you may recall from the previous chapters, healing crystals are rich in energetic vibrations themselves. When you carry a crystal or hold it near its matching chakra, geometric codes are transmitted, influencing your energetic vibration and creating a healing effect. While crystals are quite effective on their own, they are used in the context of a pattern or sacred geometry further amplify their curative properties. Using crystal grids will allow you to experience unity and harmony and will help you make the most of your healing journey.

We can connect with sacred geometry whenever we need to. We don't have to sit down and put together a crystal grid or employ it in our meditative practice. Whenever we feel out of touch with our surroundings or experience a loss in direction, we can always rely on sacred geometry for guidance. Shifting our awareness to the patterns around us and mindfully observing the shapes of the universe serves as an incredible reminder that we are perpetually connected to the universe and everything that surrounds us.

Since sacred geometry symbolizes the natural patterns in life, including movement, practicing mindful movement meditation can also be beneficial. Whether you decide to dance, walk, or move in a geometric pattern, this is a fun way to fortify your sense of alignment.

What Is a Crystal Grid?

Now that you understand what sacred geometry is and what it's good for, we're here to tell you all about crystal grids. There are two dimensions to crystal grids; physical and metaphysical. In practice, a crystal grid is often a pre-printed outline you can use to guide your crystal placement. Metaphysically, however, crystal grids employ sacred geometric shapes to best use healing stones. When you place your crystals on the grid, they form shapes that harness their energy. Not only do they connect with each other to create a strong, energetic grid, but they also connect with your intention. So, if your intention is healing, using a crystal grid will help you manifest that healing. Crystal grids, like sacred geometry, are considered a holistic healing practice. They also have meditative attributes and are guaranteed to provide a positive experience to anyone who tries them out. While the following chapters provide step-by-step instructions on how to set up and use a crystal grid effectively, trusting your intuition is the most important aspect of the process.

Crystal grids can be used in countless ways. Depending on your grid's size, you can sit inside it and feed off its healing virtues during your meditative practices. If you have a smaller crystal grid, you can observe the grids as you meditate. Both methods are equally beneficial, so it all comes down to preference.

Crystal grids aren't limited to the manifestation of personal healing. You can also use them to bring your other intentions, dreams, aspirations, and desires to live. Crystal grids have undeniable healing properties. However, they are also very powerful manifestation tools. As mentioned, all the crystals you use to set up the grid combine their energies, making them much more powerful than single-crystal use. The power of your crystal grid also comes from your intentions, your choice of crystals, and how you lay out your healing stones.

In other words, a healing grid is a special layout of healing stones that is combined with a person's intentions to manifest the desired reality. When using a crystal grid, it's important to account for your needs rather than just your wants. Ultimately, the universe makes sure to give us the things we need, even when we don't necessarily want them. This is why focusing on your needs can help you attain better results. Protection, safety, healing, abundance, health, and well-being are among the most commonly set intentions when using a crystal grid.

Using Crystal Grids

There are no strict rules or guidelines regarding healing practices and spiritual endeavors. This also applies to working with crystal grids. Allowing your intuition to guide you in using the healing stones is the best practice. Chances are you won't be able to work with your intuition the first couple of times. Fortunately, the more you work with crystal grids, the more naturally it will come to you. Using guides can be very helpful at first. However, you'll eventually come to learn that when you trust your gut feelings, that's when you yield the most fruitful manifestation and healing results. For some people, using a certain surface, such as a board, a piece of cloth, or paper, works best. Others feel like throwing in natural elements, such as flower petals, shells, or leaves, which can do the trick. Many beginners incorporate natural elements into their crystal grids because they don't have many crystals to work with. You can do this if you think the number of healing stones at your disposal is a concern. As you can tell, the practice is all about what you feel comfortable with. You will have to experiment with different tools, crystals, shapes, surfaces, and elements at first until you get a better idea of which layout works best for you.

Selecting Healing Stones

In most cases, practitioners select the stones they use to make the crystal grids based on each healing crystal's properties. If you're familiar with how healing stones work, then you probably know that each crystal is aligned with certain chakras and vibrational frequencies. This means they choose crystals that resonate with the things they wish to manifest. For instance, if they wish to set stronger boundaries in their relationships, then they may set up a crystal grid in the shape of a circle using carnelian, red jasper, bloodstone, and other red circles. If they want to become more grounded, they may create a crystal grid using stones like hematite, garnet, smoky quartz, and tourmaline.

Many others, particularly more experienced practitioners, select the stones using their intuition. Rather than prioritizing the stone's properties, they allow their gut feelings to take the reins. If you have a limited collection of stones and not a lot of leeway, you can always work with what you already have. Remember, setting your intentions is the most important step at this stage. Think of the crystals as mere tools and not the primary vehicles. Your intentions, intuition, and inner power are of utmost importance. The crystals, along with their properties, will help you get there.

The Shape of the Crystal Grid

The shape of the crystal grid also plays a great role in the effectiveness of the process. This is because the grid's power is influenced by the placement of the healing stones and not just their metaphysical properties.

Setting up a circle grid can help with boundary-setting, safety, protection, and feelings of security. A square grid is associated with the establishment of personal foundations and groundedness. It can help you feel rooted and relates to practicality. Laying out your crystals in a triangle shape can help you shift to a higher state of consciousness. The triangle is a symbol of elevated harmony and is correspondent with harmony and balance. The Star of David grid is among the most powerful, as it activates our inner grid (the one associated with the four aspects of health). This arrangement of healing stones can generate very high psychic and spiritual-energetic vibrations, facilitating healing and providing feelings of protection. This crystal grid can help you connect with the spiritual realm and aid you with manifestation. While you can feel free to meditate with this symbol, we strongly advise that you use this crystal grid under a professional practitioner's guidance.

Benefits of Using Crystal Grids

Besides their healing properties, their ability to help you achieve your goals, and the enhanced meditative experience, incorporating crystal grids into your daily practice can improve the overall quality of your life. Crystal grids allow you to cultivate positive emotions toward everything that you do. They also serve as a great opportunity for individuals to explore their own abilities. Using crystal grids allows you to practice personal healing and work on improving your general health without anyone's help. That said, you should still visit special healthcare professionals if you struggle with your mental or physical health.

Crystal grids are a great way to release negative energy from the surrounding environment. Since setting your intentions is an integral aspect of the practice, laying out a crystal grid automatically reminds you of your goals and aspirations. Using healing stones in a powerful context also allows you to let go of the emotional blockages of past events that may be holding you back.

Learning how to use these powerful tools can be incredibly empowering. You can use them to elevate numerous areas of your life. Many people use crystal grids to boost their confidence, enhance their self-esteem, and promote self-love. Others use this practice to clear brain fog, increase focus, and sharpen cognitive abilities. When used right, crystal grids can help you regain control over your life.

In addition to their aesthetic appeal, crystal grids can be employed in distance (not just personal) healing. They are also used for intention-setting and manifestation practices, incorporated into meditative techniques, and applied in ritual work. Many people even partake in crystal grid making because of the creative process involved.

Crystal grids can be used for meditative purposes.
https://unsplash.com/photos/DwJqS3QTFpo?utm_source=unsplash&utm_medium=referral&utm_content=creditShareLink

Chapter 3: Crystals and Other Tools for Gridwork

You should use the right crystals and other tools when building your crystal grid. This chapter explains the different types of materials required for making grids. We also provide a few examples of sacred geometry shapes you can use as grid layouts, such as Metatron's Cube, Flower of Life, Seed of life, and others. Finally, we include tips and tricks on how to decorate your grid.

Tools for Making Crystal Grids

Many people want to use crystals for spiritual and physical healing. When you are working with crystals for a particular purpose like love, health, or any ritual, placing them in a grid sort of style can greatly amplify their metaphysical power. You can use any crystal to create your grid, but make sure its properties match your purpose and intent. The following are the basic things you should have when you create your crystal grid:

- An appropriate location for your grid at home
- A small piece of paper
- A crystal grid plate

While some of these items come in different forms, they don't need to be special.

Selecting Crystals

It is important to choose the right crystals for your grid work. You must have at least four stones, although it is encouraged to get more. Various gemstones can be incorporated into crystal grids. For instance, you can consider gems such as tumble garnet, rough gypsum, cabbed and polished fire agate, tumbled topaz, obsidian tumbles, raw moonstone, and others. Again, ensure you get stones and crystals that align with your intention.

You can use multiple crystals of the same type depending on your goals. You must get a larger crystal to place in the center, and other stones must be small. Smaller gems are ideal for the outer part of the grid. You can use crystal points if you like, but it is not required. Crystal points do not amplify your intention, which is why they are optional.

Alternatively, you can consider different crystal combinations for your grid if you don't want to use the same type. You can try some of the following mixes to enhance your grid. For instance, you can select green and gold wealth crystals like Citrine, Aventurine, and Pyrite if you intend to create an abundance grid. When you are building a health and wellness grid, blue and purple stones such as Sodalite, Fluorite, and Angelite is ideal.

Grids specifically meant for love include green hearts and pink chakra stones. However, you can also look for other stones that align with your love intentions. If you intend to perform healing rituals, you can consider a combination of jasper, tourmaline, agate, and amethyst crystals. The stones that are commonly used to represent the seven chakras are also ideal for your grid.

An arrangement of sunstone, carnelian, and clear quartz is ideal for personal empowerment rituals. If you intend to banish someone or something negative from your life, be sure to incorporate jade, onyx, hematite, and obsidian in your grid design. When you choose crystals for your grid, there are no wrong or right stones to use. Because of this, you must trust your intuition and choose anything that appeals to you the most.

Choosing the appropriate crystals for your grid is not the end. Besides the selection process, cleaning the space where you'll be using the grid is an important step you should not overlook. You also want to cleanse the entire home of any negative energies lingering around. This will create an optimal environment to help your charged crystals fuse with your intention. A clean environment also keeps undesired elements away.

Cleansing your crystals is another important aspect of gridwork. There are different tools and methods you can use to cleanse your stones. For instance, if possible, you can place them under the full moon for the entire night. Place them outside around nightfall and remove them at about 10 AM to allow them to enjoy a few hours of sunlight.

Crystals obtained from the earth can be cleansed by burying them underground. You should leave them buried for about 24 hours. Rainwater can also be used for cleansing and charging your crystals. Just place them outside when it is raining. However, you need to know that some stones dissolve when exposed to water. You must double-check the features of the stones first before attempting to soak them in rainwater.

Saltwater is another essential component when it comes to cleansing your crystals. You can make a homemade solution or source it directly from the sea. Place the stones in this water solution and leave them for about 24 hours. When choosing this method, ensure your water is safe for the stones. Running water is readily available from your kitchen tap and is one of the most convenient and quickest methods to cleanse your crystals. Hold each stone for about one minute under running water. Whatever method you choose to cleanse your stones, make your intention clear. It is a good idea to write it down so you can refine it to suit your needs.

Grid Layout

You can choose various forms of sacred geometric shapes for your crystal grid. Essentially, sacred geometry consists of different symbols that constitute the basic things in the universe. They played critical roles in ancient Egypt, Greek, and Japanese culture since they are believed to represent the intangible and mystical elements of the universe. Sacred geometry was also used in China and India for various religious processions.

When you choose a geometric pattern, select something that suits your needs. The common ones include a pentacle, spiral, or circles. There are hundreds of sacred geometry patterns available. You can draw your pattern on paper, wood, or cloth. However, it does not necessarily mean that you should have the drawn lines in front of you. Some people have predetermined patterns in their minds, and they simply lay the crystals without drawing grids. The following are some of the sacred geometric shapes you can consider for your first grid work practice:

Triangle

Triangle.
Increase2.svg: Sarangderivative work: Dodoïste, Public domain, via Wikimedia Commons: https://commons.wikimedia.org/wiki/File:Increase_Negative.svg

A triangle is one of the easiest shapes since it represents 3, which is the number of sacred creations. In different parts of the world, particularly in Nordic cultures, this number is believed to possess mystical properties that symbolize balance and harmony. The triangle can represent father, mother, and child, but also body, spirit, and mind. When it is pointing upwards, it indicates the rising consciousness. If the triangle is pointing downward, it relates to the Divine Feminine. The Great Pyramids of Giza in Egypt famously illustrate this enigmatic structure consisting of four triangles and a square base.

Square

Square.
https://pixabay.com/images/id-422371/

A square symbolizes structure and stability. It also represents the four elements: earth, fire, air, and water. The cardinal directions (East, North, West, and South) are also represented in the number four. In other words, all the elements are equal or treated as such. You can consider this type of grid for grounding and rooting rituals.

Circle

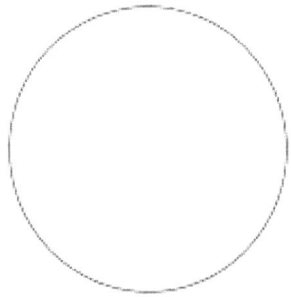

Circle

Jmarchn, CC BY-SA 3.0 <https://creativecommons.org/licenses/by-sa/3.0>, via Wikimedia Commons: https://commons.wikimedia.org/wiki/File:Circle_(transparent).svg

The circle represents the endless cycle of life, death, and rebirth in spiritual terms. It also shows oneness, and a circle often represents God. This shape is considered the base of various patterns in sacred geometry. Some of the triangle-based sacred geometry shapes, including a circle, are vectors of equilibrium and represent the grid of life.

Spiral

Spiral shapes are common in the movement of galaxies and shells, forming the basis of the golden ratio and the Fibonacci sequence. Symbolically, the spiral represents the chakras where the shifting circles form the spiral energy vortex. The pilgrimage is another essential shape that represents spiritual enlightenment.

Platonic Solids

The platonic solids comprise five shapes that are the basis of different molecules that form the entire universe. Named after Plato, they include crystal structures with three dimensions. Different symbolic attributes are ascribed to each shape. The following are the platonic solids you can consider for your crystal grid:

- **Tetrahedron:** Four-sided pyramid that represents fire.
- **Hexahedron:** Six-sided cube representing earth.
- **Octahedron:** An eight-sided figure that represents air.
- **Icosahedron:** A twelve-sided shape that represents water.
- **Dodecahedron:** Twenty-sided shape representing ether, heavens, and spirits.

Other significant geometric shapes and patterns include:

Vesica Piscis

Vesica Piscis is a Latin term meaning "fish's bladder," and it is the foundation of several sacred geometry patterns. It has two overlapping circles representing life's famine energy, birth, and union in duality.

Seed of Life

Seed of Life. Source: Sfoulkes at English Wikipedia, Public domain, via Wikimedia Commons: https://commons.wikimedia.org/wiki/File:Seed-of-Life.svg

As the name implies, the seed of life represents creation and shows the other side of God's higher consciousness. The seed of life depicts six overlapping circles, which can perfectly fit in the seventh circle. It is connected to the seven chakras and the Germ of Life forms.

Flower of Life

Flower of life.
Nickhwee, CC BY-SA 3.0 <https://creativecommons.org/licenses/by-sa/3.0>, via Wikimedia Commons: https://commons.wikimedia.org/wiki/File:Flower-of-life_(1).png

The Flower of Life is formed by replicating the Seed of Life. It reflects the creation cycle and is believed to be about 6,000 years old. It also symbolizes spiritual awakening and is believed to be a template for everything we have in the universe.

The Tree of Life

The Tree of Life has ten circles called sefirot, and it is associated with Jewish mysticism and Kabbalah. The circles in this pattern are connected by 22 lines, also known as paths. The Hebrew alphabet consists of 22 letters corresponding to each path. This pattern represents the way of creation.

Star of David

The Star of David consists of six-pointed stars that are formed from two interlocking triangles. One star faces upward, and the other down, and these star triangles are believed to show a religious connection between the creator, Tora, and the people. The shape comprising two triangles is associated with the Heart Chakra in Hinduism. It reflects the meditative state.

Metatron's Cube

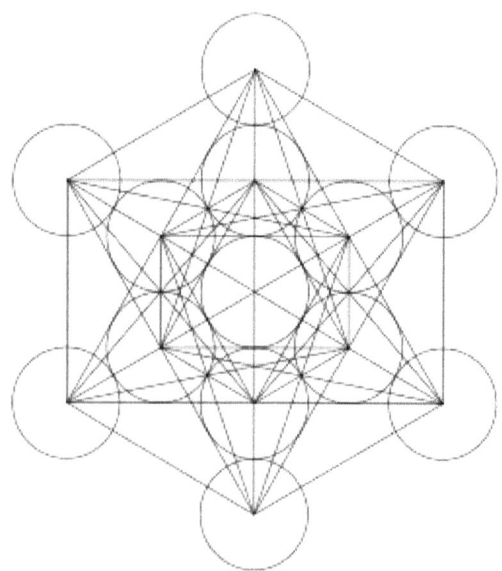

Metatron's cube.
Deathlime (at en:), Public domain, via Wikimedia Commons:
https://commons.wikimedia.org/wiki/File:Metatrons_cube.svg

The Metatron's cube has 13 circles, and it is also known as Merkaba. The circles are connected by straight lines, which form patterns that resemble two stars in a hexagon. The cube is God's geometric map since it consists of all the geometric shapes used in the universe's construction. It also has platonic solids, which form the critical components of physical matter. Crystals and DNA come in various forms in the universe, and the Egg of life is visible within the center.

Sri Yantra

Sri Yantra.
N.Manytchkine, CC BY-SA 3.0 <https://creativecommons.org/licenses/by-sa/3.0>, via Wikimedia Commons: https://commons.wikimedia.org/wiki/File:Sri_Yantra.svg

Sri Yanta is about 12,000 years old and is one of the oldest symbols in sacred geometry. Its design comprises circles and triangles based on the Golden Proportion. Tantra practitioners use the pattern as a vital tool for contemplation and meditation. It also symbolizes cosmic oneness and serves as a spiritual shield commonly used to protect people from negative energies.

Torus (Yantra)

This pattern is made up of a central axis that connects to vortexes on all ends. Energy is believed to flow from one vortex and comes out from the other vortex. The energy will then move back to the first vortex, representing the constant flow of power. The pattern reflects a balanced flow of energy among the people involved. The energy source starts off in one direction, then doubles and returns to the source.

These are some of the geometric patterns you can consider for your crystal grid, although there are several others. The section below provides various tips and tricks to decorate your grid. We also explain why it can be a good idea to create a crystal board you can use without drawing the pattern on the grid.

Making Your Crystal Grid

When you have picked your crystals and sacred geometric shape, the next step is to build the grid. For growth and spirituality, you may choose the Flower of Life. If you want, you can draw the pattern on a piece of paper or simply visualize it.

Start with placing the crystal in the center, and remember that every action you take must align with your intention. Work your way outward and place the crystals at the intersections where the lines meet. However, you do not need to place crystals on every cross-point. You can include about 4 to 20 crystals, so place them strategically. You should not place the same crystals on the same line.

However, some metaphysical schools of thought require you to work your crystal grid from outside towards the center. You must do it intentionally, no matter what method you choose to create your grid. As you place the crystals, you can enter into a trance. It is essential to begin the process by speaking about your intention. If you have a written intention, place it underneath the largest crystal in the center.

Regardless of how you place your crystals, you should be consistent. Place all the stones at even intervals. For instance, you can use an even number on each side of your grid to maintain the design's symmetry.

Sacred Geometry Adornments

Sacred geometry adornments are made from prints, jewelry, objects, clothing, and tattoos. You can use these in a spell or ritual to enhance your intention. Additionally, you can also include a sacred geometry yoga mat on your altar. You can achieve your goals if you align your intentions with different symbols that imitate sacred geometry shapes.

While people in other traditions write their intentions on paper and place them beneath the largest center stone, you may not need to do this. Others don't use physical patterns but predetermined shapes in their minds. With this type of grid, you may not have many decorations to add. However, with a physical grid, feel free to add anything you like since there is no single pattern to follow.

Drawing a Mandala

Many people draw mandalas consisting of shapes and symbols within a circle. You can see the Seed of Life or Flower of Life in a mandala, along with spirals, circles, and triangles. Mandala refers to a circle, which can be used for different purposes and to symbolize a variety of intentions.

A mandala can serve to reflect creativity and the complexity of the inner workings of your soul. You can also use it as a tool for mindful meditation to promote feelings of calmness and inner peace. Mandalas can also be employed to reduce anxiety, stress, and other issues related to mental health. A mandala is a fun and creative way of expressing your feelings and exploring your inner self. You can also use it to merge the inner and outer worlds. Lastly, it plays a crucial role since it is an effective manifestation tool that is also inspirational.

When you design a crystal grid, choose the appropriate sacred geometry symbols, and understand how to use them. You also need to select crystals that match your intention and come in different forms. Again, there is no limit to the number of stones you can use on your grid.

No matter your grid style of choice, remember it is a personal and highly subjective experience. Your design depends on your goals, intentions, and relationship to crystals. Your ability to interpret sacred geometry also determines the stones and patterns you'll use for your grid.

Another important aspect of crystal grids is that they grow with you. Because of that, your options can expand as you gather more and more stones and develop your collection. So, take your time to create a grid that serves you to the fullest. Remember to cleanse and reactivate your grid and crystals after a few days depending on your usage. The success of your intentions will depend on the effectiveness of your crystals and grid.

Chapter 4: Creating Your First Crystal Grid

Now that you know the tools required for creating a crystal grid, you are ready to make your first crystal grid. Before you begin, it is recommended to cleanse your physical body before you work with energy or do any spiritual work. You should also be relaxed and clear your mind. It is best to make your grid early in the morning, late at night, or anytime during the day when you can be at peace with no distractions.

Creating Your Crystal Grid

Seed of life printable grid.
Sfoulkes at English Wikipedia, Public domain, via Wikimedia Commons:
https://commons.wikimedia.org/wiki/File:Seed-of-Life.svg

Creating a grid is a lot easier than you may think once you familiarize yourself with the process. Make sure you follow all the instructions provided exactly as they are.

Step One: Choose the Right Space

Choosing the right space will guarantee that your crystal grid is effective and works properly. Because a crystal grid requires stability, choose a safe and sacred place where the crystals won't be disturbed or knocked over. The grid should remain in its position until you decide to take it down, build a new one, or when your intentions are fulfilled. If one of the crystals in your grid moves from its initial position, this can result in a blockage in the flow of energy.

Where you place the crystal grid should be a space that invites magic, creativity, and focus. Some people prefer placing it near a window, exposing it to lunar and solar energies. Take your time until you find the right spot for it, where it won't be moved or disturbed.

Create a comfortable space with no distractions. Turn off your cell phone and any other electronic devices in the room, dim the lights for a more relaxed ambiance, and choose a spot to place all your tools.

You can also create the grid outdoors. Just draw a circle around you in the dirt using a stick, rock, or even your finger to create the energetic space you will use for the grid.

Step Two: Cleanse the Space

After choosing a space for your crystal grid, you should cleanse it to clear your mind and prepare the space to welcome new energy. Cleansing can be done using a bowl of salt since salt is considered a powerful energy cleanser. This is a simple method: scatter some salt over the area and then sweep it. Smudging the area with sage will also do the trick. If these methods aren't available to you, you can dust and clean the area with soap and water. To get rid of old energy, open the room's window or turn on a fan for a few minutes.

Step Three: Set the Mood

Set the mood by lighting scented candles and playing soft background music. Although this step is optional, it will help create a soothing atmosphere that is conducive to successful gridwork and wellness.

Step Four: Choose the Crystals

Choose crystals that align with your intentions and the ones you feel connected with the most. There are various types of crystals and stones, each carrying a different energy type. Finding a crystal you can connect with is easy. We are naturally drawn to certain crystals the same way we are drawn to certain scents, shapes, colors, or places. We don't have to apply logic or think about why we like a certain color more than the other. The same applies to crystals. We just find ourselves gravitating towards crystals that contain the same energies we want to bring into our lives.

Instead of overthinking it, let your intuition guide you. Focus on the crystal's shape and color, and you'll find yourself going for the ones that can help manifest your intention into reality. We will also discuss various crystals for different types of intentions in the coming chapters.

Imagine the grid as a canvas; the crystals are the colors you will use to paint this canvas. It is the new life you hope to manifest for yourself. Don't use less than four crystals. You can use crystals of the same type or combine various different ones, depending on your intention. Make sure the crystal in the center is larger than the surrounding crystal.

Cleansing the crystals is also necessary. Each crystal has unique properties; by cleansing it, you guarantee that these qualities remain intact. Since different types of energy always surround us, crystals can absorb negative energies or other energetic impurities. For this reason, you should regularly cleanse your crystals and stones. You can leave them for a few hours under the moonlight or sunlight. However, be careful, as crystals shouldn't be exposed to the sun for long periods, or their colors may degrade. You can also try smudging using palo santo smoke or sage. In fact, sage smoke is a great cleanser since it kills bacteria and germs. One of the easiest methods to cleanse your crystals is by using a soft brush, soap, and water. That said, some crystals can be damaged by soap and water. We recommend you ask for a specialist's advice on the best method to cleanse your crystals or go online to see the best cleansing method for your stones. You can also cleanse the crystals by spraying essential oils, giving them healing properties.

To recharge your crystals, bury them underground overnight. After cleansing your crystals, hold them for a while, focusing on your intention.

Step Five: Set Your Intentions

Why are you making a crystal grid? Setting an intention is determining a reason for creating the grid. This is an essential step that shouldn't be put off until later. Intentions are the foundation onto which you build your grid, and they set a direction for your crystal grid to channel its energy.

An intention is a wish for something you are trying to manifest. It can be prayer, a desire, or anything else you really want. Your intention can be a better job, a new car, a bigger house, healing (for yourself or someone else), abundance, the attraction of new love, joy, and much more. Since this is your first time, you may think it is best to start with something small. However, you shouldn't hold back. Set an intention for anything you want, no matter how big it is. While setting an intention, believe deep down that you deserve whatever you are hoping for.

To set an intention, you can meditate for a few minutes. Sit quietly in a comfortable position, focus on your breathing, and clear your mind. Think about what you are hoping to achieve with the crystal grid. Make your intentions clear and to the point. Remember, you are using crystals, not a magic lamp, so avoid intentions like "I want to be a millionaire." Instead, opt for a different phrasing like "I intend to manifest better financial opportunities into my life and to find the courage to follow these opportunities." Other examples of intentions include:

- I intend to forgive those who have wronged me.
- I intend to manifest joy, peace, and happiness.
- I intend to give and receive love.
- I intend to be open to abundance.
- I intend to make healing a priority.

You can also write your intention on a piece of paper and place it on the grid. Speaking your intention out loud can also be effective, as the vibrations in your voice can attract what you want and help manifest it in the physical world. Visualization is another effective method you can use to set your intentions. Use your imagination to picture every detail of what you want to manifest as if it was real. For instance, if your intention is to acquire a new home, visualize yourself happily walking with your family into your new house. Imagine every detail of the house, like the color of the walls and the furniture. Picture what you and your family wear and your laughter as you explore your new home.

Step Six: Select a Shape for Your Grid

When selecting a shape for your grid, there are many options you can choose from. Your grid's shape should align with your intentions. For this reason, we recommend setting your intention first since this is the foundation upon which you will build your grid.

You have probably seen many fascinating shapes on social media. Each shape has a different energy. For instance, a triangle helps set boundaries, a circle grid is for courage and protection, and spirals are for expanding and reaching out. To find direction or achieve clarity, use a grid of multiples of fours, and for manifestation, use a grid of multiples of threes.

You'll find various shapes to choose from online. However, we recommend you use the seed of life shape because it is basic and easy to use. We provided a layout for you that you can print on a piece of cloth or paper and simply place the crystals on them. If printing isn't an option, use the layout as a visual aid for placing the crystals.

Step Seven: Place the Crystals

Now that you have chosen the crystals and the grid shape, you can start placing your crystals. Here is how to proceed with this step:

- **The Focus Stone:** The largest crystal should be placed in the middle, which is why it is called the Focus Stone. If you have written down your intentions, you can place them under this stone. It is one of the *most essential* parts of a grid since it absorbs the life force energy from the universe and channels it into the grid. In other words, the center stone is like a car's engine, and it is the part that powers the grid. It receives and distributes energy and helps manifest your intention by sending it out to the universe.

- **The Way Stones:** The next step is placing stones around the center stone, which are called the Way Stones. You can't create a grid without Way Stones. When the Focus Stone collects the energy, it sends it to the Way Stones through the path created. These stones work on amplifying the lifeforce energy.

- **The Desire Stones:** These are the outermost stones. They are usually placed around the Way Stones and considered the grid's final pieces. Choosing these stones mainly depends on the purpose of the grid. The Desire Stones' job is to collect the energy from the other stones and the Path. They are called the Desire Stones because they alter the lifeforce energy's tuning to fit the grid's desired results. Desire and Way Stones are usually chosen by their color rays and lattice. Whatever energy these stones collect, they amplify it to manifest your intentions.

- **The Path:** The path is basically the lines flowing through the crystal grid. They guide the energy released from the Focus Stone through the Way Stones and finally to the Desire Stones. The Path represents the journey the energy takes to help manifest our desires. These lines are the channel that depends on the geometry of the grid to align, transfer, and guide the energy to help manifest your intentions. The Path connects each stone to the patterns of life. When a grid is well-designed, the Path will allow for the energy to be easily collected, focused, and amplified.

To Sum Up:

1. Place the Focus Stone, which should be larger than the other stones, in the center of the grid.
2. Next, place the Ways Stones all around the Focus Stone.
3. Lastly, place the Desire Stones by working your way outward (around the Way Stones).

Some people also add flowers, leaves, petals, a photo, an item from someone dear to them, or any object that is related to their intention. You should be mindful while placing each stone and remain focused on your intention or even say it aloud.

Step Eight: Activate the Crystals

Activating the crystals is a crucial step that will help unify the crystals' powers and the grid. This is where you will use the wand or quartz point mentioned in the previous chapter. Feel the energy all over you as you advance through each step. Be at one with the universe and with everything it has to offer. Life and pure love energy are streaming through you and into the universe. You are an energy vessel. Hold your wand, close your eyes, and visualize all the energy inside of it flowing out. Follow these steps to activate your crystals:

1. Point your wand or quartz above the anchor while thinking of your intention. Stay still and visualize light streaming from your wand to give energy to the focus stone. Keep visualizing the light through the entire process.

4. Draw a line from the Focus Stone to the Desire Stones. Pause and repeat your intentions.

5. Next, move clockwise on the edge of the grid and draw a line to the next stone. Again, pause and repeat your intention.

6. Draw a line from this second outer stone back to the Focus Stone. Pause and think of your intention, and allow the Focus Stone to recharge your intention through your wand.

7. Trace the line to the second outer stone again. Pause for a minute, then connect it to the next stone.

8. Repeat the previous two steps (4 and 5) around the grid and finish at the Focus Stone to open all the energy channels. Your intention should be your only thought. Focus on it, and you can repeat it with every step. If your grid gets disturbed or one of the crystals moves or gets knocked over, you must reactivate it from square one.

What should you do if you want to adjust your intention or make a new one? Simply return to your grid anytime to recharge it or change the intention.

You should perform all these steps alone. However, if the grid and the intentions are supposed to help one or more people besides you, then you should activate it together.

Now, you have created and activated your grid. What's next? Your grid is working on manifesting your intentions. You shouldn't just ignore your grid or forget about it. Make it a habit to acknowledge it daily. This can be done by meditating with the grid, reaffirming your intention every time you pass by it, or simply sitting with it. You can leave your grid for a moon cycle or for long as you want. Every now and then, clean the dust off the grid to avoid energy stagnation. You can always take it down and make a new one if you wish.

However, you shouldn't just take it down after it has completed its purpose. What do you do when a friend gives you a gift? We usually say thank you and show gratitude. The same goes for your crystal grid. Show gratitude by thanking it for everything it has done.

Don't remove all the crystals at once; instead, remove them one by one. We recommend you cleanse them before you store them using any of the cleansing methods mentioned earlier. After you remove all the crystals, cleanse the space where you placed the grid using incense or white sage. This will clear out any built-up energy in the area.

Ultimately, a crystal grid is a powerful tool to help manifest your intentions to the universe. Be patient and give it time to work. Make sure to follow all the steps detailed here and prepare yourself physically and mentally for this process, just like you should prepare the crystals and the area where you'll place the grids. Believe in the crystals and their power, and remove any doubt from your heart and mind. Trust in the universe; it is working for you.

Chapter 5: Crystal Grids for Love and Relationships

Who doesn't want to find love? Many people dream about meeting their soulmates and finding their life-long companions. Crystals can help get you closer to what you are looking for. Love crystals are like a compass that can guide you to manifest what your heart desires. When it comes to matters of the heart, you'll find a crystal for everything like self-love, healing from past wounds, unblocking the heart chakra, and attracting new love. Now that you know how to make a crystal grid, we can focus on more specific grids like love and relationships.

Love Crystals

Creating a love and relationships grid requires love-related crystals. Here is a list of various crystals to bring balance to your relationships, help you heal, and find love.

Rose Quartz Stone

Rose quartz.
Parent Géry, CC BY-SA 3.0 <https://creativecommons.org/licenses/by-sa/3.0>, via Wikimedia Commons: https://commons.wikimedia.org/wiki/File:Quartz_rose_cristallis%C3%A9_sur_quartz_(Br%C3%A9sil)_3.JPG

When it comes to love stones, no one is as prominent as the Rose Quartz. With its gentle pink color associated with romance, this stone emits feminine energy, compassion, tenderness, and sensuality. It helps bring trust, unconditional love, and tolerance. Old wounds can prevent people from moving on and falling in love again, but Rose Quartz crystals can help heal and free your heart, so you are open and ready to attract new love. It also unblocks the heart chakra, so all kinds of love, whether self-love or romantic passion, can flow through you once again.

Rhodonite Stone

There is a reason this beautiful rose stone is a favorite among many crystal enthusiasts. Rhodonite can help manifest forgiveness and romantic love in your life. Although love is blind, and we are all guilty of getting swept away in the magic of new beginnings, the Rhodonite stone helps open our eyes to the harsh reality of love. It makes you aware that love can have its share of painful moments and not-so-happy endings. This realization grants you the confidence and inner strength to forgive yourself and the other person, so you can heal from heartbreak and release negative emotions like anger, disappointment, or fear.

Pink Kunzite Stone

Another pink-colored stone, the Pink Kunzite, is often called "the woman stone." This crystal can manifest wisdom, inner peace, and deep love with its nurturing and loving energy. This delicate stone can help your heart heal and tear down the walls you have erected to protect yourself from emotional harm. It can bring trust back to your life, so you can build healthy and strong relationships with people worthy of your love.

Moonstone Stone

Like its namesake, the moon, the Moonstone is also associated with femininity. This stone emits feminine energy that can bring divine adaptation and balance to your life. Do you have any newlywed friends? The Moonstone will make the perfect gift for the happy couple as it is known to bring good luck. Are you looking to reunite with an old partner? The Moonstone can help reunite estranged lovers, emotionally and physically. It is associated with abundance, new beginnings, fertility, and renewals.

Fun Fact: According to ancient folklore, if two people wear the moonstone at the same time on a full moon, they are destined to fall madly in love.

Amethyst Stone

Are you ready to meet the love of your life? Amethyst can help prepare you for your next love story. With its gentle purple color, the Amethyst stone is considered one of the most powerful stones for promoting peace, healing, and self-worth. Many people seek this stone's healing properties after experiencing a harsh heartbreak.

Amber Stone

Another stone known to bring good luck to newlyweds, the Amber stone emits energetic and calming vibes to balance a lover's heart. This stone can bring sensuality, protection, healing, and good luck in all areas of love.

Pink Tourmaline Stone

The Pink Tourmaline stone can prompt abundance, new love, and comfort to the heart. This stone can unblock the heart chakra so that love energy can flow through your body and heal old wounds. It emits compassionate and calming energies that can quiet your troubled heart. Whatever fears or pain you carry from your past relationships, Tourmaline can help you face them, so you are open to attracting new love into your life. This stone has healing powers to mend your broken heart so you can overcome emotional trauma.

Rhodochrosite Stone

This beautiful pink and white stone is a compass that will guide you to your greatest love story. Since it emits various vibes through its many layers, Rhodochrosite helps you uncover all the layers of yourself so you can better understand any past issues or negative emotions preventing you from finding love. Simply put, it encourages emotional healing and invites new love into your life. It helps you prioritize your needs while opening your heart to self-love.

Agate Stone

The Agate stone comes in many colors and shades, each carrying its own set of healing properties. For instance, the Moss Agate is known to encourage self-love and heal the heart chakra to find love. When in a relationship, the Moss Agate can bring balance and peace to your love life. The Blue Lace Agate can manifest truth, harmony, and love. Do you want to bring passion and sensuality into your life? This stone can ignite the fire of passion in your love life, so you and your loved one cannot keep your hands off each other.

Aventurine Stone

As green as the heart chakra's color, Aventurine can help you activate and connect with your heart chakra. It is considered a good luck charm and emits success energy which can come in handy for a new relationship. The Aventurine stone can bring love, passion, and compassion into your life. It can also promote calmness so you can withstand all the problems and misunderstandings that occur at the beginning of a relationship.

Lapis Lazuli

How can you make a relationship work? You talk things out with your partner and find ways to communicate your feelings and needs to each other. The Lapis Lazuli stone is associated with communication due to its connection to the throat chakra. It encourages you to be honest about your feelings and gives you the confidence to be your most authentic self in a relationship. We thrive in relationships when our feelings are acknowledged, and *we feel heard*. Ruled by Venus, the Lapis Lazuli stone can bring love and harmony to your love affairs. It can also help you think clearly when you are in love since it keeps the heart and head in balance. After the end of a relationship, this stone can bring healing and inner peace to a broken heart.

Garnet Stone

This red-shaded stone is associated with trust, devotion, love, passion, and desire. It can balance your sex drive and promote healing and positive energy. The Garnet Stone gives you the courage to be honest about your needs and feelings to have an open and healthy relationship with your partner.

Ruby Stone

If you are looking for a stone to make you feel confident and empowered, look no further than the Ruby stone. This crystal, which is connected to the root chakra, can manifest self-love into your life, especially for those who tend to put themselves last in a relationship.

Malachite Stone

The Malachite stone connects you with the heart chakra, encourages you to let go of any doubts, and brings trust into your life. It will open you up to attract new love, which is why this stone is considered a love magnet.

Citrine Stone

Citrine emits joy and bright energy and can serve as a reminder that love is a wonderful feeling that brings happiness and comfort. Unfortunately, many people who were hurt in a past relationship tend to forget that love is a beautiful, warm, and magical feeling. They see the world from a cynical point of view and lose the spark in their eyes they once had. The Citrine stone can bring back joy and positivity to your heart and soul.

Chrysocolla Stone

Chrysocolla isn't only unique because of its eye-catching color; it is also connected to the heart and throat chakras. It opens these two chakras so that energy can flow from the heart to your tongue, allowing you to communicate your feelings and desires. This stone can foster communication, love, and growth and help you attract new love. At times, it seems the universe only sends the wrong people our way, which begs the question, when will we meet the one? The Chrysocolla stone will convey your intention to the universe and help bring the right person into your life.

Obsidian Stone

If you have ever seen an Obsidian stone, you may be wondering what a black stone has to do with love. Obsidian can bring feelings of safety and protection to our hearts. This can make you trust in yourself and believe that you deserve unconditional, real love.

Opal Stone

Opal has been associated with good luck all throughout history. Although some people deem this stone unlucky, the Romans considered it one of the luckiest stones out there. So, don't believe the rumors that Opal can cause misfortune. In fact, this stone can bring desire, love, and passion into your life. It is associated with romance and openness, granting you the courage to be passionate and fulfill all your sexual dreams and desires with your partner. This stone brings loyalty and good communication and stabilizes your emotions as well.

Carnelian Stone

Dressed in the color of love, this red stone brings courage, endurance, and joy to your relationships. The Carnelian stone helps connect us to the sacral chakra so we can develop healthy relationships. It also brings passion into our love life while keeping us grounded.

You may have noticed that these stones have a few things in common besides healing and attracting new love. Many of these stones are either pink or red, which are colors closely associated with love and romance. These stones are also connected to the heart chakra, which is the only chakra associated with romantic love, self-love, and platonic love. Certain stones are also connected to the throat chakra, which is responsible for helping us communicate our feelings and express ourselves in relationships.

Creating Crystal Grids for Love and Relationships

Now that you know which crystals are associated with love, you are ready to use these stones to make love and relationship grids. As you know, there are various shapes of grids, but to make a love gird, we recommend using any of these formats:

- The Metatron's cube
- The flower of life
- The shape of a heart
- The seed of life

Let's start making grids. Remember to follow all the instructions in the previous chapter, like cleansing the crystals and choosing the right area for your grid.

Self-Love Grid

Tools and Crystals
- A photo of yourself
- 8 Rose Quartz
- Any grid format of your choice

Instructions
1. Sit in a relaxed position in a quiet place with no distractions.

2. Focus on your thoughts, and ask yourself: "What is my one true desire?" and "Do I want love, support, or acceptance?"

3. Now, focus on your feelings, and ask yourself: "What does support feel like?" "What does self-love feel like?" "What is self-acceptance?"

4. Now, set an intention that you will love, accept, and support yourself.

5. Put your photo in the center of the grid.

6. Start placing the crystals one by one around your picture while visualizing white light flowing from the universe through you and into the grid.

7. Sit for a few minutes with your grid while remaining focused on your intention.

Healing Past Wounds

Tools and Crystals
- 6 Pink Opal stones
- 6 Amazonite stones
- 1 large Rose Quartz stone
- Seed of life grid

Instructions

1. Set your intentions for healing past wounds, like "I intend to heal the wounds of the past, so my emotional body is healthy and balanced."
2. The Rose Quartz will serve as your focal stone. Place it at the center of the grid while repeating your intention out loud.
3. The six Amazonite stones will serve as the way stones. So, place them around the focus stone. They represent empathy and compassion.
4. The six pink Opal stones will serve as the desired stones and will be placed around the Amazonite stones. These stones represent forgiveness and emotional healing.
5. Now, activate the grid with a wand or a clear Quartz crystal point using the same activation method discussed in the previous chapter while repeating your intention.

Attracting Love

Crystals
- 1 Large Rose Quartz stone
- 6 Green Aventurine stones
- 6 Clear pointers of Quartz stones
- Any grid format of your choice

Instructions

1. Set an intention that you want to attract love, romance, and new possibilities into your life. You can also write it on a piece of paper and place it under the focus stone.

2. Clear your mind and focus on your intention. You can keep repeating it or hold the paper close to your heart.

3. Place the Rose Quartz at the center of your grid. This focus stone will work on bringing new love into your life.

4. For the way stones, place the six green Aventurine stones around the Rose Quartz stone. They will help charge the grid with love and attract new opportunities.

5. The six clear Quartz are the *desire* stones, which you'll place around the six green Aventurine stones. They will intensify the energy of the other stones.

6. Activate the grid.

Now that you know how to make a grid, you can customize your own using different love stones mentioned earlier. Each stone has a function, so you can either use different pieces of the same stone or combine various types. For instance, if you want to attract new love and heal from a past wound simultaneously, you can use Rose Quartz for the focus and way stones since they can fulfill both purposes. Or you can use Rhodonite as way stones to manifest forgiveness and help you heal. You can use clear pointers of Quartz stones as desired stones. Experiment with different types of grid shapes, arrangements, and crystals, and remember to always follow your heart when practicing gridwork.

Love is all around us. All you need to do is set your intention, place your crystals, and let the universe do the rest. Open yourself up and prepare your heart to give and receive love. Have faith in the universe and believe you are worthy of healing and unconditional love from yourself and others.

Chapter 6: Crystal Grids for Money and Career

When we think of money, the colors green and yellow immediately come to mind. While it's true that yellow and green healing stones can help us manifest wealth and prosperity, our financial stability and career success are also associated with various other colors and crystals.

Several red healing stones can be used to help us manifest financial stability. Red is the root chakra color, which is essentially responsible for our feelings of security, protection, and satiation. Those with an imbalanced root chakra may become greedy. Rather than pure selfishness, this sense of greed is instigated by the fear that they will run out of money and struggle financially. These individuals typically grew up in an environment where money was a concern. If you wish to manifest abundance, you must first release all blockages and let go of all the beliefs and behaviors that hold you back. Using healing stones to balance your root chakra is one way to do so.

An imbalanced solar plexus chakra may lead to procrastination, especially regarding financial matters. Money management issues are among the most prominent symptoms of a blocked solar plexus chakra. The affected individual often finds themselves buried beneath a mountain of debt and experiencing the consequences of poor financial decisions. Using yellow healing stones can help you develop a more mindful mindset when it comes to your personal finances.

You may be surprised to learn that green is the heart chakra color. Most people think this chakra has to do with matters of the heart, but this isn't always the case. While the heart chakra governs our ability to give and receive love, this energy center is also related to how we make our money choices. When our heart chakra is balanced, we don't let our emotions guide our purchases. Since green and pink are the colors of this chakra, associated healing stones can help you make professional and monetary decisions rationally.

People with blocked throat chakra typically struggle with debt because they have trouble asking for help. We all struggle with our finances at times. Knowing when it's time to ask for advice can help us keep our heads above water. Using blue crystals can help us admit that we need to improve how we manage our money.

Activating the third-eye chakra can help us visualize financial abundance and promote wise spending habits. This chakra is also associated with our intuition, inspiration, and creativity, which means nurturing it is essential when seeking professional success. Purple healing stones can help you activate your third-eye chakra.

In this chapter, you'll find out which healing stones you can use to achieve abundance, wealth, prosperity, and success in your career. You will also discover which layouts work best for these purposes. Here, you will find step-by-step instructions on how to set up your crystal grids.

Crystals for Wealth, Prosperity, and Career Success

Pyrite

It is no surprise that Pyrite is one of the best crystals for manifesting wealth and abundance. After all, it is popularly known as "Fool's Gold." While this healing stone may not be worth as much as actual gold, it can help you achieve prosperity. This stone can also help you experience career success as it allows you to unleash your skills, improve your communication, and release all the blocks that lie on your path. You can work on building self-trust and diminishing self-doubt, as well as building a robust professional network by using Pyrite.

Citrine

If you take a glance at a Citrine crystal, you'll immediately sense that this crystal can attract wealth and abundance into your life. This bright yellow healing stone can be a confidence booster, especially regarding fulfilling financial plans. Citrine is also known for radiating positivity. Placing this crystal near a window in your workspace can greatly contribute to your professional success.

Sunstone

This is another healing stone that can help you overcome your self-doubts. Nothing can halt your career as much as a lack of faith in your abilities. Using a Sunstone can help you maintain optimism throughout your professional journey. It can also help you become a better communicator, leader, and decision-maker.

Sodalite

Sodalite is the perfect crystal to bring balance to matters of the mind and the heart. When you are at a crossroads and can't decide whether to go with your emotions or let logic take the reins, use this healing stone to achieve some clarity. Sodalite can help you enhance your problem-solving skills and adopt a positive thinking philosophy in life. This stone can be very useful when taking a stand in your career. It promotes confidence and ensures that you communicate your views effectively.

Green Jade

Green Jade has been associated with wealth, abundance, and prosperity for centuries. It promotes harmony in several aspects of life, making it easier for you to keep your composure and think logically and clearly. These are all essential aspects of manifesting wealth and financial stability.

Malachite

Malachite is another crystal that is associated with confidence, resilience, and strength. You can benefit from using this stone when you seem to be experiencing numerous life changes. Malachite will give you the strength to keep advancing towards your goals even when challenges come your way. This stone corresponds to the heart chakra, meaning it will help you stay passionate in terms of your monetary goals. Working toward achieving financial abundance is not an easy journey. You may feel compelled to give up on your goals. That said, Malachite will ensure that you stay on track.

Amethyst

Amethyst.
MAURO CATEB from Brazil, CC BY 2.0
<https://creativecommons.org/licenses/by/2.0>, via Wikimedia Commons:
https://commons.wikimedia.org/wiki/File:Brazilian_amethysts_(6330378228).jpg

Amethyst can help you restore peace and balance to your life. It can also diminish your stress and anxiety, allowing you to get in touch with your ultimate life purpose. This healing stone will allow you to stay connected to your spirituality even when you get all caught up in financial issues. This way, you can remain focused on the bigger picture and stop dabbling in areas that don't serve you.

Carnelian

Carnelian can help you work toward a successful future. This healing stone can grant you the motivation you need to get things done.

Green Aventurine

This stone is known for its ability to attract good fortune and abundance. When you use Green Aventurine, you'll find opportunities springing up wherever you go. This healing stone can help you manifest your financial goals and guide you toward a successful career. Green Aventurine teems with positive energy and can aid with communication. Use this stone if you need help discovering your passions in life.

Rose Quartz

Rose Quartz is another heart chakra healing stone that can help you open yourself up to rewarding opportunities. Opening your heart chakra opens you to receiving abundance, light, love, trust, and good fortune. It allows you to accept promising options that you may have turned your back on in the past.

Amazonite

Amazonite is one of the most effective stones for abundance and success, making it particularly effective for manifesting monetary satisfaction, happiness, and professional success. Use this stone to boost your work ethic, remain focused on your goals, and maintain positive emotions.

Clear Quartz

Clear Quartz is a very special crystal that magnifies the energy you surround it with. You can use this to your advantage whenever you're laying down your financial goals or setting abundance and wealth-related intentions. Keep a Clear Quartz around when planning how to achieve these goals. For best results, combine this crystal with another money and wealth healing stone.

Tiger's Eye

Tiger's Eye is believed to bring good fortune and luck into one's life. It can also give them the strength, patience, resilience, and best of all, determination to stay on the path to achieving financial stability and career advancement. Using a Tiger's Eye can help you stay rooted and grounded, reminding you of the things that matter the most. Many people think carrying it around can help you get promoted, make better decisions, become a superb communicator, and grasp a better sense of the present.

Garnet

A Garnet can help you improve your overall quality of living. This stone is associated with abundance, wealth, and aspirations. A Garnet can help you release all negative energy, garner strength, and enrich your soul. Working with this stone will remind you of your capabilities and your ability to make great things happen. It is rich with passion, joy, wonder, and positivity.

Agate

Agate is commonly used to replenish your self-confidence and boost your courage. Using this stone can encourage you to take steps toward inner healing. By obtaining this sense of stability, you'll eventually be able to take risks. Whether these risks drive you to invest in the stock market, chase your dreams, or ask for a promotion, Agate will undoubtedly help you achieve prosperity.

Peridot

At times, our own negative emotions and insecurities in life can stop us from improving our financial status. Getting rid of these blockages is the most important step in manifesting abundance and wealth. If you're looking to do so, Peridot is the right crystal for your needs.

Selenite

Selenite is ideal for energy cleansing practices. It releases negative energy from the space around it while bringing in the positive energy to help you connect with the highest aspect of yourself. Using this stone can help free your mind and heart from issues that no longer serve you, so you can make space for better opportunities. Selenite will help you focus on what matters to your financial and professional success. By driving away all the negative aspects of your life, whether they're people, situations, or even places, you'll open yourself up to the abundance that awaits you.

Crystal Grids

As you now know, creating a crystal grid is not a complicated endeavor. Besides the crystals, you don't need many supplies to get started. You will need around 35 to 40 crystals to set up the crystal grids we'll mention below. However, if you don't have that many crystals at your disposal, don't let this stop you! You can use any elements of nature, such as flowers, petals, leaves, or even shells instead. If you have more than the ones required in each grid, you can use more if you'd like to.

We will mainly use Citrine, Clear Quartz, Yellow Jade, Pyrite, Mahogany Obsidian, Tiger's Eye, Amethyst, Blue Lace Agate, Golden Labradorite, Polychrome Jasper, Red Jasper, Green Jade, and White Agate. That said, you can still incorporate any of the other stones mentioned above. Remember to allow your intuition to guide you. So, if you feel inclined to use Malachite instead of Blue Lace Agate as one of the grids, you're free to do that. Choose the stones that align with your purpose and the ones you believe will yield the best results for your needs. The most important thing is that you set your intention clearly.

Using crystal grids with pre-printed sacred geometry is much easier to follow, especially for beginners. It's also said that combining sacred geometry with crystal grids amplifies their power. If you don't have ready-made templates, you can set your crystals directly on a surface or use a crystal grid cloth. Adding candles, incense, and essential oils that are relevant to money matters can also be of great help.

There are numerous crystal grids to help you promote career advancement and abundance. However, we recommend using the following layouts:

- The Flower of Life
- The Octagram
- The Tree of Life
- Triangle, Octagram, and Circle

Prosperity and Abundance Crystal Grid

Tools and Crystals

- 8 Clear Quartz crystals
- 3 Pyrite Tumble stones
- 3 Yellow Jade Tumble stones
- 1 large Citrine

This crystal grid is a combination of the Octagram, which can help you open yourself up to growth, development, prosperity, and abundance, and the Flower of Life, which can aid with manifesting.

Instructions

1. Set your intention: "I am using this crystal grid to attract prosperity and abundance into my life."
2. Use the large citrine crystal as the central stone.
3. Place the 3 Yellow Jade stones in the shape of an upright triangle around the central stone.
4. Place the 3 Pyrite stones in the shape of a downward-facing triangle around the central stone.
5. The Yellow Jade and Pyrite Stones should create a circle around the Citrine.
6. Use 4 Clear Quartz stones to shape a square around the other stones (one at each corner).
7. Use the other 4 Clear Quartz to shape a diamond surrounding the square you just formed.

Crystal Grid to Attract Wealth

Tools and Crystals

- 6 Clear Quartz stones
- 1 large Pyrite stone

This is a Flower of Life crystal grid. As you know, this is a powerful, universal, all-purpose grid and manifestation tool.

Instructions

1. Set your intention: "I am using this crystal grid to attract wealth into my life."
2. Set the Flower of Life Crystal Grid in front of you.
3. Place the large Pyrite in the center of the grid.
4. Use the Clear Quartz as the support stones, laying them out on the grid to create a circle around the Pyrite.

Crystal Grid for Success

Tools and Crystals

- 8 Mahogany Obsidian stones
- 3 Pyrite stones
- 1 large Tiger's Eye stone

This crystal grid combines three symbols: the Triangle, which boosts creativity and helps with manifestation, the Octagram, which keeps you determined and promotes success – and the Circle, which is needed for commitment and focus.

Instructions

1. If you want, find a picture of the diagram, and place it in front of you to amplify the results of the grid.
2. Set your intention: "I am using this crystal grid to attract success into my life."
3. Place the large Tiger's Eye stone in the center.
4. Place the eight Mahogany Obsidian stones around it in the shape of a circle.
5. Use the three Pyrite stones to form a triangle around the circle.

Balance and Prosperity Crystal Grid

Tools and Crystals
- 1 Amethyst stone
- 1 Blue Lace Agate stone
- 1 Citrine stone
- 1 Golden Labradorite stone
- 1 Polychrome Jasper stone
- 1 Red Jasper stone
- 1 White Agate stone
- 1 Green Jade stone
- 1 Orange Calcite stone
- 1 Black Tourmaline stone
- 1 Green Aventurine Stone

This crystal grid is in the shape of the Tree of life. It's a very powerful tool to manifest balance, prosperity, and healing.

Instructions

1. Place the Tree of Life grid card in front of you.
2. Set your intention: "I am using this crystal grid to attract balance and prosperity into my life."
3. Place the Green Jade in the second to last spot down the center of the diagram.
4. Moving clockwise, place the Orange Calcite in the spot next to it.
5. Continue moving in the same direction, placing the Red Jasper, followed by the Black Tourmaline, White Agate in the top center, then Green Aventurine, Blue Lace Agate, and then Amethyst.
6. Once you reach the center, place the Golden Labradorite below the Green Jade and the Citrine above it, followed by the Polychrome Jasper.

Attracting wealth and job success into your life requires you to work with your root, solar plexus, heart, throat, and third-eye chakras. Fortunately, there are numerous stones that you can incorporate into your daily practice to yield the desired results. Now that you understand which geometrical shapes and crystal grids work best for this purpose, you can use your intuition to create your own combinations of healing stones.

Chapter 7: Crystal Grids for Health and Healing

Arranging crystals in a specific pattern to channel the vital life force during the healing process is far more efficient than using individual stones. This is because you have at your disposal the collective healing vibrations of all the stones you use in your grid. These vibrations resonate on much higher levels. When combined with a powerful healing intention, crystals in certain geometrical formations can cleanse the mind, body, and soul. They can also alleviate the symptoms of many diseases or injuries far better than individual stones can. The latter feature can come in handy when distance healing is needed. The more power you can combine with your intention, your healing session will be more effective. Naturally, you can also use crystal grids to empower yourself or your loved ones in person by relieving physical or mental symptoms. Crystal can be used for clearing mental blocks, finding spiritual peace, or simply a way to freely express your creativity.

The placement of the stones can determine their effect, and in more ways than one. As we established earlier, placing crystals in different layouts gives them diverse empowerment forms. Besides making them stronger, their healing and nurturing effects will also depend on which patterns are used. For example, there are different grids to chase away depression, soothe a restless mind, or establish an overall sense of well-being. Moreover, where you put the grid will also impact its effect on your mind, body, and soul. You can put them under the table when working someone's chakras, instruct them to put them under their beds, or place them under your pillow while sleeping. In any case, forming a crystal grid is a spiritual act, and it involves the manipulation of energy. Cleansing your space and tools before a session is always a good idea. However, when using crystals for healing, you must be even more vigilant about the purity of the energy you are nurturing them with. It will be up to you whether you use smudging or any other cleansing method.

Recommended Crystals for Health and Wellness

Since healing can mean many things, the number of crystals you can use in healing grid work is also significant. The crystals play a crucial part in the grid work, so make sure to choose the most appropriate ones for your intention. If your goal is to enhance health and well-being, the crystals you choose to incorporate should align with that purpose. As for the colors, purple and blue crystals work best for health and wellness but feel free to choose white and stones in a color linked to a particular chakra you are trying to heal. If the intention is to soothe someone's nerves, use light blue and clear stones as these have more relaxing effects.

Here are some of the most commonly used healing crystals and their effects:

- **Obsidian:** Useful for protection against physical and emotional traumas and to help process the emotions and experiences that come with these conditions. It can show you the pathway to find your inner strength and clear any emotional blockages.

- **Sodalite:** By encouraging rational thought formations, this stone brings peace to your mind. It helps verbalize your emotions and speak your inner truth. This can help you avoid stressful situations and depression due to an inability to express your desires.

- **Clear Quartz:** Thanks to its ability to cleanse the entire energetic system, this stone is often considered one of the most powerful healers. Clear quartz can alleviate the symptoms of multiple chakra blockages by amplifying the positive energy that enters your body. It also helps cognitive function.

- **Jasper:** Nurtures the spirit and helps keep it high during stressful times, allowing you to combat stress, anxiety, and other consequences of being under pressure. It acts as a shield against negative energy and promotes positive thought processes, no matter how tough the situations you find yourself in.

Jasper.

Linas Juozėnas, CC BY-SA 4.0 <https://creativecommons.org/licenses/by-sa/4.0>, via Wikimedia Commons: https://commons.wikimedia.org/wiki/File:Picture-jasper.jpg

- **Rose Quartz:** While typically used to encourage love and trust in relationships, this stone can also help you overcome the loss of your loved ones. It also promotes self-love, which is essential for spiritual and mental health.

- **Citrine:** By opening the avenues of creativity, this stone can spark your enthusiasm for life, allowing you to be emotionally stable. It's also a concentration booster, which helps you become more productive and experience a sense of fulfillment.

- **Ruby:** Restores vitality, giving you more energy for all the activities you need to do to keep yourself healthy and happy. In parallel, it brings you emotional awareness and the ability to differentiate truth from fiction.

- **Turquoise:** Soothes painful emotions and helps you understand what you can't change. It's often used in grounding exercises or when the goal is to strengthen physical and emotional immunity.
- **Sapphire:** Like the previous stone, this blue stone is also used to attain spiritual relaxation and prosperity. It provides you with the wisdom you need to keep your health in check.
- **Moonstone:** Promotes inner growth and builds up strength for new beginnings. Use this stone to envision a positive outlook instead of stressing out about unfamiliar experiences, so you can embark on new ventures with clear mental health.
- **Tiger's Eye:** A great motivation booster, this stone eliminates fear, self-doubt, and other negative emotions that hinder your mental productivity. It helps you find spiritual balance and make well-informed decisions about your health.
- **Bloodstone:** By encouraging the flow of the vital life force towards and within your body, this stone promotes blood circulation and the flow of constructive ideas. It eliminates impatience and lets you focus on the solution instead of the problem.
- **Prehnite:** Effective against restlessness and disturbed nerves, it lowers the heart rate, allows you to breathe deeply, and achieves clarity of the mind.
- **Smoky Quartz:** Helps dispel trepidation and anxiety, chases away nightmares, and replaces them with dreams where your mind processes emotions and thoughts more healthily.
- **Howlite:** This stone can absorb negative energy from your body, bringing you comfort and a worry-free mind and spirit.

- **Celestite:** Channels a gentle stream of positive energy to release all worries and fears without overwhelming you with the sudden energy shift.
- **Lepidolite:** Relieves symptoms of stress, anxiety, and depression. It is particularly effective for fighting off nightmares and other sleeping disorders.

Geometrical Patterns to Use

The most common geometrical patterns used for crystal grids are square, spiral, circle, triangle, and rhomboid. There are also more complex patterns, such as the five platonic solids. Here, we explain which of these are the most helpful for healing and why.

Cube

A cube symbolizes the earth's grounding energy and your experiences in the physical environment, catering to basic human needs for safety and reassurance. It may also represent the connection between the physical body and the rational mind. This ability is often used to release mental stress through the body. If your goal is to create a foundation for a healthier life or clear the existing one of negative influences, the cube is the perfect pattern to use in gridwork.

Metatron's Cube

An upgraded version of the previous pattern, Metatron's cube, is associated with an angel. Whether you use Metatron as your spiritual guide or another entity, this layout will help you reach out to the spiritual realm and connect to them. Upon doing this, you are opening your soul to new experiences, leaving behind any limiting beliefs and negative thought patterns that cause your restlessness. This will help you find your purpose and embrace it, establishing a healthy mindset that can be calmed anytime you want it to be relaxed.

The Flower of Life

Just as a flower has many seeds that can grow into unique plants, the Flower of Life layout teaches us that although each of us has the same exact biological blueprint, we are still different from one another. It can help you accept that it's all right to process emotions in a certain way, as long as it brings you a sense of inner balance. This has a generally calming effect on your mind, body, and soul.

Circle

The circle represents an infinite polygon that's often equated with wholeness and eternity. It may also symbolize perfection, but only in a spiritual capacity. It's used by those wanting to ascend to a higher spiritual level. For this to happen, you must first embrace all the qualities lying within the circle. The layout is used to move forward and release emotional baggage when viewed as a circle in motion.

Icosahedron

The icosahedron is the simplest one of the five platonic solids, which is used to clear away limiting beliefs. It can teach you how to accept the natural flow of life and embrace all your experiences, good or bad. The layout may also help unblock your creativity and find ways to express your thoughts and emotions. It gives back control over everything you want to communicate with yourself and the outside world, balances your feelings, and transforms your life into a more purposeful one.

Dodecahedron

The dodecahedron is perpetually linked to the vital life force. This makes it ideal for when you need empowerment through spiritual wisdom. Due to this, its use is often combined with meditation or other mindfulness techniques. Since it is already attuned to natural frequencies, the grid raises your vibrations more efficiently. It also helps transform the energy of the space you are using it in, creating the perfect environment for relaxation. In this state, you can identify chakra imbalances, blockages, and even physical issues that must be addressed to restore one's health.

Merkabah

The Merkabah layout creates an incredibly powerful energy field. It can assist with stronger blockages when you need more force to recreate the balance between the opposing energies. This specific arrangement raises vibrations to the levels required to heal physical and mental traumas or achieve spiritual growth. The high frequencies facilitate the connection with your inner strength, even if you haven't been aware of this power before.

Octahedron

The octahedron typically resonates with your feelings, both positive and negative ones. It helps you uncover hidden desires and see what emotions these bring out. It may also allow you to explore the reasons behind certain emotional reactions to events, objects, or people in your environment. The octahedron can open up your heart to new experiences, including unconditional love toward yourself. You can learn how to forgive yourself and stop worrying over past actions. This layout nurtures your essence and stimulates emotional creativity when included in a spiritual healing process.

Tetrahedron

The tetrahedron symbolizes groundedness and unity, often considered the most stable of the platonic solids. Its frequencies enhance manifestation, spiritual awakening, and protection against malicious intent. Since one of its ends always points to the sky, it's also used for achieving mental clarity and enlightenment. Moreover, the grid provides a firm foundation for emotional development and spiritual connections. It's often combined with different forms of quartz crystals and sodalite, as these enhance its ability to connect to higher frequencies and experience a complete spiritual awakening.

Reiki Symbols and Crystal Healing

Crystal grids can be combined with many other alternative healing techniques and tools, including Reiki. This can be especially useful when using the distant healing symbol or Hon Sha ze Sho Nen. Reiki practitioners use this symbol for sending restorative energy across time and space. So, what better to ensure the power gets to its rightful destination than empowering your Hon Sha ze Sho Nen with vibrations from a crystal grid?

There is also a pattern called the Reiki grid. It uses 14 crystals (12 outside, 1 in the center, and 1 for the master stone) that align with the intention of channeling Reiki energy towards the body. The stones are aligned according to a pattern that brings peace and health or a Reiki symbol, such as Sei he ki.

Grid Suggestions for Health and Wellness

The number of grid and stone combinations you can implement in your healing practice is virtually limitless. Here are some suggestions for healing grid recipes to try.

A Grid for Soothing a Restless Mind

More often than not, your brain will want to process every stimulus before resting. If it can't do this, you may find your mind racing with thought after thought just when you are getting ready to sleep. This grid recipe can help you soothe your mind and enjoy better sleep.

You'll Need

- Rose quartz
- Clear quartz
- Smoky quartz
- Howlite
- Amethyst
- Lepidolite
- Celestite
- Prehnite
- Moonstone
- A grid with a pattern for releasing stress, such as Cube or Metatron's Cube

Instructions

1. Select your crystals and cleanse them before arranging them on the grid.
2. Place the formations under your bed or on your nightstand before going to sleep.
3. Enjoy your night's sleep while your crystals spread relaxing energy around you.

A Grid for Fending Off Depression

There is no better way to fend off depression than by connecting to nature through an empowering crystal grid. The grid below will help with this, as well as being used for replacing negative thoughts with positive ones.

You'll Need
- A Flower of Life grid pattern
- Pieces of white cloth
- Howlite
- Lepidolite
- Tiger's eye
- Citrine
- Bloodstone
- Rose quartz

Instructions
1. Place the crystals on your grid and charge them with your intention. Do this in an area where you spend most of your time but where the stones won't be displaced.
2. Leave the grid in plain sight to remind you of your intention to chase away negative thoughts and fend off symptoms of depression.

A Grid for Alleviating Physical Symptoms

While crystals are typically geared towards spiritual healing, the sacred geometry used in gridwork can also be the perfect tool for alleviating physical symptoms. It is best combined with other methods devised for physical healing, such as Reiki hand placement or chakra balancing methods.

You'll Need
- A dodecahedron pattern
- Jasper
- Amethyst
- Bloodstone
- Obsidian
- Clear quartz
- Ruby

Instructions

1. Cleanse your stones thoroughly before forming the grid.
2. Perform the healing technique you are combining the grid with.

A Grid to Promote Overall Well-Being

You can benefit from crystal healing even if you don't suffer from any health conditions. This grid is designed to boost your immune system, cognitive function, and emotional and spiritual stability so you can prevent injuries and keep illnesses at bay.

You'll Need
- Bloodstone
- Ruby stones
- Smoky quartz
- Clear quartz
- A square piece of red paper or cloth
- A square piece of green paper or cloth
- An Icosahedron grid

Instructions

1. Place the red piece of cloth on the area you are working on. Put the green one on top of the red one by aligning it diagonally.
2. Gather your supplies and cleanse them before arranging your stones according to the pattern.
3. Create an intention that affirms your positive state of health. This will help you keep it that way.
4. Activate the grid and let it be until you feel the need for its restorative energy.

All crystal and grid suggestions are optional. The number of stones you need depends on the pattern you are using. You can replace or add other crystals if you feel a connection (or lack thereof) to a particular stone. Feel free to do the same if you think certain healing stones will help you set your intention better than others.

Chapter 8: Crystal Grids for Psychic Development and Protection

Using your psychic abilities requires a high concentration level that you'll only achieve through spiritual development. There are many ways to enhance your abilities, and one of them is to ask for the assistance of a spiritual guide. They can also provide the protection you need when communicating with the spiritual realm. This chapter is dedicated to the different spiritual benefactors and using crystal grids to work with them. Remember, the layouts and the stones you implement into your psychic practice have just as much bearing on your development as the guides themselves.

Working with Spiritual Guides

Everyone has their spiritual guides, beings that accompany you during one or more periods of your life. Some are only there for a short time, while others stay longer and can be contacted whenever you need guidance or protection. Sometimes, they will even send subtle signs of their presence or a message they want you to acknowledge. Other times, you will need to reach out on your own and get to know your spiritual guide more before they can assist you.

Common Spirit Guides

Ascended Masters

Ascended Masters are spirits that have achieved the highest levels of spirituality through devotion, practice, and teaching of their craft. They continue to empower the next generation of practitioners from the spiritual world. Their spirits are typically contacted by those who focus on energy work and can assist several people during one session.

Angels

There are several types of angels that can empower your psychic development, beginning with your own guardian angel. Since they are dedicated only to you, they will be the easiest to contact. There are also helper angels, who are willing to help out anyone in need in case their own guardian is not around or if they haven't found it yet. Finally, there are the archangels, the leaders of the angelic world. They only work with empaths and people who have transcended to the highest levels of spirituality.

Ancestral Spirits

These are the souls of your loved ones who continue to watch over you after departing from this world. You may have several ancestor guides at your disposal, but you'll receive assistance from those who can help you in each situation. Sometimes, it will be a relative with whom you had a close connection in their lifetime and who has just recently passed away. Other times, you may receive a visit from a long-dead ancestor you never met but who wishes to guide you, nevertheless.

Common Guides

These are typically the spirits you first encounter when contacting the spiritual world in search of a guide. They can appear in many forms, although they are usually known for taking the shape of the spiritual guidance you need or are looking for. After guiding you to a particular path and letting you familiarize yourself with the spiritual world, they will either reveal your true guide or show you how to contact them yourself and then move on to help someone else.

Animal Spirits

Like departed ancestors, animal spirits also linger around to keep you company and shepherd you in your spiritual development. These can be the souls of deceased pets or even animals you haven't ever seen before. The former are great helpers when you need spiritual empowerment to overcome grief or similar difficulties. The latter will appear when you need guidance on a larger scale of life or protection from powerful malicious spirits.

Discovering Your Spiritual Guide

If you are yet to establish a connection with your spiritual guide, you may find this process a little challenging because when getting to know a person you are trying to build a relationship with, you must establish trust and develop some ground rules. Here is a little exercise to find your spiritual guide and get to know what they like and how they communicate:

- Find a quiet place, take Obsidian (or any crystal that helps you form a spiritual connection) into your hands, and sit comfortably.

- Close your eyes and take a few deep breaths until you feel completely grounded.

- Now, start focusing on the different stimuli you perceive in your environment.

- Take notice of anything you may hear, see, or smell. This could be a subtle message your guide sends you to help you find the gate to the spiritual world.

- Visualize this gate and enter, but stay close to it and wait for your spiritual guide to come to you.

- When they do, ask them if they are your guide. If the answer is yes, you may ask questions about them and discuss how they can help you. Ask them to take you to your guide if they aren't your guide.

- When you feel you've learned everything you can about your guide, thank them for their assistance and visualize yourself traveling back to the physical world.

- Put the crystal you used under your pillow. Your spiritual guide will recognize it as the tool you used to contact them, and by seeing you keep it close, they will know that you are interested in working with them.

Crystals for Protecting and Enhancing Your Intuition

There are many crystals for enhancing psychic powers and empowering your intuition. While all have their advantages, the ones you will be using must feel right for you as this is where you start to rely on your intuitiveness.

Here are the best crystals for spiritual protection, communication, and psychic development.

Black Obsidian

Black Obsidian.
The High Fin Sperm Whale, CC BY-SA 3.0 <https://creativecommons.org/licenses/by-sa/3.0>, via Wikimedia Commons: https://commons.wikimedia.org/wiki/File:Black_obsidian.JPG

Black Obsidian is one of the best stones to use for reconnecting with your intuitive powers. It helps create balance in your energetic system, heal you all the way around, and prepare you for a higher purpose. Black Obsidian is great for clearing out negative energy before you get in touch with your spiritual guides, so they can't prevent them from intercepting your messages. It can also be a mediator to heal traumas suffered by your ancestors, which were passed on to you, creating a bond between you. Lastly, the stones elevate your consciousness to a level where the use of psychic abilities comes to you naturally and effortlessly.

Amethyst

By removing energetic blockages, Amethyst makes you more receptive to the messages sent by your spiritual guide. It also helps you get in touch with higher knowledge (including your guides) and learn how to trust your gut. With the help of this stone, you become more aware of the truth, the one you are looking for when using your psychic abilities. By preparing you on how to react to changes in your energy system, the stone enhances your powers of clairvoyance, revealing the path towards profound insight.

Blue Apatite

Blue Apatite is one of the best crystals for communicating with your ancestral spirits. By providing insight into your ancestors' lives, this stone can help you understand them better. This will allow you to understand their messages each time you contact them. It will also enable you to send clear messages about wanting protection, guidance, or answers to your divinatory questions. Blue Apatite is also beneficial for releasing any mental blocks caused by the past transgression of your ancestors. This will provide you access to the next level of psychic consciousness.

Lapis Lazuli

A stone is known for its ability to promote spiritual revelations, starting from your own inner wisdom. Once you pass the stage of self-discovery, you can practice using the stone to develop your intuition and contact your spiritual guides. It teaches you to listen to how your body reacts to energetic changes when receiving spiritual messages. Through this, Lapis Lazuli allows you to pick up hints from your environment, strengthening your psychic abilities in the process.

Sodalite

Sodalite calms your mind and allows you to see things more clearly, including what was unknown until then. It stops you from overanalyzing everything, notably the messages you get from your spiritual benefactors. By encouraging you to accept them as they are, the stone elevates your spirit to a higher level of consciousness. When working with Sodalite, you also learn how to pick up subtle frequencies, which is an essential skill for developing your abilities in clairvoyance.

Labradorite

When you want insights into your past life rather than your ancestors' lives, you should call on the powers of Labradorite to assist you. This stone can open your mind to revelations about your spiritual purpose, including the reasons for your present gut feelings. It will help you understand how your intuition works, so you can learn to trust it regarding divination, telepathy, and other psychic practices.

Serpentine

This is a gemstone recommended for developing your intuitions. It works by realigning your chakras to restore the uninterrupted energy flow throughout your body. Every time you receive a message from your spiritual benefactors, you can rely on this stone to translate it and answer appropriately. Whether you need guidance, help with divination, or anything else, Serpentine will place the answer into a higher perspective, eliminating all the confusion. This will elevate your spirit once you understand what's inevitable and what you can change with actions.

Kyanite

Kyanite is another gemstone believed to enhance one's abilities in clairvoyance. It can help you channel energy, reveal divination, and amplify your intuitive powers. Through this, Kyanite will let you uncover hidden spiritual gifts and talents. It also facilitates communication with your spiritual guide and lets them know when you need protection or an answer to a pressing question.

Clear Quartz

Clear Quartz is one of the most commonly used crystals for cleansing your energy system, which allows you to see everything more clearly. By incorporating this stone into your grid, any spiritual message you receive will bring you closer to a higher purpose. It's often applied for dream divination, as this is the best time for you to access its cleansing powers. In your dreams, you can let go of any misconception, prejudice, or unproductive thought pattern that prevented you from reaching your full psychic potential. When you wake up, you'll be ready to listen to your intuition and accept whatever is telling you as truth.

Sacred Layouts to Empower Your Psychic Development

Each sacred shape has its own way of helping you develop your intuition. Below are listed the most beneficial layouts for this purpose. Some are more suitable for those with a higher spiritual development level, while newbies can also use others.

Triangle

As one of the simplest of all grid layouts, a triangle can be a handy tool for practicing the use of psychic abilities. It already symbolizes a higher level of consciousness, as you can see from it pointing upward. The triangle can help you open the gates of spirituality through balance represented by its sides.

Tetrahedron

Because it is connected with the fire element, the tetrahedron is the ideal layout to relight the inner fire of your intuition. This will fuel your inner desires, allowing them to be realized, become fulfilled, and empower you spiritually. These patterns can also help you accept responsibility in your practice, including in your relationship with your spiritual guide. All sides of the tetrahedron point to the higher levels of spirituality, indicating that the only way is up.

Dodecahedron

The dodecahedron is known for increasing vibration levels to a higher spiritual plane, making it perfect for those wanting to hone their psychic abilities. As the universal symbol of the sky and the heavens, the patterns allow you to form deeper bonds with your spiritual guides.

Merkaba

Although a more complex shape, the Merkaba is one of the most effective tools for enhancing physical powers. Its shape symbolizes opposing energies, which need to be balanced for you to obtain deeper levels of spiritual development. It can help you channel your abilities in the right direction. Even if you are looking for a grid for different purposes, you are reaching out to the most sacred of symbols by turning to this first.

Tips for Choosing the Appropriate Pattern

When it comes to healing, the secret to choosing the appropriate layout to connect with your spiritual guide is to set an intention for this. You can do this through meditation, grounding exercises, or even by using individual crystals as empowerment tools. If you are just starting your spiritual journey, you can begin by setting your intention for healing in general. This will help you get in touch with your intuition and listen to it when choosing the stones and layout for your grid. Rediscovering your intuition is also the first step on your journey toward psychic development. Each time you use grids to tap into your intuition, you also elevate your psychic abilities to a new level. And the more these grow, the more they will help you on your spiritual journey, including communicating with your spiritual guides.

Once you learn how to listen to your gut feeling, you can also set your intention on grounding or protection. The first will bring you closer to the spiritual world, and the second will establish contact with a helpful spirit or your personal guide. To do this, it's best to use stones like Smoky Quartz, Hematite, Bloodstone, or Red Jasper. These will block out the negative energy from your space and set a balance for you to develop your psychic abilities. Use stones like Selenite or Clear Quartz in the center of your grid to elevate your vibrations and get in touch with your spiritual guide.

Chapter 9: Crystal Grids for Spirit Communication

Besides reaching out to your spiritual guides for assistance with divination and healing practices, spiritual communication skills can also serve other purposes. For example, you can have a simple conversation with loved ones who recently passed away. It is believed that the souls of the departed linger in the spiritual world for some time before moving on. However, some souls remain for a longer period and may need a little encouragement on your part to help them to move on. This dedicated chapter will show you how to get in touch with your loved ones' spirits and keep their memory alive.

Communicating with Spirits through Gridwork

There are many reasons you may choose to contact the soul of your loved one and just as many reasons for them to contact you. Some spirits cannot move on, living very close to the border of the realms. When given the opportunity (for example, in your dreams), they will cross the border or send a message through other spirits who can do it for them. Either way, you will feel their presence, which can be rather intimidating. While your loved souls can't hurt you, they may be accompanied by other spirits that negatively influence them. Your loved ones' souls are more vulnerable to bad vibes, and they can very quickly transfer them over to you. For this reason, a significant part of your communication efforts should focus on providing protection from malicious spirits. Having done that, you can communicate with your loved ones more freely. Some just don't cross to the other side because they fear the unknown, have something left to say, or are reluctant to leave you behind. You can help your loved ones' souls by hearing the message they have yet to convey to you. You can also reassure them that moving on will be spiritually fulfilling for them and for you.

Unlike spiritual guides who are typically ready to be contacted or know how to reach out to you, the souls of your loved ones may not be familiar with spiritual communication. Now, unless they were versed in it during their lives or have lived in the spiritual world for a long time, communicating with you won't come as easy to them. So, to hear them, you must elevate your consciousness to a higher level and calm your mind so it can focus on the subtle messages it receives. Crystal grids can quickly lift your vibrations, allowing you to get in touch with their spirit and inquire about the reasons for staying in the spiritual world. Grids can be combined with any other remembrance, gratitude, and healing practices. They provide plenty of opportunities to connect to your loved ones' spirit.

Not only do crystal grids elevate your vibrations, but you can also use them to prompt the spirits to lower theirs, so you can meet in the middle.

The most straightforward way to communicate with spirits is to meditate beside a crystal grid you just charged with your intention.

Crystals That Facilitate Spiritual Communication

Plenty of crystals can naturally facilitate spirit communication and clarity to help you receive and understand the messages given to you. Here are some of the most commonly used ones.

Obsidian

As mentioned earlier, you will need plenty of protection when contacting the spiritual world. Obsidian can safeguard your energy from negative influences and ground you during and after the communication process. It also helps you develop your intuition, making it easier to decipher messages you have received from the spiritual world.

Jet

Jet is another crystal with a substantial grounding ability. It can serve as a tool for protection, especially if you are expecting a message when traveling either physically or spiritually. Jet brings you back to the present carefully, so you are not as confused after your arrival.

Selenite

Selenite is primarily used for cleansing your energetic system before communicating with the spiritual realm. However, you can make use of it during your communication as well. This stone will also cleanse the energy of the spirit you are reaching out to, facilitating your interaction.

Clear Quartz

Clear quartz.
Timon Jähnert, CC BY 2.0 <https://creativecommons.org/licenses/by/2.0>, via Wikimedia Commons: https://commons.wikimedia.org/wiki/File:Natural_Clear_Quartz_(48341137417).jpg

Just like the previous stone, this gemstone also purifies your energetic system. However, Clear Quartz also can amplify and channel your energy toward your intention. It can also create a passageway between this world and the spiritual realm, making it easier for you to contact the spirits and for them to reach out to you.

Charoite

Not only will this stone allow you to communicate with spirits, but it also channels all your energies in the right direction, so they can meet in the middle. Whether you prefer to receive messages through sounds, sights, smells, or impressions, Charoite will help you make it happen.

Blue Lace Agate

Unlike many other gemstones, Blue Lace Agate doesn't aid spirit communication by directly affecting your vibes. Instead, it balances out your emotions, making it easier for you to elevate your vibrations on your own and receive the appropriate messages from spirits.

Celestite

Celestite is typically used for establishing a connection with the spiritual world. It has a soothing effect, effectively dismissing the worries that often distract you when attempting to communicate with spirits. It can also gently transition you from being awake into a dream and allow you to perceive spiritual messages when sleeping. When you wake up, you'll be able to recall and interpret the information you've received.

Apophyllite

Apophyllite is another fantastic crystal for communicating with the spirits of your loved ones. It connects you with the spiritual world and enhances your ability to manifest during meditation practice. It also helps you remember the dreams that contain messages from spirits. This is because Apophyllite improves your cognitive functions, allowing your mind to rest and process your dreams during sleep. You will wake up with mind clarity and know what to do to help your loved ones' spirits.

Amethyst

By opening up your higher chakras, this gemstone allows you to reach a higher level of consciousness and awareness during spiritual communication practices. Amethyst will let you focus, so you and whatever spirit you are contacting can have a meaningful conversation, even if this happens during your dreams. When combined appropriately, this crystal also can protect your emotions.

Sacred Geometric Shapes to Use

In parallel, the sacred shapes of geometry will also come in handy when communicating with different spirits. Here are the most commonly used geometric patterns for crossing the barrier between this world and the spiritual realm.

Circle

The easiest way to connect to any spirit is by using a simple circle layout for your crystal grid. A circle symbolizes eternity and the endless continuation of life cycles. This can help you and the soul you are speaking to with the understanding that their departure is not the end of their journey. It's merely the gateway to another life; the sooner they move on, the sooner they can start life anew.

Flower of Life

While the flower of life grid is suitable for many other healing purposes, it works exceptionally well for spiritual communications. Because it facilitates forming a meaningful connection with any departed soul, both beginners and experienced practitioners can use it. Whether you knew the person well or not during their life, and whether you have experience establishing a spiritual connection, the flower of life will guide you through the process with ease.

Merkaba

Merkaba symbolizes body, light, and spirit. It requires you to pay attention to the communication ritual, teaching you the importance of each individual element. By learning how to cleanse and prepare this grid, you'll understand what helps you properly convey messages to and from the spiritual world and what not to do to avoid negative external influences.

Seed of Life

While the seed of life pattern is already contained within the flower of life, taking it out and using it as a standalone grid enhances its powers. In it, you'll find the symbols of creation, the harmonious cycles that reassure you about the continuation of life throughout the many realms of the universe. So, even if a soul isn't meant to return to this world right away, it will have a purpose elsewhere.

Tree of Life

The roots of this tree have a grounding effect and will raise your vibration to higher levels. This heals your energetic system and opens up your mind for spiritual communication with yourself and other souls inhabiting the spiritual world. On the other hand, the top of the tree depicts one's unity with the universe, which includes even the spiritual world. There is a strong parallel between this and the view of our psyche as a map with interconnected branches.

Metatron's Cube

With its spheres depicting feminine energy and its interconnecting straight lines representing masculine energy, Metatron's cube is the ultimate symbol of spiritual balance. By working together as a unified energy field, these opposing powers will teach you how to balance your thoughts and emotions and become more receptive to spiritual communication.

Vesica Pisces

This layout is a complex pattern full of similarities and differences. It includes several overlapping circles, representing the connection between this world and the spiritual one. The fish in the center of the Vesica Pisces symbol represents the creator of the universe who can help you get in touch with any soul inhabiting the spiritual world.

Celtic Knot

An empowered version of the circle and the infinity symbol, the Celtic knot layout represents the interconnectedness of different worlds and lives. It's another helpful reminder that our souls have a purpose and that our mission through all our life cycles should be to fulfill this purpose.

Icosahedron

Closely tied to the water element, Icosahedron represents our creativity and emotions. It's recommended for situations when you struggle to find common ground with a departed soul through traditional means like mediation, spells, ritual, and individual crystals. This layout will help you find other creative ways to exchange messages with them without running the risk of breaking your bond.

Pentagram

Lastly, the Pentagram is one of the oldest pagan symbols, commonly associated with Wiccan practices. It has five points depicting the five senses, emphasizing their importance in spiritual communications. After all, a spirit you haven't yet communicated with may not contact you in the way you expect them to. The pentagram grid will help you pick up on any hints they are dropping.

Additional Tips for Communicating with Spirits

If you are just dipping your toes into spiritual communication, it's advised that you start with simple grid shapes and only a few crystals. Using too many tools will confuse you and the soul you are trying to get in touch with and will only result in stress and disruptive behavior. Crystals are receptive to all types of energy. So, until you learn how to protect both yourself and your tools, using too many crystals will only raise the risk of exposing yourself to negative influences.

Listen to your intuition when picking out your stones, and focus only on the ones that truly speak to your vibrations. Sometimes, this is an early sign of a spirit trying to reach out to you. Apply the same principle when choosing which soul you will respond to. Communicating with spirits that hold too many negative emotions and refusing to let them go is not in your best interest. Focus on those who you can help and who will uplift your spirit.

In the beginning, you'll need to put in extra effort to stay focused on your intention of reaching out to a particular spirit. However, after a while, being intentional will be like second nature to you, and gridwork will help you with that. You just have to let it guide you to the basics of spiritual communication and embrace the positive messages you receive.

For newbies, besides having the grid beside you, it's also helpful to hold a grounding stone while communicating with a spirit. If they don't respond to you immediately, keep the stone in your hands for a few more minutes to see if they get back to you. At first, the messages you receive will come with much higher vibrations than your body is used to handling. You will need the grounding stone to stabilize your energy and keep your head clear, allowing you to interpret the messages correctly. This is because souls (especially those that recently passed on to the spiritual world) have a lot of emotions to process, and this causes them to have higher vibrations. It may take some time until they learn that they must slow down for you to understand them.

Spirits can contact you in many ways. You can wait until you hear back from the spirits you want to contact while meditating, or you can ask them to send their message later throughout the day. However, even after you reach out to them through your preferred means, there is no guarantee they will send the message back right away through that same channel. They may send it afterward, in your dreams. Those who recently passed away often find this to be the easiest way to communicate with those they left behind, knowing their messages will be received calmly without disturbing the recipient's emotions. Place the communication grid under your bed and prepare yourself to listen to your dreams. You may want to have paper and pen ready beside you to write or sketch what you saw in your dreams as soon as you wake up.

Chapter 10: Crystal Grids for the Home

Your home is your safe space and haven. It should be abundant in nurturing and protective energy. When your home is free of negative energy, it allows you to recharge from the complexities and stresses of the outside world. Tending to your home is also an act of self-care. At the end of the day, you get to go back to a calming retreat where you can pull the plug on the external world.

As you already know, healing crystals have been used in homes to get rid of negative emotions and pent-up bad vibes in all rooms and spaces and promote better sleep, prosperity, and abundance. Your home is where you can unwind and interact with the people you love the most. Using crystals and arranging them in mindful ways can help you communicate effectively with your family and housemates, protect your home from negative vibes that visitors may carry into your home, and promote a cozy, homey environment.

Since energy is easily transmitted, we can unintentionally bring negative energy into our homes after we've had a stressful work day or an argument with a loved one. Using protective healing stones to make crystal grids can help prevent this. When crystals secure your home, you can cultivate protective boundaries, keep yourself in an upbeat mood, create a loving and compassionate environment, promote creativity, and encourage positive interactions. When your home absorbs negative energy, it becomes dreary and triggers intrusive thoughts and feelings like frustration, anger, and sadness.

There are many ways you can use protective crystals to protect your home. While wearing them or carrying them around can be effective, we recommend placing them in your home's entryways to prevent bad energy from coming through. Crystal grids are, of course, one way to make the most of your protective crystals.

Healing stones can serve more than one purpose. You've probably come across most of the crystals we'll mention here in the previous chapters, too. In this one, you'll find a combination of stones that can help you block out negative energy and ones that carry attributes like safety and peace. Black crystals are typically the strongest protective healing stones. This is because they can endure negativity and maintain their prowess and stability. Black crystals can also shield your aura from toxic and negative energy, especially ones that may wish to bring problems to your home.

In this chapter, we will recommend healing stones that will beautify your home and ensure that it remains protected. You will also find out which crystal grid layouts you can use to enhance their properties.

Home Protection Healing Stones

The following are some home protection healing stones and how you can use them effectively:

Black Tourmaline

Keep near windowsills and doorways for protection.

Black Tourmaline has protective and healing energies. It can keep you grounded and help you eliminate negative energies in the environment. Keeping this crystal in your home, particularly beside windows and doorways, can make you feel safe whenever you enter your home. This stone will ensure that your home's energy remains protected regardless of the energy your visitors may carry.

Rose Quartz

Use this stone to ease connections and instill trust and compassion when tension arises.

This heart chakra healing stone radiates positive, compassionate, and gentle energy. If your family or roommates struggle to get along, Rose Quartz can help everyone open up. Working with this stone can heal the heart and elicit positive qualities like trust, tolerance, and empathy. This nurturing crystal can help dissolve tension and facilitate connection.

Blue Lace Agate

Keep near beds to promote tranquility and peaceful sleep.

Blue Lace Agate is as relaxing and calming as it looks. It emanates tranquility, and since it's associated with the throat chakra, it promotes effective communication. This healing stone can help alleviate your stress. Placing it near your bed can encourage a good, regenerative night's sleep.

Citrine

Use this stone for positive energy and abundance, especially during winter.

This bright, cheery healing stone will undoubtedly draw positive energy into your home. Citrine alleviates the mood of everyone around and is as effective as a good luck charm. Keep this crystal in your home to attract abundance and sunshine. If your home gets darker around winter, you can combat seasonal affective disorder by working with Citrine.

Amethyst

Work with Amethyst whenever you feel anxious or stressed and whenever you want to connect with your higher spiritual self.

Amethyst can help alleviate feelings of stress and anxiety, promoting an overall serene environment. This healing stone can help you combat brain fog and allow you to connect with the highest aspect of yourself. Keep this stone around your home when things get stressful to prevent negative energy from spreading indoors. If you're reading this book, then you're probably embarking on a spiritual or psychic journey. Working with this stone can be incredibly beneficial at a time like this.

Aquamarine

This healing stone can help keep you and your home safe in times of trouble. You can also use it to enhance your sleep.

Did you know that sailors were believed to carry Aquamarine for protection? It was said that this crystal could keep them from drowning. You can do the same with your own home! Whenever troubles come your way, you can use this stone to navigate safely through the rising tides. It's a superb tool for combating stress and overcoming toxic events. If you struggle with insomnia or other sleep-related issues, keep this stone beside your bed to help you fall asleep.

Selenite

Use this crystal whenever your home feels dark and out of balance.

If the vibes in your home have been feeling blocked lately, it's time to clear out this negative energy by using this crystal. Selenite can help you eliminate the heaviness in the air, bringing light and joy into your home. This stone not only unleashes its airy and positive metaphysical properties but also allows the natural light to shine through whenever the environment feels dull and dreary.

Carnelian

Use it when your house lacks joy, creativity, and nurturing homey energy.

This fiery, passionate healing stone brings warmness and optimism into the home. Use this stone whenever you're yearning for a spark of creativity or wish to hear laughter filling up this space. Carnelian is a nurturing, grounding, and comforting stone that can make your house feel more like home. Keeping it on the south side of your house can help you attract abundance into your life.

Clear Quartz

Keep in all rooms to manifest safety, protection, and positive energy.

Clear Quartz is the ideal cleansing and healing stone. It can help you bring your home protection and safety manifestations to life. Since Clear Quartz can help you achieve your desired things, you must set your intentions while working with this stone. You can make the most out of this crystal's energy by placing it in every room. This way, you'll ensure your entire space abounds with positive energy.

Green Aventurine

Keep Green Aventurine at home to boost productivity and promote healthy interactions.

Green Aventurine is widely known as the crystal of luck and opportunity. Its metaphysical properties gleam with positivity and comfort. This healing stone can help bring peace of mind and strengthen your bonds with others. It can help drive out negative energy, increase focus, and enhance memory. Place it near your desk or workspace to make the environment more productive. You can also use it whenever your housemates lack healthy interactions.

Lapis Lazuli

Lapis Lazuli.
Teravolt at English Wikipedia, CC BY 3.0 <https://creativecommons.org/licenses/by/3.0>, via Wikimedia Commons: https://commons.wikimedia.org/wiki/File:LapisLazuli.JPG

Lapis Lazuli can protect your home from harmful energies and support your spiritual practices.

Many ancient cultures used this blue-shaded stone to ward off psychic attacks. Lapis Lazuli was also associated with art, creativity, and royalty. Use this healing stone to maintain emotional balance or even support your dreamwork endeavors. This crystal can help you keep your home protected from energy vampires and other intrusive energies.

Hematite

Keep Hematite at home to protect its energy at all times and benefit from its focus-driven, encouraging attributes.

Hematite is associated with vigor and magic. Working with this crystal can instill determination, give you courage and strength, and boost your willpower. Hematite can protect your home because it works to eliminate potentially harmful energies. It is rich in grounding energies and can help you stay focused and on task.

Smoky Quartz

Use Smoky Quartz whenever you need to get rid of excess negative energy.

There is no better crystal for eliminating bad vibes than Smoky Quartz. This healing crystal is rich in grounding, positive, and cleaning energies. It can help you free your mind from negative thoughts. It can also help you ease up on all that unfavorable self-talk and the bad energy that radiates from it. It will ensure your environment never experiences the impact of your harmful habits.

Labradorite

Work with Labradorite if you want your home to feel like a safe haven.

While this healing stone has its magical qualities, it never fails to keep you in touch with your authentic self. Labradorite is ideal for cultivating deep and strong relationships with one's inner self. This stone is linked to the third-eye and throat chakras, meaning it can help you refine your intuition and improve your communication. Placing this crystal at home can help encourage free and effective self-expression and communication, ensuring that everyone gets along and feels heard. Labradorite can help you make your home feel like a safe space for you to speak your mind and talk openly about your feelings.

Pyrite

Pyrite is a good luck charm you can use to attract abundance and prosperity into your home. Use it to promote the home's inhabitants' general well-being and spark creativity.

Pyrite is known for its potent and stable energy. It is associated with prosperity, abundance, and good fortune in numerous areas of life, including wealth, health, and quality of thought. Keeping this healing stone in your home can attract good luck and ensure your family's well-being. Pyrite will help you ward off negativity to make space for greater opportunities. If you wish, you can keep it near your home office, workspace, or even art corner to spark creative energy and trigger innovative ideas.

Black Obsidian

Placing Black Obsidian at your home's windows and doorways can help you catch and release negative energy.

Black Obsidian is as mystical as its appearance. This crystal boasts vigorous qualities that can help keep you and your home protected from negative energies and foreign psychic attacks. This healing stone works best when placed in your home's doorways and windows. This way, it can guarantee that no bad vibes penetrate your home, making sure that any stuck negative energy is fully acknowledged so it can safely exit your home.

Onyx

Onyx can help you leave anxiety, worries, stress, and bad vibes behind when you close your home's front door. It is ideal if you're embarking on your healing journey or need help overcoming detrimental patterns.

If you're prone to anxiety, you may carry this energy home with you. This also applies to other negative emotions. If things have been stressful at work lately, this nervous and restless energy will also seep into your home. You can combat this by keeping Onyx at your front door. This crystal acts as a protective barrier, allowing you to leave your stress, fears, worries, and phobias behind. Onyx encourages healing and can help you overcome past hurts. It also promotes joy and good fortune and can allow you to take mindful moments to reflect and meditate. It is particularly helpful for anyone who is going through major changes or grievances in life. This crystal can help you eliminate bad thought patterns, decisions, and behaviors that keep you stuck in your old wounds.

Home Protection Crystal Grids

You can use any of the abovementioned healing crystals to create the following crystal grids. Go with your intuition or choose the ones that align with your intention. For instance, if you wish to dissipate the tension between family members, we recommend using Rose Quartz. For protection against adverse energies and psychic attacks, go with Black Obsidian.

There is never a wrong choice when it comes to selecting crystals. All crystals work in harmony, meaning their energies can't conflict with each other. That said, one must be careful when using several powerful crystals at once because they may feel overwhelmed when many things happen simultaneously.

When employing protective crystals, remember that they may need to be changed often. This is because they're constantly picking and breaking down bad energy. Cleansing and charging them is essential if you want them to stay effective. Leave them in moonlight or around Clear Quartz, Selenite, or other charging crystals.

The following are the recommended crystal grid layouts for home protection:

- The Square
- The Cross
- The Diamond

Home Cleansing Crystal Grid

You can use this grid to cleanse the energy of a specific room or your entire home. If you plan to cleanse your entire house, use the ground home to place your grid.

Tools and Crystals

- Four natural Selenite wands
- Four large Black Tourmaline tumble stones

This crystal grid combines the Cross, which protects against negative energies, the Square, and the Diamond, which provides environmental support.

Instructions

1. Say your intention: "I am using this crystal grid to keep my (room or home) constantly purified, balanced, and cleansed."
2. In the corners of your ground floor room, place the four large Black Tourmaline tumble stones.
3. Place the four natural Selenite wands at the center of your wall. They should be in the middle, between each 2 Black Tourmaline stones.

Crystal Grid for Blessing Your Home

Like the grid above, you can use this layout to bless the energy of a specific room or your entire home. If you plan on cleansing your entire house, use the ground floor to place your grid.

Tools and Crystals

- Four large Citrine Crystal Points

This crystal grid is a combination of the Square and the Cross. It provides support and can help you connect with spiritual energies.

Instructions

1. Say your intention: "I am using this crystal grid to attract blessings and high vibrational positive energy to my (room or home)."

2. In the corner of your ground floor or targeted room, place the Citrine crystal points. They should be pointing inward, so they form a cross shape.

Crystal Grid for Home Protection

You can use this grid to cleanse the energy of a specific room or your entire home. If you plan on protecting your entire house, use the ground floor to place your grid.

Tools and Crystals

- 1 Large Red Tiger's Eye
- 4 Large Black Tourmaline crystal points

This grid combines the Square and the Cross to create safe boundaries and yield protection.

Instructions

1. Say your intention: "I am using this crystal grid to protect my (room or home) and all who live here from any type of harm."

2. In the corner of your ground floor or targeted room, place the Black Tourmaline crystal points, either standing up or pointing outwards.

3. Place the Red Tiger's Eye near the front door so that it's visible when you step in.

These protection healing stones can help you build a safe space where you can live peacefully. Having a home that fosters positive energy and allows you to easily communicate and express yourself is of utmost importance. These stones and crystal grids can help you rid your home of any unwanted energy and keep it balanced.

Chapter 11: Crystal Grid Uses and Maintenance

In this final chapter, we guide you on using and maintaining the crystal grid once you create it. We explain different aspects you should know about, such as activating the grid and charging the objects in the grid. Finally, we discuss how you can take care of your grid over time.

How to Use Your Crystal Grid

Make sure the space where you want to use your crystal grid is purified and energized. You can smudge or cleanse the room where you want to set up your grid to eliminate the negative energy that can affect your desired outcomes. Burning sacred herbs and incense around the room helps clear it of negative powers.

When you lay down your printed geometric design, you can start placing your crystals in the desired pattern. Since there are different forms of geometric formations, you need to get the best pattern that suits your needs. You can also consider drawing a mandala grid base if you fail to use one of the common designs. Make sure you use anything with symmetry as long as it suits your desires.

You can also build your crystal grid on a piece of wood or tray so you can move it when you need it. You need to keep your grid intact since you can use it again, depending on your intention.

When placing crystals on your grid, start with the biggest in the center and work your way outward. Place the stones at even intervals on each side of the grid to create balance in the energy. You can also work with color symmetry, but this may not be necessary if you don't have sufficient stones. The smallest gemstones must be placed on the edges of the crystal grid.

You can use different stones on your grid, which helps build a powerful effect. Your intention determines the stones to include. You can use Rose quartz and other stones related to love if your intention is based on this subject. There is no single formula concerning grid work, so feel free to experiment.

Other people write their intention or goal on a small piece of paper before working on their desired crystal layout. The paper is then placed underneath the big stone in the center. However, this is optional since it does not reduce the effectiveness of your grid if you choose not to include it.

Activating a Crystal Grid

Activating your crystal grid is more crucial than creating it. Before using your grid, you must properly activate it so that your outcome is clear. Without activation, you may not achieve your desired goals. The first step to activating the grid is to take a moment to observe its layout. Admiring your work is one of the best ways of showing appreciation in the spiritual world.

The next step is to outline your intention. During the creation process of your grid, you already have your intention in your mind, but you need to define it for the last time before starting your ritual. State your intended outcome and close your eyes while at the same time taking deep breaths to finalize the intention. Open your eyes and begin tracing the invisible line from the stone in the center using your finger. Make sure you touch all the stones when you perform the activation process.

The major purpose of activating your grid is to ensure that all the stones are attuned and connected to others. To achieve your goals, all the crystals should work together. You may not be able to manifest your intention using a single stone, which is why activating crystals is critical. Crystal grid intentions deal with different aspects such as love, luck, attraction, career, or anything that affects your life.

Crystals constantly absorb energy and lose it, weakening them after a few days. This means you need to charge your stones regularly, and you must keep your grid in a safe place for optimum performance. You need to reactivate your stones after three days, and you should perform this activity with your intention in mind. You can repeat the process of reactivating your stones until the time you get mental clarity. Reactivating your stones usually takes less than five minutes. Your stones can work against you if you fail to tend to them.

Crystal Grid Intentions

You can ask your crystal grid for anything you wish to achieve in life, and there is no limit. However, remember that you cannot use your crystal grid for evil intentions like causing harm to someone or wishing them ill. Additionally, your crystal grid cannot protect you from inevitable things in life like death.

Crystals have a higher frequency vibration than human experiences. Therefore, they cannot cause low vibratory experiences to the users like bringing diseases or disharmony. Crystals provide high vibratory experiences such as protection from harm, amplification of positive emotions, alignment with destiny, and greater opportunity.

Your intentions mainly determine the results you'll get from using your crystal grid. Carefully select vocabulary and focus on one intention at a given time. Focus on your intention as if you are watching a movie. A certain type of vocabulary is recognized by the universe which you should use. Avoid negative words since the law of attraction only aligns with positive outcomes.

In the spiritual realm, everything is positive, so you must not think of negativity. The universe listens to everything you say, so you should avoid negations. Instead, you must use affirming words that resonate with your intentions. Think in the positive to bring about a positive outcome. You can also use a wordless intention where you visualize yourself in the position you desire. If you intend to get a new home, picture yourself living in a better place than where you currently are.

How Do I Charge the Objects in a Grid?

Before using your stones, you should cleanse them of negative energy and charge them with positive power. Cleansing your stones is not all about making them physically clean but removing negative energy.

There are plenty of methods to cleanse and charge crystals, including smoke, earth, water, intention, and the full moon, which is the most effective. The moon is a powerful method to clear old energies and reset your stones for new work. Apart from resetting your stones, cleansing can absorb certain energies. For instance, stones like obsidian and tourmaline are specifically meant to combat negativity and can also benefit from a regular recharge.

Using a Full Moon to Recharge Your Stones

Using the full moon is the simplest method to charge and cleanse your crystals. All you need to do is leave the stones in an open space with access to the light from the moon. Multiple stones should not be piled up, so try to separate them. You can leave your crystals overnight to allow the entire process to occur naturally. If you live in an apartment, you can leave your crystals on a windowsill. There is no need to hold a ceremony or a special ritual to cleanse your stones. Moonlight is enough, and the process is natural. It does not require your direct intervention.

The light from the moon will saturate the stone with the vibrations associated with it. You can charge your crystal for cooperation, challenging norms, and boosting intuition with an Aquarius moon. Since the moon is strongly associated with collaboration, you can also use your crystal grid to charge and cleanse multiple stones at once. Let your intuition guide you and allow the stones to amplify each other's energies in a circular pattern.

You can set your intentions if what the moon offers differs from what you have in mind. However, you should do this additional work after the moon has done its cleansing. It is vital to cleanse the stones first before charging them. You need to hold your crystal in your hand and focus on your breath, the stone, and your intention when you charge your crystal. Simply breathe on the stones and visualize.

Some prefer to use visualization of light or breathing into the stone. Any comfortable image is good, so you must consider your intention. You can leave your crystal in the moonlight for a few hours and then meditate on its charging. Other people prefer to charge it the following day. You can do as you wish, depending on your desired goals.

A few things can go wrong when you cleanse and charge your stones. Like missing the full moon, setting the stone in the wrong place, or overcharging it. Fortunately, there are other ways to charge the stones. Sit under the moonlight, meditate on your stones, or find a quiet indoor space. Other crystals can be overwhelmed by sunlight or easily damaged when cleaned with water. Others are soft and break easily, so try to find a gentle method of charging that does not affect them. When you choose your crystals, you should understand different methods to cleanse them.

Maintaining Your Crystal Grid

When creating your crystal grid, you need to maintain it, and you can do this by taking different measures. If you bring your grid from somewhere outside, you must cleanse it of any negativity it might have picked up. The following are some of the methods you can use depending on your stone:

- Hold it under running water.
- Dip it in seawater.
- Place it under moonlight or sunlight.
- Cleanse your stones with sage or other herbs.

If you want crystals to work well, the mental clearing of negative energies is ideal. Clear the skepticism about the capability of your stones that you may have. You must respect the crystals and have faith in their potential and what they can do for you.

Your stones will collect negative energy each time you use them. Because of this, you must clear your stones at least once every month. If you feel that a particular stone is feeling heavier, you need to cleanse it. Others can cleanse their stones after a few days. Find the cleansing method that resonates with your intention and interests. Something that works for you may not work for another person, so choose the cleansing method that will suit your needs.

After cleansing, your stone should feel lighter - physically and energetically. When your stones have been cleansed, make sure you keep them in an appropriate and safe place. For instance, keep them near plants or windows where they can absorb natural healing energy. You can also place the stones in your home or any space in which you are, as long as it aligns with your intentions.

Crystal grids are used for different purposes, but they cannot be substituted for medication. They are effective in activities like spiritual healing and other aspects that can affect your life, like love, luck, and career. If you are skeptical about the healing powers of crystals, they may not do you any good. Fortunately, crystals do not cause harm. While no scientific evidence supports the efficacy of crystals in healing, many people believe in their power. If you try them, you may be in for a pleasant surprise.

Conclusion

As you've learned from this book, a crystal grid is nothing more than the intentional arrangement of precious stones in a geometric design. This design enhances the crystals' energy due to their natural mineral composition. This energy is created by the vibration caused in their structure, just like the vibrations made inside your body. Crystals use energy to connect with any natural element around them. For example, crystals can help you ground yourself in nature and harness its life force, healing your own energy system. Each crystal has its own vibrational frequency, granting them different healing abilities.

When charged with specific intentions, a crystal will connect to a chakra associated with the same mineral color the stone is made of. The chakras are centers that focus on the subtle energy flowing through your body. They represent the easiest way to scan a person's energy system. Crystal grids grant even more straightforward access to the chakras and quicker resolution to your health issues. Besides the stones themselves, grid work only requires a few other tools you can easily acquire or craft yourself.

Grids can be as simple or complex as you want them to be - as long as they fit your intention. Of course, simple patterns are always the safer options for those just dipping their toes into grid work. They will teach you how to prepare your mind to connect with several crystals at once. Make sure to also learn each crystal's functions while practicing and avoiding combining unsuitable ones.

Once you have mastered the basics of gridwork, you can move on to learn how to make crystal grids for specific purposes. You can, for instance, create a grid to attract love into your life or form healthy and nurturing relationships. Either way, the focus will be on enhancing your ability to express your emotions and recognize other people's feelings. You can also attract money, good fortune, and better career prospects.

Another way to use crystal grids is to connect spiritually with your ancestors or spiritual guides. They can be contacted for protection, guidance, or to answer specific questions. Through crystals, you can ask for protection for yourself, your loved ones, or anyone who reaches out to you, or for a property you feel can be in danger from malicious intent. Likewise, working with crystal grids contributes to your own spiritual development. The more time you spend connected to healing stones, the more your vibrations will be elevated. You can continue until you can finally raise them all the way up to your upper chakras.

Of course, you will only be able to reap all these benefits if you take good care of your crystals. Just as they can store, channel, and enhance positive energy, so can they accumulate negative energy. Make sure to cleanse them regularly to avoid mixing energies. If a grid is used over a longer period of time, you need to channel more energy into charging them before their activation. You may also have to repeat your intention every few days. Otherwise, they may lose power before their purpose has been fulfilled, forcing you to repeat the process one more time.

Appendix 1: A-Z Crystals and Their Properties

The number of healing crystals your practice can benefit from is much larger than what was covered in the previous chapters. This appendix lists the different types of healing stones practitioners from various cultures and spiritual beliefs use in grid work or individually. They can be used for healing, divination, guidance, spiritual connections, and much more. Remember, each of them must be charged with a proper intention to reach their full potential.

Here is a list of crystals along with their healing attributes:

Agate - Linked to groundedness, a calm and centered state of mind, the crown chakra, self-acceptance, and letting go of misplaced loyalties for social norms and unhealthy relationships.

Alexandrite - Associated with an understanding of one's purpose, spiritual and wisdom, cleansing, renewal, longevity, and finding joy and happiness in spiritual transformation.

Amber - Used for energetic protection during rituals, divination and healing practices, spiritual cleansing or the reduction of stress symptoms, and physical alignment with one's inner values.

Amethyst - Linked to stress relief, protection for one's personal space, tools and energy system, proper mood regulation, cognitive functions, better sleep, and the crown chakra.

Andara - Helps establish connections with entities that emit high-frequency vibrations, allows you to manifest your inner desires, express your authenticity, and reveal the appropriate spiritual path.

Angelite - Promotes careful attunement to nature's energy and the spiritual world, facilitates communication with ancestral spirits, and helps both the living and the souls of the departed to move on if needed.

Apophyllite - Used for enhancing your intuition, teaches you how to develop and listen to it, leading to high vibrations, a spiritual awakening, and improving endocrine system functions.

Aquamarine - Known for its ability to bring good luck and abundance. It also has a calming and cooling effect on the body and soul, balances the throat chakra, and provides the chance for introspection.

Auralite - Allows the soul, mind, and body to all become still and serene, slow down, and enjoy simple things, relieving oneself from the burden of stress.

Black Tourmaline - Provides energetic protection for your body, working space, and those around you, absorbs negative energy from the chakras, and safeguards against negative influences over your chakra system.

Bloodstone - Commonly associated with patience, better sleep, healthy circadian rhythm, energetic cleansing, stronger immune system, improved blood and lymphatic circulation, and the heart chakra.

Blue Lace Agate - Provides self-confidence, vibrations for relaxation, communication with the spiritual realm, and a cooling effect on your body and nervous system after a stressful experience.

Blue Topaz - Can aid in letting go of past hurts, painful memories, and unhealthy relationships, finding a life path and true humility, and balancing and unblocking the throat chakra.

Boji Stone - Has a mild grounding effect, allowing you to connect to nature's life force, and remain in the present without getting distracted by worries about the past or future.

Calcite - Helps dissipate irrational fears, alleviates the symptoms of anxiety and depression, and soothes pain in the stomach area, nausea, vertigo, and ground during journeying.

Cathedral Quartz - Often associated with high vibrational frequencies and elevated consciousness. It promotes the effects of meditative and other mindfulness exercises, pain relief, and a general sense of well-being.

Celestite - Known for its ability to facilitate attunement to spiritual activities and provide spiritual guidance. It also supports all the energy centers and unblocks or heals the crown, third eye, and throat chakras.

Citrine - Represents monetary wealth and prosperity, spiritual advancement, divine energies, the solar plexus chakra, optimal digestion, and a well-balanced diet.

Clear Quartz - Linked to spiritual protection, energetic cleansing, problem-solving, charging other spiritual tools, the empowerment of the chakra system, communication with the spiritual realm, and immunity.

Dendritic Agate - Associated with spiritual and material growth, pain relief, emotional release, a healthy nervous system, and abundance in spiritual riches.

Desert Rose - Helps protect you and those around you from negative spiritual influence, scrub all the low-frequency energies away, overcome phobias and gain motivation and self-confidence.

Diamond - As the symbol of eternal love, spiritual commitment, strength, fidelity, and clairvoyance, it's often used for the protection and cleansing of all chakras and to attract good fortune.

Emerald - The symbol of renewal and growth, youth, hope, fertility, emotional and spiritual healing, the heart chakra, nature, and divine masculinity.

Flint - Can assist with developing deeper understanding and communication skills, establishing integrity, expressing emotions, hidden desires, and one's spiritual values.

Fluorite - Used as a shield against artificial vibrations, emotional and psychological manipulations, or to provide mental clarity, better communication, and creative expression skills.

Garnet - Linked to balance in relationships, passion, good fortune, professional success, financial gain, and love that withstands the test of time.

Golden Topaz - Often reveals a new, unusual source of energy and provides ways to soothe your nerves, as well as motivation to move past life's hurdles and purpose in life.

Green Tourmaline - Improves cognitive functions and your ability to channel the vital life force towards your body. It also represents masculine energy and love from a male point of view.

Hematite - Associated with grounding, restful sleep, soothing the symptoms of blood disorders, finding your confidence, inner voice, and the ability to remain calm in times of stress.

Herkimer Diamond - Symbolizes creative endeavors, gut feelings, open communication, the throat chakra, commitment, and loyalty in one's personal and professional life.

Jasper - Associated with cleansing all the main chakras, flushing out negative energy from the body, elevated organization and problem-solving skills, vivid imagination, clairvoyance, and clairsentience.

Jet - Provides energetic protection, balances the chakra system, uplifts your mood, helps you combat negative emotions and thought processes, and calms all fears.

Kunzite - Linked to heart activation, throat chakra unblocking, breaking down emotional walls, opening one's mind, and improved mood and endocrine system regulation.

Labradorite - Linked to spiritual alignment, a clear view of one's inner values, the balance between intuitive wisdom and rationale, and energetic protection for all chakras.

Lapis Lazuli - Often applied due to its calming effect, attunement to the spiritual world, source of pure, serene energy, and ability to soothe migraines and pains throughout the body.

Larimar - Linked to high vibrational levels, elevated consciousness, spiritual and physical awareness. It improves the reflexes and neuromuscular links, opens the upper chakra, and ensures uninterrupted energy flow through them.

Lepidolite - Helps protect yourself from artificial vibrations, break unhealthy patterns, leave relationships, and mend your spiritual and mental issues.

Magnetite - Associated with strength, faithfulness, and unwavering commitment. It also contributes to reducing inflammation levels and balancing organ and chakra functions.

Malachite - Used to reduce swelling and inflammation and provide energetic cleansing while detoxifying the body. It may also help break unhealthy cycles and relationships with spiritual elevation.

Moonstone - Useful for calming an upset stomach and relieving other digestive issues, protection during traveling and spiritual journeying, finding joy in little things, and establishing clear communication.

Morganite - Associated with virginity, innocence, divine love, compassion, pure energy, open heart, and the elevation of the spirit, alongside raised vibrational levels.

Obsidian - A powerful protection crystal with a grounding effect and the ability to confront your inner demons and reveal dark truths before they taint your energy.

Opal - Used to find inner peace, means to express oneself through art and magical practices, love and loyalty in a relationship, truthfulness in others, and balance for the throat chakra.

Orange Carnelian - Known for its ability to provide a boost of pure energy when needed, charge other crystals on the grid, stimulate spiritual growth, and support reproductive health.

Peridot - Helps dissipate negative emotions like anger, stress, jealousy, insecurity, disruptive thought patterns, and negativity from the heart chakra.

Petalite - Causes high vibrations, the fast opening of the upper chakras, raised consciousness, and spiritual preparation for different purposes.

Phenacite - This stone also leads to elevated vibrational frequencies but helps with grounding when the upper chakras are opening to a sudden stream of fresh energy.

Pink Tourmaline - Linked to divine feminine energy, fertility, improved heart chakra functions and unblocking, the opening of the heart, and a constant and positive energy flow.

Rhodochrosite - Associated with finding unconditional love and opening one's heart for compassion, joy, peace, tenderness, and the ability to heal emotional wounds.

Rhodonite - Activates the heart chakra, opens the heart, heals emotional scars, reliefs the symptoms of stress and anxiety, and teaches you how to love yourself just the way you are.

Rose Quartz - Associated with love, compassion, and other positive emotions, spiritual and emotional dedication to loved ones, the opening of the heart (both the chakra and spiritually), and improved blood circulation.

Ruby - Symbolizes established goals, passion for work, life, play, relationships, and hobbies, promotes improved circulation, sexuality, and the balancing of the heart chakra.

Selenite - Facilitates making high-frequency connections with spirits and guides, grounding oneself to nature, attracting higher energy, and finding one's true spiritual purpose.

Smithsonite - Helpful for emotional healing, developing compassion and ways to combat all the negativity surrounding you, resolve any conflicts peacefully and calm your mind, body, and soul.

Smoky Quartz - Linked to energetic cleansing, body detoxing, clearing of the mind, absorbing negative influences from the energy system, grounding, connecting to nature and the universe, and the root chakra.

Tiger's Eye - Associated with abundance, good luck, universal wisdom, inner knowledge, integrity, fidelity, courage, and the ultimate power source, the highest of the spirits.

Turquoise - Linked to stress relief, the freedom to let go of pent-up negative emotions, empowerment, travel protection, and pain relief, as well as better pulmonary functions.

White Topaz - Known for granting clarity of mind, better sleep, improved cognitive skills, organizational skills, motivation to find purpose, and open-mindedness.

Appendix 2: A-Z Crystals and Minerals

Amazonite: Yin/Yang balance, protection, intelligence, communication, truth.
Chakra: Throat and Heart chakras
Planet: Uranus
Star Sign: Virgo
Amber: Healing, cleansing, stability, renewal, confidence.
Chakra: Solar plexus chakra
Planet: Sun
Star Sign: Aquarius
Amethyst: calmness, balance, peace, patience, meditation.
Chakra: Third Eye chakra
Planet: Uranus
Star Sign: Aquarius
Agate: Love, healing, financial gain, concentration, perception.
Chakra: Heart chakra
Planet: Saturn
Star Sign: Pisces
Aquamarine: Good communication, mental clarity, wisdom, prosperity, trust.

Chakra: Throat chakra.
Planet: Uranus
Star Sign: Gemini
Auralite: Tension relief, anger dissipation, intuition, communication, serenity.
Chakra: Crown chakra
Planet: Venus
Star Sign: Gemini
Azurite: Psychic protection, mental clarity, positivity, purification, energy.
Chakra: Crown chakra.
Planet: Uranus.
Star Sign: Taurus
Aventurine: Happiness, protection, grounding, calming, and peace.
Chakra: Sacral chakra.
Planet: Sun
Star Sign: Taurus and Gemini.
Bloodstone: Financial abundance, success, tension relief, courage, creative energy.
Chakra: Sacral chakra.
Planet: Mars and Pluto.
Star Sign: Leo and Scorpio
Carnelian: Courage, protection, trust, stability, positive attitude.
Chakra: Heart chakra
Planet: Saturn and Mars.
Star Sign: Scorpio and Sagittarius.
Chrysocolla: Emotional balance, fertility, communication, self-realization, level-headedness.
Chakra: Throat chakra.
Planet: Venus.
Star Sign: Cancer.

Citrine: Financial abundance, prosperity, creativity, confidence, self-improvement.
Chakra: Solar plexus chakra.
Planet: Mercury
Star Sign: Libra and Scorpio.

Clear Quartz: Grounding, psychic ability, healing, energy, balance.
Chakra: All chakras.
Planet: Earth.
Star Sign: All signs.

Chrysoprase: Inspiration, creativity, emotional balance, healing, self-love.
Chakra: Heart chakra.
Planet: Jupiter and Venus.
Star Sign: Aries and Leo.

Druzy: Personal growth, peaceful expansion, psychic protection, stress relief, love.
Chakra: Heart chakra.
Planet: Sun.
Star Sign: Gemini and Cancer.

Emerald: Wealth, love, tranquility, success, money.
Chakra: Solar plexus chakra.
Planet: Venus.
Star Sign: Virgo and Libra.

Fluorite: Psychic ability, confidence, dreamworld mysticism, purity of mind, love.
Chakra: Heart chakra.
Planet: Mercury, Venus, and Mars.
Star Sign: Aries and Sagittarius.

Gypsum: Antidepressant, calming, healing, cleansing, Yin/Yang balance.
Chakra: Heart chakra.
Planet: Sun.

Star Sign: Cancer and Taurus.

Hematite: Stress relief, healing, protection, balance, good communication.

Chakra: Root chakra.

Planet: Mars.

Star Sign: Libra and Aries.

Herkimer Diamond: Money, good fortune, protection, love, creativity.

Chakra: Crown, Heart, Third eye chakras

Planet: Venus.

Star Sign: Gemini and Libra.

Iolite: Good luck and protection, increased success and wealth, mental clarity, serenity.

Chakra: Throat chakra.

Planet: Neptune.

Star Sign: Aquarius and Capricorn.

Jade: Healing, honesty, calmness, restful sleep, soothing.

Chakra: Heart chakra.

Planet: Venus.

Star Sign: Cancer and Leo.

Jasper: Protection, courage, strength, good luck, business success.

Chakra: Root chakra.

Planet: Mars.

Star Sign: Aries and Capricorn.

Kunzite: Healing, protection, healing of old wounds, confidence, divine love.

Chakra: Heart chakra.

Planet: Sun

Star Sign: Libra and Libra.

Lapis Lazuli: Courage, protection, love, strength, and mental clarity.

Chakra: Third eye chakra.

Planet: Venus.

Star Sign: Cancer and Scorpio.

Malachite: Self-expression, courage, balance in all aspects of life, protection, purification.

Chakra: Heart chakra.

Planet: Jupiter and Venus.

Star Sign: Leo and Aries.

Moonstone: Protection, healing, love, emotional balance, Yin/Yang balance.

Chakra: Throat chakra.

Planet: Moon.

Star Sign: Cancer and Pisces.

Pearl: Connection with all life, support, emotional balance, focus, truth.

Chakra: Crown chakra.

Planet: Pluto.

Star Sign: Taurus and Scorpio.

Peridot: Luck, protection from evil spirits, psychic ability, aura strength, peace.

Chakra: Solar plexus chakra.

Planet: Mercury.

Star Sign: Aquarius and Aries.

Petrified Wood: Protection against negativity, strength, inner transformation, balance, relaxation.

Chakra: Root chakra.

Planet: Mars.

Star Sign: Scorpio and Sagittarius.

Pyrite: Protection, good fortune, positive life energy, Yin/Yang balance, aura fortification.

Chakra: Heart chakra.

Planet: Venus.

Star Sign: Cancer and Capricorn.

Rose quartz: Love, healing, peace of mind, tranquility, happiness.

Chakra: Heart chakra.
Planet: Venus.
Star Sign: Cancer and Pisces.

Rutilated Quartz: Luck, courage, success in business, clear communication, anti-anxiety.
Chakra: Throat chakra.
Planet: Uranus.
Star Sign: Taurus and Gemini.

Smoky Quartz: Inner strength, wisdom, protection, healing of old wounds, heart-opening.
Chakra: Heart chakra.
Planets: Saturn and Pluto.
Star Sign: Aries and Scorpio.

Snowflake Obsidian: Protection against negativity, good luck, protection from evil spirits, creativity, purification.
Chakra: Root chakra.
Planet: Venus.
Star Sign: Gemini and Aquarius.

Sodalite: Creativity, clarity of thought, serenity, peace, decision making.
Chakra: Third eye and throat chakras.
Planet: Mercury.
Star Sign: Aries and Scorpio.

Spectrolite: Protection, creativity, spirit guide connection, channeling, honesty.
Chakra: Third eye and Throat chakras.
Planet: Uranus.
Star Sign: Libra and Pisces.

Turquoise: Shielding, protection, grounding, clearing of old issues, tranquility.
Chakra: Solar plexus chakra.
Planet: Mercury.
Star Sign: Aries and Libra.

Unakite: Scrying, happiness, work/life balance, vision, grounding.
Chakra: Third eye chakra.
Planet: Venus.
Star Sign: Cancer and Aquarius.

Variscite: Anti-anxiety, joy, Yin/Yang balance, clarity of thought, compassion.
Chakra: Third eye and Crown chakras.
Planet: Venus.
Star Sign: Leo and Capricorn.

Vesuvianite: Inner peace, emotional healing, peace of mind, sleep aid, clarity.
Chakra: Heart chakra.
Planet: Moon.
Star Sign: Taurus and Cancer

Yttrium: Healing, prosperity, good luck, growth, protection.
Chakra: Heart chakra.
Planet: Venus.
Star Sign: Aries and Taurus.

Zircon: Protection, grounding and calming, spiritual healing, aura fortification.
Chakra: All chakras.
Planet: Uranus.
Star Sign: Taurus and Pisces.

Here's another book by Silvia Hill that you might like

Free Bonus from Silvia Hill available for limited time

Hi Spirituality Lovers!

My name is Silvia Hill, and first off, I want to THANK YOU for reading my book.

Now you have a chance to join my exclusive spirituality email list so you can get the ebooks below for free as well as the potential to get more spirituality ebooks for free! Simply click the link below to join.

P.S. Remember that it's 100% free to join the list.

~~$27~~ **FREE BONUSES**

- 9 Types of Spirit Guides and How to Connect to Them
- How to Develop Your Intuition: 7 Secrets for Psychic Development and Tarot Reading
- Tarot Reading Secrets for Love, Career, and General Messages

Access your free bonuses here
https://livetolearn.lpages.co/crystals-and-crystal-grids-paperback/

References

Alexander, Skye. 2019. Magickal Astrology. Red Wheel/Weiser.

Costelloe, Marina. 2010. The Complete Guide To Crystal Astrology. Forres: Findhorn Press.

Godden, Patricia. n.d. Astrology, Crystals, And Spirituality.

Hall, Judy. 2017. Judy Hall"s Crystal Zodiac. Octopus Publishing Group.

Harold, Edmund. 1992. Crystal Healing. Ringwood, Vic.: Viking.

Kunz, George Frederick. 1989. The Curious Lore Of Precious Stones. New York: Bell Pub. Co.

Leavy, Ashley. n.d. Cosmic Crystals.

Lilly, Simon. n.d. The Crystal Healing Guide.

Lilly, Sue, and Simon Lilly. 2005. The Power Of Crystals And Crystal Healing. London: Southwater.

Lyne, Cynthia. n.d. Beginner's Guide To Crystals.

Mégemont, Florence. 2008. The Metaphysical Book Of Gems And Crystals. Rochester, Vt.: Healing Arts Press.

Permutt, Philip. 2021. The Modern Guide To Crystal Healing. La Vergne: Ryland Peters & Small.

"Signs Of The Zodiac: A Reference Guide To Historical, Mythological, And Cultural Associations."1998. Choice Reviews Online 35 (08): 35-4240-35-4240. doi:10.5860/choice.35-4240.

Simpson, Liz, and Leslie Kenton. 2005. The Book Of Crystal Healing. London: Gaia Books.

Van Doren, Yulia. 2018. Crystals. Quadrille Publishing, Limited

Lazzerini, E. (2017). Crystal grids power: Harness the power of crystals and sacred geometry for manifesting abundance, healing, and protection. Createspace Independent Publishing Platform.

Khan, A. (2020, April 28). The Basics of Subtle Energy: Nadis, Chakras, and the Aura. Well Into Life Massage & Bodywork - in Richmond VA. https://wellintolife.com/the-basics-of-subtle-energy-nadis-chakras-and-the-aura/

Faurote, A. (2020, October 31). The Benefits of Crystal Healing. Coveteur: Inside Closets, Fashion, Beauty, Health, and Travel. https://coveteur.com/2020/10/31/crystal-healing-benefits/

]Murray, B. (2017, September 5). A beginner's guide to using crystals. Harper's BAZAAR. http://www.harpersbazaar.co.uk/beauty/fitness-wellbeing/a43244/crystal-healing-beginners-guide/

Kelly, A., & Thomas, S. S. (2018, April 9). What Are Healing Crystals? Popular Crystals & Their Meanings. Allure. https://www.allure.com/story/healing-crystals-for-beginners

Crystal Visions Store. (n.d.). An introduction to crystal Grids. Crystal Visions Store. https://crystalvisions.net.au/blogs/an-introduction-to-crystal-grids/an-introduction-to-crystal-grids

Destination Deluxe. (2020, May 29). Sacred Geometry explained. Destination Deluxe. https://destinationdeluxe.com/sacred-geometry-explained-healing-benefits/

Flower, S. (2018, November 16). Platonic Solids Meaning - Sacred Geometry. Soul Flower Blog. https://www.soul-flower.com/blog/platonic-solids-meaning-sacred-geometry/

Sacred geometry: Unlocking the secret structures of the universe. (2020, July 11). Ancient Origins. https://www.ancient-origins.net/history-famous-people/sacred-geometry-0013969

The benefits of using crystal grids. (n.d.). Rylandpeters. https://rylandpeters.com/blogs/health-mind-body-and-spirit/the-benefits-of-using-crystal-grids

Todic, S. (2020, October 23). Everything you need to know about crystal grids. Conscious Items. https://consciousitems.com/blogs/practice/everything-you-need-to-know-about-crystal-grids

Wigington, P. (2018, July 5). How to make and use a crystal grid. Learn Religions. https://www.learnreligions.com/how-to-make-a-crystal-grid-4171722

Gemstones for crystal grids or healing layouts - Arkansas crystal works. (2014, June 24). Arkansas Crystal Works - Genn John.

https://arkansascrystalworks.com/arkansas-crystal/extras/crystal-for-grids-or-healing-layouts/

Sam, T. +., & Wander, T. (2022, January 24). What are sacred geometry symbols, and how to use them? Two Wander. https://www.twowander.com/blog/what-are-sacred-geometry-symbols-and-how-to-use-them

Destination Deluxe. (2020, May 29). Sacred Geometry explained. Destination Deluxe. https://destinationdeluxe.com/sacred-geometry-explained-healing-benefits/

10 intentions to set for your most authentic life. (2015, January 11). Mindbodygreen. https://www.mindbodygreen.com/0-16947/10-intentions-to-set-for-your-most-authentic-life.html

Cassie, P. by. (n.d.). How to create a crystal grid in 7 steps. Zennedout.Com. https://zennedout.com/how-to-create-a-crystal-grid-in-7-steps/

Davis, F. (2021, May 1). How to make a crystal grid: Steps, tips & best practices. Cosmic Cuts. https://cosmiccuts.com/blogs/healing-stones-blog/how-to-make-a-crystal-grid

de Pietro, M. C. (2018, October 2). How to use crystal grids to maximize positive energy in your home. Well+Good. https://www.wellandgood.com/how-to-do-crystal-grids/

Fisher, J. (2020, February 27). Crystal Grids 101: How to make a crystal grid to supercharge your life. Sage Crystals. https://sagecrystals.com/blogs/news/crystal-grids-101-how-to-make-a-crystal-grid

Formtastica, M. (2021, June 17). 5-step guide to making crystal grids. House of Formlab. https://houseofformlab.com/5-step-guide-to-making-crystal-grids/

Guide to crystal grids. (2013, November 8). Crystal Vaults. https://www.crystalvaults.com/crystal-grids/

Hosking, J. (2021, December 9). How to Make a Crystal Grid. Mystic Doorway. https://www.mysticdoorway.com/how-to-make-a-crystal-grid/

How crystals can help you stay connected to your intentions. (2016, March 31). Mindbodygreen. https://www.mindbodygreen.com/0-24297/how-crystals-can-help-you-stay-connected-to-your-intentions.html

How to make a crystal grid: The easy step-by-step guide. (n.d.). Betterly. https://www.betterly.com/uk/blog/how-to-make-crystal-grid

How to set up A crystal grid. (2019, December 16). THE MYSTIC CAT. https://themysticcat.com/info-hub/crystal-grids/setting-up-a-crystal-grid/

Lazzerini, E. (2022, January 24). Crystal grid central stones, focus stone, centre stone. Ethan Lazzerini. https://www.ethanlazzerini.com/crystal-grid-central-stones/

Leavy, A. (2021, July 19). How to create and use a crystal grid (step-by-step) - love & light school of crystal therapy. Love & Light School of Crystal Therapy. https://loveandlightschool.com/how-to-create-use-a-crystal-grid-step-by-step/

The how-to guide for crystal grid use. (2021, February 8). Serena Loves. https://serenaloves.com/the-how-to-guide-for-crystal-grid-use/

This crystal grid is the key to unlocking your inner badass. (2017, May 16). Mindbodygreen. https://www.mindbodygreen.com/articles/crystal-grid-how-to/

Wigington, P. (2018, July 5). How to make and use a crystal grid. Learn Religions. https://www.learnreligions.com/how-to-make-a-crystal-grid-4171722

(N.d.). Almanacsupplyco.Com. https://almanacsupplyco.com/blogs/articles/how-to-make-a-crystal-grid

Davis, F. (2021, September 20). Create a crystal grid for love with these crystals & tips. Cosmic Cuts. https://cosmiccuts.com/blogs/healing-stones-blog/crystal-grid-for-love

Faber, L. (2019, October 30). Why are some gemstones associated with bad luck? The Gemmological Association of Great Britain. https://gem-a.com/gem-hub/gem-knowledge/why-are-some-gemstones-associated-with-bad-luck

February. (n.d.). GEMSTONES FOR LOVE: Crystals that support & attract romance ♥. Mexicali Blues. https://www.mexicaliblues.com/blogs/our-stories-mexicali-blues-blog/gemstones-for-love-crystals-that-support-attract-romance

Leavy, A. (2020, February 23). Crystal grid for emotional healing recipe - love & light school of crystal therapy. Love & Light School of Crystal Therapy. https://loveandlightschool.com/crystal-grid-for-emotional-healing-recipe/

M., X. (2021, February 3). Best crystals & gemstones for love & seduction. Villagerockshop.Com. https://www.villagerockshop.com/blog/crystals-for-love-seduction/

Rogers, J. S. (2016, February 5). Create a crystal grid for nurturing support and self-love. Jodi Sky Rogers. https://jodiskyrogers.com/2016/02/05/create-a-crystal-grid-for-nurturing-support-and-self-love/

Zelikson, A. (n.d.). 8 powerful gemstones for valentine's Day love. INAYA. https://inayajewelry.com/blogs/news/74748165-8-powerful-gemstones-for-valentines-day-love

(N.d.-a). Tinyrituals.Co. https://tinyrituals.co/blogs/tiny-rituals/8-gemstones-that-will-manifest-the-love-life-of-your-dreams

(N.d.-b). Tinyrituals.Co. https://tinyrituals.co/blogs/tiny-rituals/8-gemstones-that-will-manifest-the-love-life-of-your-dreams#Kunzite

Camille. (2021, September 30). 6 simple crystal grid layouts for abundance. Crystal Healing Ritual. https://www.crystalhealingritual.com/crystal-grid-for-abundance/

Chee, C. (2021, September 27). 10 best crystals for money: Stones to attract wealth & prosperity. Truly Experiences Blog; Truly Experiences. https://trulyexperiences.com/blog/crystals-for-money/

Dhiman, P. L. (2020, August 9). 3 ways you can use your chakras to make more money. Linkedin.Com; LinkedIn. https://www.linkedin.com/pulse/3-ways-you-can-use-your-chakras-make-more-money-pooja-l-dhiman/

Lazzerini, E. (2017). Crystal grids power: Harness the power of crystals and sacred geometry for manifesting abundance, healing, and protection. Createspace Independent Publishing Platform.

Lazzerini, E. (2018, March 24). Crystal grid for success in business, work, and career. Ethan Lazzerini. https://www.ethanlazzerini.com/crystal-grid-for-success/

Omstars. (2019, September 17). How your Chakra energy could be affecting your Financial freedom. OmStars. https://omstars.com/blog/business-of-yoga/how-your-chakra-energy-could-be-affecting-your-financial-freedom/

Shrimali, N. (2021, June 4). 9 best crystals for career success and Good Luck in life. Tocrystal. https://tocrystal.com/blog/best-crystals-for-career-success/

Tree of life crystal grid. (n.d.). Crystal Life. https://www.crystal-life.com/product/crystal-grid-tree-of-life/

Want to manifest more money? Make sure you have the right crystals. (2017, April 24). Mindbodygreen. https://www.mindbodygreen.com/0-29486/want-to-manifest-more-money-make-sure-you-have-the-right-crystals.html

Which Chakra is Related to Career? (n.d.). Phoebegreenacre.Com. https://phoebegreenacre.com/blog/chakra-related-to-career/

(N.d.). Tinyrituals.Co. https://tinyrituals.co/blogs/tiny-rituals/crystals-for-money-17-stones-to-create-true-prosperity

Rekstis, E. (2022, January 21). Everything You Need To Know About Healing Crystals and Their Benefits. Healthline. https://www.healthline.com/health/mental-health/guide-to-healing-crystals

Leavy, A. (2021, February 9). A Crystal Grid Recipe for Wellness. Love & Light School of Crystal Therapy. https://loveandlightschool.com/a-crystal-grid-recipe-for-wellness/

Estrada, J. (2021, February 16). 10 Types of Crystals for Healing, Self-Love, Energy Clearing, and Positivity. Well+Good. https://www.wellandgood.com/types-crystals/

Davis, F. (2020, December 21). The Spiritual Meaning of Sacred Geometry Shapes & Platonic Solids. Cosmic Cuts. https://cosmiccuts.com/blogs/healing-stones-blog/sacred-geometry-shapes

M., X. (2019, December 16). Crystal Grid Kit for Healing. Villagerockshop.Com. https://www.villagerockshop.com/blog/crystal-grid-kit-for-healing/

M., X. (2020, February 25). Stones for Sweet Dreams - Crystal Grid for Sleep. Villagerockshop.Com. https://www.villagerockshop.com/blog/crystal-grid-for-sleep/

Brewer, S. (2021, July 12). How to Use a Crystal Grid for Mindfulness. STEAM Powered Family. https://www.steampoweredfamily.com/brains/how-to-use-a-crystal-grid-for-mental-health/

Davis, F. (2021, February 2). 10 Crystals for Intuition & Psychic Ability: Tap Into Your Innate Power. Cosmic Cuts. https://cosmiccuts.com/blogs/healing-stones-blog/crystals-for-intuition-psychic-ability

Wigington, P. (n.d.). 4 Types of Spirit Guides You Should Know. Learn Religions. https://www.learnreligions.com/what-is-a-spirit-guide-2561758

Deluxe, D. (2020, May 29). Sacred Geometry Explained. Destination Deluxe. https://destinationdeluxe.com/sacred-geometry-explained-healing-benefits/

Aletheia. (2018, February 5). 7 Types of Spirit Guides (& How to Connect With Them). LonerWolf. https://lonerwolf.com/spirit-guides/

Richardson, T. C. (2021, March 17). 6 Types Of Spirit Guides & How To Communicate With Them. Mindbodygreen. https://www.mindbodygreen.com/0-17129/how-to-effectively-communicate-with-your-spirit-guides.html

Todic, S. (2021, July 6). Sacred Geometry: Symbols and Shapes and Healing Benefits Explained. Conscious Items. https://consciousitems.com/blogs/lifestyle/sacred-geometry-healing-explained

How to Make Your Own Crystal Grid. (n.d.). Energymuse.Com. https://www.energymuse.com/blog/crystal-grids

Hunter, D. (2017, July 17). Seven Stones for Summoning Spirits. Llewellyn Worldwide. https://www.llewellyn.com/journal/article/2641

Healing Crystals, www. healingcrystals.com. (n.d.). Crystals for Spirit Communication. Healingcrystals.Com https://www.healingcrystals.com

Lapidos, R. (2019, March 26). How To Communicate With Spirits, According to a Medium. Well+Good. https://www.wellandgood.com/how-to-communicate-with-spirits/

Snider, A. C. (2018, March 20). Sacred Geometrical Patterns That Will Make You One with the World. Culture Trip; The Culture Trip. https://theculturetrip.com/north-america/usa/articles/sacred-geometrical-patterns-that-will-make-you-at-one-with-the-world/

Kahn, N. (2018, December 25). Here's exactly where you should be keeping your crystals at home. Bustle. https://www.bustle.com/life/where-should-i-keep-my-crystals-heres-a-room-by-room-guide-for-which-crystals-work-best-in-your-home-15525339

Lazzerini, E. (2017a). Crystal grids power: Harness the power of crystals and sacred geometry for manifesting abundance, healing, and protection. Createspace Independent Publishing Platform.

Lazzerini, E. (2017b, October 20). Home Protection Crystal Grid with black tourmaline. Ethan Lazzerini. http://www.ethanlazzerini.com/home-protection-crystal-grid/

Neese, A. (2016, October 4). How to use crystals in your home. Parachutehome.Com; Parachute Home. https://www.parachutehome.com/blog/four-crystals-for-home

Tips and trick in storing crystals at home. (n.d.). Stonebridge Imports. https://stonebridgeimports.com/a/658-gemstone-display-and-storage-tips-and-tricks

Your A-Z guide to at-home crystal healing during times of stress. (2017, June 20). ELLE. https://www.elle.com/uk/life-and-culture/culture/articles/a31572/what-are-healing-crystals-how-to-use-them/

(N.d.). Tinyrituals.Co. https://tinyrituals.co/blogs/tiny-rituals/protection-crystals-for-the-home

(N.d.). Healingcrystalsco.Com. https://www.healingcrystalsco.com/blogs/blog/crystal-grids-complete-guide

Nunez, K. (2020, July 14). Throat chakra stones: What are they, and how to use them. Healthline. https://www.healthline.com/health/health-benefits-of-throat-chakra-stones

Moore, R. (2021, August 13). Full moon and charging your crystals. Quirk Books. https://www.quirkbooks.com/full-moon-and-charging-your-crystals/

Healing Stones Guide - A Complete List. (n.d.). Moonmagic.Com. https://moonmagic.com/blogs/news/healing-stones

emilygardner. (2021, February 8). The How-To Guide for Crystal Grid Use. Serena Loves. https://serenaloves.com/the-how-to-guide-for-crystal-grid-use/

Murray, B. (2017, September 5). A beginner's guide to using crystals. Harper's BAZAAR. http://www.harpersbazaar.co.uk/beauty/fitness-wellbeing/a43244/crystal-healing-beginners-guide

www.ingramcontent.com/pod-product-compliance
Lightning Source LLC
Chambersburg PA
CBHW070325010526
44107CB00004B/419